FUTURE FINANCE

FUTURE FINANCE

Legal Geographies of Financial Centres and the Asset Economy

SABINE DÖRRY

agenda
publishing

First published in 2025 by Agenda Publishing

Agenda Publishing Limited
PO Box 185
Newcastle upon Tyne
NE20 2DH
www.agendapub.com

ISBN 978-1-78821-734-7

British Library Cataloguing-in-Publication Data
A catalogue record for this book is available from the British Library

Typeset by Newgen Publishing UK
Printed and bound in the UK by 4edge

EU GPSR authorised representative:
Logos Europe, 9 rue Nicolas Poussin, 17000 La Rochelle, France
contact@logoseurope.eu

CONTENTS

PREFACE

What if the financial system no longer reflects the real economy, but instead functions as a mirage – one that expands the closer we examine it? How can there be four times as much wealth circulating in global financial markets as the total annual value of goods and services produced? If finance is intended to support productive investment, why has it increasingly turned towards speculation, inflating asset prices while leaving wages stagnant and economies sluggish? These contradictions lie at the heart of financial capitalism. We are told that the global economy is expanding, yet much of this growth occurs on paper – through financial instruments that generate wealth without necessarily creating value. Since 2000, the world's total assets – including real estate, stocks, bonds and bank deposits – have grown at a pace far exceeding that of GDP. In just two decades, this inflation of asset values has produced approximately $160 trillion in "paper wealth": a figure that dwarfs the productive capacity of the real economy (McKinsey Global Institute 2023). Until the turn of the millennium, global net worth expanded more or less in tandem with GDP. Since then, however, the financial sector has become increasingly decoupled from the real economy, reshaping resource allocation, social organization and our understanding of ecological value.

Future Finance contends that finance no longer merely reflects economic activity; it has become a system unto itself, fuelled by legal and institutional innovations that sustain its own expansion. Economic orthodoxy teaches that financial markets efficiently allocate resources – but reality suggests otherwise. The gap between financial speculation and economic productivity has widened dramatically, raising urgent questions: What does it mean when price formation is detached from real-world value? How does this growing financial abstraction shape inequality, sustainability and political decision-making? And what are the implications for a world grappling with climate crises and social upheaval?

Economic coordination is now increasingly shaped by financialization – a process that extends far beyond banking and investment, reorganizing economies and societies according to financial logics, often speculative in nature (Christophers 2015; Epstein 2005b). Under financialization, uncertainty itself has become a source of value, while price – no longer a proxy for productive worth – has emerged as the defining measure of economic reality. The 2001 Enron scandal exemplifies this logic: through "legal accounting tricks and illegal fraudulent financial statements", the company's stock prices were inflated without any corresponding growth in productivity (Mazzucato & Collington 2023: 63). Such episodes are not anomalies, but symptoms of a deeper transformation within financial capitalism – one in which financial instruments, derivatives and synthetic assets generate self-referential loops increasingly detached from material conditions. As Baudrillard (1994) might suggest, financialization has produced a form of "hyperreality", wherein finance no longer represents the economy, but constructs its own.

Crucially, finance is not a passive or neutral mechanism; it constitutes an active system of power, anchored in financial centres such as London, New York and Hong Kong – global hubs that do not merely host financial activity, but actively produce and sustain it. Often characterized, in economic terms, as the production sites of finance, these international financial centres (IFCs) function as dense agglomerations of financial institutions, encompassing both banking and non-banking entities, financial infrastructure such as exchanges and clearing houses, as well as auxiliary professional services including brokers, dealers, insurers, and the legal and accounting firms collectively referred to as financial and advanced business services (FABS).

Together, these actors form dynamic business ecosystems, instrumental in shaping the structural logic and arbitrage-driven nature of contemporary finance. Financial production systems – just like complex automotive production systems with several tiers of suppliers, industry standards and specialized labour markets – are inherently spatial. They involve networks, interdependencies and institutional arrangements that manifest in spatially distributed clusters: financial centres. IFCs are not merely venues for economic transactions; they are sites of coordination, organization and production. Accordingly, their influence extends well beyond the financial sphere into previously non-financial domains, through legal geographies where law is shaped, contested and mobilized as an economic resource, such is the central hypothesis of this book. Financial centres are thus active architects of global financial structures, wielding power that is both spatial and political (Allen 2003; Massey 2005, 2007). As Massey (2004) contends, power is inherently spatial, and finance is no exception: it must be continuously generated, anchored in particular places, and sustained through specific legal and institutional configurations.

One of the principal mechanisms through which finance sustains its expansion is "legal bricolage" – the adaptive and innovative repurposing of legal structures to create new financial opportunities (Engelen *et al.* 2010; Fourcade & Savelsberg 2006; see also Potts 2024). Legal bricolage is a distinct instrument closely tied to broader trends of economization. At its core, economization (Çalışkan & Callon 2009) refers to the active construction of the "economic" through social and material processes. It involves framing actions, devices and representations as "economic" by market actors and analysts, shifting attention from the economy as a given system to the *practices* through which it is made. In this sense, economization applies economic logics to domains not traditionally governed by them – such as law, nature (particularly its ecological services) and nursing homes. One modality of economization is marketization, which highlights how markets are constructed through socio-technical arrangements – rules, conventions, devices and calculative practices (Çalışkan & Callon 2010). Others, like commercialization and capitalization, focus more directly on the financial valorization of things, nature and people. Assetization, a related yet distinct process, refers to the transformation of things – land, data, infrastructure or future income streams – into assets that can be owned, valued and managed (Birch & Muniesa 2020). Unlike marketization, which centres on exchange, assetization emphasises the creation of long-term value-holding entities capable of generating predictable future income. While it overlaps with capitalization (which assigns present value to future returns), assetization also entails the institutional and legal infrastructures – accounting norms, intellectual property rights, regulatory frameworks – that make such *valuation* possible (Doganova 2024).

Closely linked is financialization (see Epstein 2005a; Mader *et al.* 2020): the increasing dominance of financial motives, markets, actors and institutions across the economy. It describes a shift where value creation is increasingly driven not by production or trade, but by financial operations – especially the leveraging and trading of asset-based income streams. Financialization builds upon assetization, amplifying the role of finance in everyday life and consolidating power in the hands of asset managers and institutional investors. This book draws primarily on the concepts of economization, assetization and financialization to explain the creation of immense paper wealth, much of it driven by rising asset prices. In economic orthodoxy, price is seen as a reflection of value: without value, there is no price. These and other dynamics are foundational to the management of assets – now a globally dominant and increasingly powerful industry.

Legal bricolage underpins the very logic of what can be called *synthetic* finance, whereby legal and institutional innovations enable the continual creation of novel asset classes, derivative instruments and opportunities for regulatory arbitrage. It is through such processes that finance has prospered – not by driving productivity-led growth, but by leveraging newly created opportunity spaces through legal innovation. Financial expansion, in this sense, is propelled by co-constitutive dynamics: financial centres profit from the emergence of lucrative legal economies, key to the rise of "paper wealth" (McKinsey Global Institute 2023) and the concurrent growth of "paper geographies" (Haberly *et al.* 2019).

In pursuit of further expansion, finance has increasingly adopted the rhetoric of sustainability. IFCs now position themselves as key mediators in green finance and net-zero transitions. Yet their role remains profoundly paradoxical. Having long been complicit in exacerbating economic inequalities, these same financial actors now assert their leadership in advancing environmental and social responsibility. The rapid proliferation of so-called "green financial centres", which brand themselves as pioneers of sustainable finance, raises pressing questions: are they genuinely contributing to a just transition and the achievement of the Sustainable Development Goals (SDGs) – "a universal call to action to end poverty, protect the planet, and ensure that by 2030 all people enjoy peace and prosperity" (UNDP nd) – or are they merely repackaging financialization under a green narrative? Recent findings suggest the latter (e.g. Bogart & Chaudhary 2019; Bridge 2008; Dorn *et al.* 2022; Dörry & Schulz 2024; Lai 2025; Lang & Mokrani 2013).

Future Finance situates financialization within its legal geographies, arguing that financial centres function as sites where law, economy and space converge to forge new financial frontiers. Offering a critical, interdisciplinary perspective, it bridges legal studies, political economy and financial geography to explore how finance has evolved into a system wherein law itself becomes a mechanism for private wealth creation. While finance purports to drive economic growth, it increasingly operates through self-perpetuating legal and institutional innovations that entrench economic hierarchies. If finance is to contribute to a truly sustainable future, we must first confront its systemic contradictions. *Future Finance* challenges mainstream economic assumptions, presenting a novel framework for understanding financialization – not as a passive backdrop to economic life, but as a dynamic, evolving force that actively shapes our world. *Future Finance* does not deny the existence of industrial systems, services or production – the foundations of the real economy. On the contrary, the asset economy depends on them. Yet over the past decade, the dynamics of financialization and assetization have expanded disproportionately, raising concerns that the resources needed to address challenges like climate change are being diverted or depleted. *Future Finance* highlights the industrial scale of assetization – now a powerful and globally dominant industry in its own right – arguing that it demands more scrutiny. Geopolitical and geo-economic upheavals – such as the tariffs introduced by the Trump administration – will undoubtedly impact both systems. These developments emerged after this book was finalised and could not be incorporated. However, as events continue to unfold, the global socio-economic structures shaping the asset economy will still influence how it operates and how it might be transformed. This book focuses on unpacking those underlying structures.

By examining finance through the lens of legal geographies, *Future Finance* unpacks how financial capitalism is territorialized, regulated and contested in both spatial and legal terms. It argues that to comprehend finance, one must understand law – and to understand law, one must also grasp geography.

ACKNOWLEDGEMENTS

Future Finance emerged from my keen academic curiosity and years of living in and researching various financial centres. As an economic geographer, I could analyse the many spatial dynamics of finance, but I quickly realized that a crash course in forensic accounting or law would have been a godsend. After all, dissecting an industry as complex as asset management – responsible for everything from our pensions to financing the socio-ecological transition – is no small feat. Tracing investment funds – those elusive creatures of the asset management world – through a maze of financial hubs, both offshore and onshore, proved to be quite a challenge. This book would not have been possible without the generosity of my expert interview partners, who welcomed me into the nerve centres of finance in cities such as Amsterdam, Dublin, Frankfurt, London, Luxembourg, Philadelphia, San Francisco, Singapore and Wilmington. Their insights provided much of the empirical foundation of this work, and I remain deeply grateful for their time and trust.

Beyond my own disciplinary bubble, engaging with diverse research groups and subjecting parts of this book to critical scrutiny has been invaluable. I sincerely appreciate the invitations to workshops and seminars, particularly during the book's writing process, from The Hague (October 2023), Helsinki, Stavanger (both December 2023), Zhuhai (March 2024), near Paris (April 2024) and Brussels (June 2024). The generous feedback and thoughtful discussions from these exchanges have profoundly shaped my arguments. Naturally, any shortcomings remain mine alone.

Over the years, my research has been supported by numerous funding bodies, most notably the Luxembourg National Research Fund (FNR), which also covered the open access fees for this book (FNR/FWO/16/11312037/FinWebs). The idea for *Future Finance* first took shape during my Marie Curie postdoctoral fellowship at the University of Oxford (2013–15), generously funded by the European Commission. My collaboration with Ben Derudder and Gary Robinson on the FINWEBS project (2017–23) was instrumental in refining and developing this work further. I am also grateful to my Luxembourg-based colleagues – Paolo Balmas, Sara Benceković, Elena Emrick-Schmitz, Brian Longobardi, Nicolas

Hercelin, Markus Hesse, Christian Schulz and Thomas Sigler – for their valuable support and stimulating discussions. At LISER, a special thanks goes to Camille Perchoux, Marie Valentova, Magdalena Gorczynska-Angiulli, Olivier Klein and Martin Dijst, who kept my motivation high throughout the writing process. A heartfelt thanks to Isabelle Bouvy, Bérengère Darud and especially Benoît Lanscotte for transforming my complex ideas into clear, accessible illustrations. Our conversations helped sharpen and refine the book's messages in ways I could not have achieved alone. I am deeply grateful to those who bravely read and generously commented on (some very early) drafts of this book, including Paolo Balmas, Jan Germen Janmaat, Adam Leaver, Jean-Philippe Robé, Christian Schulz, Michiel van Meeteren and Matti Ylönen. Their critical yet encouraging feedback helped make this book leaner, clearer and more readable. I also extend my gratitude to the anonymous reviewers, whose insightful advice was instrumental. At Agenda Publishing, Alison Howson and Camilla Erskine displayed incredible patience, keeping me on track with a firm but kind hand throughout this book's journey. Thank you also to Clare Owen and Victoria Chow for their kind support in production. The editors have encouraged me to engage a broader audience, not only by transcending disciplinary boundaries but also by reaching beyond established researchers to include students and readers outside academic circles. I have endeavoured to keep this in mind, striving to make the discussion accessible while remaining true to the complexity of the subject.

For over a decade, I have had the privilege of teaching geography and economics students – mainly at the universities of Bonn and Luxembourg – blending topics such as sustainable finance, global production networks of finance, and financing sustainable regions for the future. Their enthusiasm and curiosity were the true spark behind this book. But I also recognize that these topics can leave students feeling uneasy, even pessimistic, about the future. I dedicate this book to them, in the hope that it inspires and empowers them to build a financial system that is resilient, inclusive and meets their aspirations head-on.

Finally, a special thanks to Jennifer Johns and Sarah Marie Hall, who edited the marvellous all-female collection *Contemporary Economic Geographies* (Johns & Hall 2024). When they invited me to contribute to the project, they suggested the chapter title "Future Finance" – a title that sparked my imagination and has stayed with me ever since.

Sabine Dörry
Esch-sur-Alzette/Belval

ABBREVIATIONS

ABS	Alternative business structures
AUM	Assets under management
Big Four	Reference to the four largest accountancy/consultancy firms: Deloitte, Ernst & Young (EY), Pricewaterhouse Coopers (PwC), and Klynveld Peat Marwick Goerdeler (KPMG)
CIT	Corporate income tax
EEC	European Economic Community
ESG	Environmental, social and governance (investment criteria)
ESM	European Single Market
ESMA	European Securities and Markets Authority
ETF	Exchange-traded funds
EU	European Union
FABS	Financial and advanced business services, including finance, accounting, banking, and legal services
FDI	Foreign direct investment
FMC	Fund management company
FoFs	Fund of funds
GDP	Gross domestic product
GFN	Global financial network
GHG	Greenhouse gas (emissions)
GP	General partner (in a limited partnership responsible for the day-to-day operations of the fund or portfolio)
GPN	Global production network
GVC	Global value chains
IF	Investment fund
IFC	International financial centre
IMF	International Monetary Fund
LBO	Leveraged buyouts
LLC	Limited liability company

LLP	Limited liability partnership
LP	Limited partner (limited partnership in corporate law or a limited partner in a PE fund)
NAV	Net asset value
OJ	Offshore jurisdiction
PE	Private equity
RoI	Returns on investment
SDGs	Sustainable Development Goals
SNA	System of National Accounts
UCITS	Undertakings for Collective Investment in Transferable Securities
UHNWIs	Ultra-high-net-worth individuals (individuals with investable assets of at least $30 million or more)
UK	United Kingdom
US	United States
VC	Venture capital

1

SYNTHETIC FINANCE

Financialization and climate inertia: the structural paradox

In recent decades, the pervasive influence of finance has reshaped capitalism's institutional, spatial and socio-political architectures. What was once considered a specialized sector of the economy now defines its dominant logics. From the transformation of state power and corporate governance to the commodification of nature and social life, financialization has permeated every facet of contemporary life. It is no longer just finance within capitalism, but rather capitalism articulated *through* finance.

Social scientists have consistently developed new conceptual frameworks to capture the shifting contours of contemporary capitalism, with financialization being central to this analysis (see Epstein 2005a; Mader *et al.* 2020). Financialization reflects the expanding influence of financial interests on political structures and extends to encompass the ascendancy of shareholder value, the spatial restructuring of the global economy, the transformation of class and social relations, and even shifts in cultural identity and self-perception. As a governing rationality, financialization crystallizes the outcomes of earlier ideological and policy-driven shifts (Slobodian 2018; Tooze 2018), exposing both their enduring legacies and the material sites of their manifestation. Nevertheless, financialization is neither historically unprecedented nor unique to contemporary capitalism. Rather, it represents a renewed phase of financial expansion (Christophers 2015), in which financialization is not simply about "more finance", but about how finance reorganizes society, reshapes power relations and redefines value – an argument reinterpreted and developed in this book.

Far from being abstract, the consequences of financialization are acutely material: rising inequality, the erosion of public goods and, most pressingly, the intensifying climate crisis. Despite the scientific consensus on the urgent need for decarbonization and systemic transformation, private capital continues to flow disproportionately into extractive and speculative sectors. Finance thus appears as both culprit and potential saviour: widely implicated in driving eco-logical breakdown while simultaneously being positioned as an essential lever for climate mitigation and adaptation.

Climate finance mechanisms – green bonds, environmental, social and gov-ernance (ESG) metrics, sustainability-linked investments – now form the bed-rock of major global policy frameworks such as the UN Sustainable Development Goals (SDGs) and the European Green Deal.[1] Yet these instruments – meant to drive sustainability – remain embedded within financial logics of rent extraction, short-term valuation and speculative gain. Kate Raworth's *Doughnut Economics* (2017) challenges this paradigm by compellingly advocating for an economic model that respects planetary boundaries while ensuring healthy socio-ecological foundations, and her intervention stresses the dissonance between prevailing financial architectures and the socio-ecological realities they purport to address. Indeed, the global entrenchment of financialization has intensified both environmental degradation and social inequality, not least because the extractive dynamics underpinning the wealth of the global North have not only ravaged ecosystems all over the globe but also deepened divides between the global North's own neighbourhoods, cities and nation-states. Even as calls to reduce greenhouse gas (GHG) emissions by 2050 grow more urgent, and the causal link between fossil fuel combustion and climate change becomes indis-putable, coordinated global action to halt the planet's rapid warming and avert ecological collapse remains elusive.

Consider the fossil fuel sector. Despite mounting evidence of its role in cli-mate breakdown, capital continues to flood into oil, gas and coal projects.[2] The June 2024 sale of Saudi Arabia's Aramco shares – which attracted overwhelming international demand exceeding available stock within hours, with projections reaching up to $13.1 billion – exemplifies the enduring allure of fossil fuel assets to global investors. This paradox – wherein the very financial systems fuelling ecological collapse are simultaneously tasked with delivering sustainability – lays bare the structural contradictions at play. Wildfires in California and cata-strophic flooding in Pakistan render these contradictions viscerally evident.

This is not just a failure of coordination or policy design; it is symptomatic of the deep structural entrenchment of financial power. Over the past decades, asset managers, private equity (PE) firms and pension funds have emerged as key architects of the global energy landscape. BlackRock, for instance, ranked as the second-largest institutional investor in fossil fuels in 2024, with expos-ure exceeding $400 billion (see ClientEarth 2024). While some institutions have divested from fossil fuels, these assets have not been eliminated – in most cases, they have merely changed hands, often shifting into opaque PE portfolios that evade robust regulatory oversight (Fitch Ratings 2021; Petry *et al.* 2021).

Consequently, the average pension saver in the global North may unwittingly underwrite the very climate catastrophes that threaten their own future. This "irony" was starkly illustrated during the December 2024 wildfires in Los Angeles, where pension funds were revealed to be indirectly invested in the industries exacerbating local climate disasters. Indeed, for decades, the fossil fuel industry – a vast global oligopoly of resource-rich countries and corporations – has shaped geo-economic dependencies and geopolitical realities (IEA 2024; Mitchell 2023). Nonetheless, political mobilization is growing. In the US, Vermont has spearheaded legislative efforts to hold fossil fuel firms financially accountable. Following suit, New York State enacted the Climate Change Superfund Act, requiring major emitters between 2000 and 2018 to contribute approximately $3 billion annually for 25 years to finance climate adaptation (Jones Day 2025). This signals a possible shift – nearly a decade after the 2015 Paris Agreement – towards the long-anticipated "stranding"[3] of fossil fuel assets and a reversal of longstanding economic privileges that have enabled the externalization of gigantic social and environmental costs.

Yet, the paradox endures: private finance remains indispensable to any serious attempt at climate mitigation and adaptation. The sustainability transition demands vast capital investment – not only in renewable energy and sustainable infrastructure, but also in climate resilience and adaptive capacity. The 2030 Agenda for Sustainable Development, particularly SDG 17, identifies finance as a critical enabler of systemic transformation. Estimates suggest that achieving the SDGs will require between $5 trillion and $7 trillion annually, with an emphasis on unlocking $1 trillion in private capital (UNDP 2020). In this context, private financial institutions are positioned as key actors. In 2023, global investment in clean energy reached a record $1.8 trillion, yet the International Energy Agency (IEA 2023a) insists this must rise to $4.5 trillion annually by the early 2030s to meet net-zero targets.

However, the prevailing structure of global finance remains misaligned with equitable, long-term ecological outcomes. Sustainability metrics such as ESG criteria have too often been diluted, co-opted or politicized (Pollman 2024), while regulatory regimes constantly lag behind financial innovation. The fundamental question, then, is not simply how to attract more capital to green initiatives, but *whether the existing financial architecture is even capable of enabling a just and sustainable transition.* Finance is a means of implementation and a central pillar of the global development agenda. While it undergirds all 16 SDGs, it is especially foregrounded in SDG 17. Alongside financial mobilization, the agenda calls for technological innovation, capacity-building and inclusive trade to create enabling environments – particularly in the global South – while "tackling climate change and working to preserve our oceans and forests".[4] Numerous initiatives aim to steer financial investments toward sustainable outcomes,[5] among them the UN Principles for Responsible Investment (PRI), the Climate Bonds Initiative, the Global Reporting Initiative, UN Environment Programme Financial Initiative's Principles for Responsible Banking and Sustainable Insurance, the Task Force on Nature-related Financial Disclosures (TNFD) and the efforts of major development banks.

The issue of climate finance is inextricably linked to the broader trend of financialization, which has historically facilitated the transfer of wealth from public to private hands – often with far-reaching social and ecological consequences. Previous waves of privatization have shown that PE models tend to prioritize short-term returns over long-term investment in essential maintenance (Pike *et al.* 2016, 2019). This has, at times, undermined critical public assets, including utilities (Deruytter *et al.* 2022), local authorities (Brackley & Leaver 2024), housing (Christophers 2023; Goulding *et al.* 2023) and entire communities (Feldman & Kenney 2024). Contemporary climate finance strategies, such as those underpinning the European Green Deal, now seek to mobilize private capital, predominantly through PE, to deliver green infrastructure vital for a sustainable future. This includes investment in public transport electrification, data centres for the green and digital economies, and energy infrastructure – from wind turbine production to grid expansion and storage.

What may seem straightforward often obscures the complexity of the infrastructure underpinning the green and digital transition. Private capital is being directed into existing, deeply interconnected networks that support this twin shift. For instance, investment in data centres extends beyond physical facilities and includes entire energy systems – such as (nuclear) power plants and other energy sources – required to power these energy-hungry operations. Similarly, the electrification of public transport involves far more than vehicles; it encompasses digital ticketing and data systems, integration with smart city technologies, and links to smart energy grids and storage infrastructure. In short, private finance is entering vast, intricate and deeply interconnected infrastructure systems whose complexity and public significance demand careful scrutiny. After all, privatization also entails a transfer of control – over infrastructure maintenance, data security and more. With substantial public funding gaps, PE has taken a leading role in financing green infrastructure systems. Financial centres such as Luxembourg and Dublin, home to clusters of PE firms, position themselves as key hubs for channelling large-scale green investment. Yet, as in many other financial sectors, a significant number of these firms are of US origin, highlighting European IFCs' key dependency on the US private capital and other financial markets.

While the involvement of private capital is crucial to addressing climate change, it also raises pressing concerns about its growing influence over the foundational systems of future societies – or, more bluntly, the risk of unravelling the social fabric amid the life-threatening crisis of climate change. Hence, although these efforts collectively seek to align private capital with environmental imperatives, the proliferation of paper wealth – partly under the guise of climate finance – combined with the limitations of prevailing adaptation and mitigation models, warrants critical scrutiny if we are to overcome the structural inertia that continues to hinder meaningful climate action.

Law and financial infrastructure

Beneath the surface of global finance lies a vast legal machinery; one that not only stabilizes markets but also actively shapes and enables them. Law is not a neutral backdrop to the architecture of the economy; it is a generative force, capable of producing, legitimizing and safeguarding an increasing number of specific financial arrangements.

Textbooks generally attribute profit to entrepreneurial activity and technological progress, traditionally seen as drivers of innovation and economic development. Financial innovation – ranging from ATMs to banking apps – has contributed to this trajectory. Over time, however, innovation has increasingly become endogenous to finance, shifting from financing production to innovations within finance itself. More recently, a new form of legal innovation has emerged: the strategic reconfiguration of institutional frameworks to create new opportunities for financial activity. This legal innovation has not only facilitated financial expansion but has also become a commercial activity in its own right, underpinning the growth of legal and other services in major financial centres.

The central hypothesis here is that legal innovation is far from a benign technical process – it functions as a strategic instrument of financialization. Legal frameworks, such as contracts, property rights and corporate structures, not only define the contours of market activity but also determine what qualifies as an asset, who controls it, and how rights and responsibilities are distributed. The notion of the firm as a "legal fiction" (Coase 1937), for instance, masks the fact that corporations are legal persons: they hold rights, enjoy protections and frequently act as privileged vehicles for wealth accumulation. One key example is the doctrine of limited liability, which has long shielded firms and their shareholders from the broader socio-ecological consequences of corporate conduct, including pollution, environmental destruction and climate-related harm. This legal insulation in economic orthodoxy has far-reaching implications: it facilitates the externalization of risk, the evasion of accountability and the continuation of business models premised on socio-ecological harm.

To be sure, legal frameworks are also mobilized in the public interest. Under the right political and regulatory conditions, law has the capacity to protect collective goods, enforce environmental standards, and foster more equitable economic arrangements. However, in practice, legal infrastructures remain largely aligned with the interests of capital. The challenge lies not only in gaps in regulation or inconsistent enforcement, but also in the ways legal frameworks may, at times, contribute to the persistence of financial and environmental inequalities.

Moreover, legal innovation has become a domain of fierce global competition. Financial centres now specialize not only in financial services but also in jurisdictional engineering – crafting legal regimes that attract capital by offering favourable tax, regulatory and corporate governance frameworks. The proliferation of offshore financial centres and incorporation hubs exemplifies this trend, as states compete to offer bespoke legal infrastructures tailored to the demands of global finance. As a consequence, law firms, accountancy practices and financial intermediaries act as architects of these environments, reinforcing the reach and durability of the financial industry. Yet these processes remain largely obscured in mainstream climate finance discourse. Prevailing assumptions suggest that financial markets can be reoriented towards sustainability via disclosure regimes, market incentives and voluntary commitments. However, such efforts often neglect the legal scaffolding underpinning financial expansion – structures that, unless fundamentally reformed, will continue to obstruct meaningful climate action. In short, legal form is not incidental to finance; it is constitutive. If climate finance is to serve as a genuine driver of transformation rather than a vehicle for greenwashing, the legal architectures that govern financial markets and industries must be subjected to the same level of scrutiny as the capital flows they facilitate.

Originating primarily in the Anglo-American sphere, assets have become a central organizing principle of contemporary capitalism, recasting the system around an asset logic. This logic prioritizes financial return, shifting economic orientation from production to value generation through the manipulation and capitalization of assets. Although related to the commodity form, an asset differs in that it does not have to satisfy a social need to possess exchange value (Marx 1990 [1867]). Instead, assets – tangible or intangible – are capitalized as revenue streams (Boltanski & Chiapello 2006; Boltanski & Esquerre 2020), with *expected* future earnings discounted to their present value (Muniesa 2023; Muniesa *et al.* 2007). This mechanism transforms future income (expectations) into present wealth and renders assets durable sources of economic rent, enabling extraction of value independent of production. The longevity of these revenue streams, however, depends on the specific attributes inherent to the asset itself.

One critical attribute of assets is their role as "boundary objects between financial actors and financial infrastructures" (Golka 2025: 75). This framing underscores how assetization – a process through which land, cultural goods and public assets are rendered legible to financial markets – both relies upon and reshapes financial infrastructures. Assetization reconfigures social relations by converting cash flows into discrete, tradable objects designed to attract more capital. Golka (2025) argues that assets operate as bridges between distinct social worlds, while maintaining a shared infrastructure enabling interaction across groups. As assetization becomes institutionalized through these cross-cutting relationships, it evolves into both a financial and social organizing mechanism. Assets thus function not merely as financial instruments but as mediators of social relations – linking, for instance, smallholder farmers in the global South (Ouma 2015) with traders on Wall Street, but ultimately serving the interests of the latter.

The asset form creates a taken-for-granted reality in which anticipated returns eclipse the socio-ecological and socio-economic conflicts that underpin asset value. At the heart of this issue lies ownership. Legally, ownership is more accurately understood as a "bundle of rights" *to* property, encompassing the rights to use, lease, transfer or sell an asset (Robé 2011). Yet these rights entail not only entitlements, but also responsibilities and obligations – to maintain property, respect the rights of others, uphold accountability and safeguard the environment. Across disciplines, property rights – or ownership – are often conflated with *possession*, leading to conceptual confusion (see Robé 2020: 47). Such responsibilities are particularly crucial for the future-oriented green infrastructure envisaged by the world's many green deal initiatives. Yet in practice, the state's protection of individual and corporate property rights has often undermined these ethical obligations. The asset form – central to contemporary capitalism – is itself a legal construct. Assets generate value not through use, but through ownership and expected returns. Assetization, then, is not merely a technical or financial process, but a profound socio-legal transformation. Yet, even the most abstract forms of capital remain materially grounded.

While economic orthodoxy treats large firms, including financial firms, as legal fictions (Coase 1937), in reality corporations are legal persons, which hold both rights and responsibilities: legal personhood provides the legal structure through which business strategy is executed (Robé 2011). To be precise, the concept of the *firm* – as an economic organization – differs from that of the *corporation* (or other legal structures), which is "a specific form of legal person to legally structure most large firms" (Robé 2020: 31). Traditional economic theory, exemplified by Friedman's (1970) focus on profit maximization, has long upheld the firm's right to financial return while eliding its broader social obligations. Limited liability, coupled with robust protection of private property rights – rigorously enforced yet often blind to wider duties to society and the environment – has entrenched this logic (Robé 2020). It has thereby weakened principles such as "polluter pays" and reinforced a narrow, shareholder-centric conception of property ownership. Although legal scholars have begun to bridge the gap between legal practice and orthodox economic assumptions, economic theory remains largely detached from the socio-legal realities shaping contemporary market practice.

This detachment also illuminates McKinsey's (2023) analysis of the disproportionate rise in paper wealth relative to real economic growth, introduced in the preface of this book. In contexts where asset prices are inflated through speculation rather than productive investment, asset prices may acquire fictitious – or synthetic – characteristics: financial markets become detached from economic fundamentals, and the appreciation of speculative asset values blurs the line between productive and fictitious capital. Both are ultimately managed as assets by large institutional investors, and understanding this distinction is key to explaining why global assets have expanded at a pace far exceeding global GDP (McKinsey Global Institute 2023).

Fictitious capital is capital that does not represent real, productive activity, but the present valuation of anticipated future income (Marx 1990 [1867]; Durand 2017; Norfield 2017). Key instruments include stocks, bonds and derivatives. In contrast to industrial capital, which derives value from labour and production, fictitious capital accrues value from expectations and is traded as if equivalent to tangible wealth. It plays a critical role in decoupling financial accumulation from material production, fuelled by speculation, magnified by leverage and stabilized through legal abstraction. Fictitious capital also reflects a broader ontological shift within capitalism: a movement from value as substance to *value as anticipation* (Doganova 2024), increasingly animated by projected returns on intangible assets, imagined profits and algorithmically generated sentiment. This is not merely the outcome of deregulation or financial innovation – it is a defining feature of rentier capitalism (Christophers 2020). The result is a proliferation of paper wealth, increasingly detached from productive activity, that can expand or collapse on the basis of narrative, algorithm or collective belief. In the realm of climate finance, the significance is particularly pronounced. Green bonds, sustainability-linked derivatives and climate risk insurance instruments may appear to internalize environmental concerns. Yet they do so within the same logics of abstraction, speculative valuation and monetization that characterize the broader financial system. As such, these instruments risk entrenching the very dynamics – of extraction, enclosure, inequality – that underpin climate and ecological breakdown.

A final analytical distinction worth highlighting is that between fictitious capital and interest-bearing capital (Alves 2023; Dymski 2024). Interest-bearing capital generates income through lending – its value is tied to an actual monetary transaction. Fictitious capital, by contrast, derives its worth from expectations of expectations, making it far more volatile and speculative. Both forms of capital are central to the machinery of financial centres. These forms of capital are produced, priced and traded in financial nodes where legal authority and economic valuation intersect. Financial centres, in this sense, are not neutral intermediaries but spaces where fictitious – or synthetic – value is stabilized and projected as real. If financialization shapes the logic of capitalism, and assetization reshapes the form of value, then financial centres are where these processes are spatially anchored and strategically enacted. Far from being mere sites of transaction, financial centres function as assemblages of legal, infrastructural and epistemological authority and power[6] – the command hubs of global financial capitalism.

By synthesizing the quantitative and qualitative dimensions of financialization, namely, the expansion of finance ("too much finance") (Arcand *et al.* 2012) and the rise in speculative activity ("too much speculation") (Shaxson 2018), it becomes evident that finance has come to dominate not only economies but societies. A principal driver of this shift since the 1980s has been financial deregulation. One of the most consequential examples was the repeal of the Glass–Steagall Act, which – having already been significantly weakened through a series of incremental reforms – had previously enforced the separation between retail and investment banking. Its removal enabled financial institutions to integrate traditional banking activities with high-risk speculative practices, thereby prioritizing short-term returns over long-term stability (Thiemann 2018; Tooze 2018), while portraying many extractive activities as adding value to national balance sheets (Assa 2017).

Moreover, the ongoing commercialization of legal and accounting practices, coupled with the commodification of state sovereignty (Picciotto 1995, 1999), has given rise to prolific financial and para-financial ecosystems (FABS). Many of these ecosystems – arguably non-productive[7] in these economic settings – generate vast economic wealth through legal, accounting and financial services. Financialization has indeed produced "a swathe of new services and 'products' for both corporations and individuals, which are bought because they allow the purchaser to make a future gain, stemming from outperformance, wise custodianship or superior risk abatement" (Blackburn 2006: 41). In response, legal scholars have raised concerns about the financialization of legal knowledge itself (Cornut St-Pierre 2023), drawing attention to the expanding epistemological authority of legal *professions*, which, in turn, reinforces the epistemic authority of legal *professionals*. These scholars caution that legal practice is increasingly being instrumentalized for economic gain. Indeed, consultancy engagements of legal scholars frequently serve private interests, despite the continued authority of their opinions in shaping legal outcomes (Raitasuo & Ylönen 2022). More broadly, entire branches of law risk being transformed from socially facilitative structures into instruments of economic leverage – or, indeed, into economic resources in their own right.

Assetization and the redefinition of value

The expansion of financial capitalism has been propelled not only by the pro-liferation of capital flows but by the systematic transformation of things into assets. This process – assetization – is fundamental to understanding the logic of contemporary finance: a logic no longer (only) anchored in production, but oriented towards rent, yield and speculative return. Assets differ from commodities. While commodities are consumed, assets are held and capitalized (Birch & Muniesa 2020). Their value lies not in use, but in ownership and control – the capacity to generate income through the promise of future revenue streams. This includes physical infrastructure, intellectual property and natural resources, as well as, increasingly, the environment itself. Forests, water ecosystems, biodiversity and carbon emissions are gradually being rendered as financial assets, inputs for markets in which projected future income can be traded in the present. Assetization therefore depends upon two interlocking infrastructures: *financial engineering* and *legal abstraction*. The former enables the bundling, slicing and pricing of expected future income; the latter constructs property rights, insulates investors from liability and renders socio-ecological goods legible to capital. Assets are therefore not "natural"; they are *produced* – socially, legally and spatially.

Crucially, assetization entails a profound redefinition of value. Dominant economic thought, shaped by marginal utility theory (Kauder 2015), reduces value to price: typically, the price someone is willing to pay based on anticipated returns. In this narrow economic framework, value becomes speculative and forward-looking: it is severed from social utility or ecological function and anchored instead in the asset's capacity to yield income. This logic marginalizes alternative conceptions of value – cultural, ecological, communal – and obscures forms of life that resist commodification. Commodification takes real, formal and fictitious forms – pricing, transforming and monetizing goods and services (Marx 1990 [1867]; see also Hermann 2021). Fictitious commodification applies market logic to non-market domains like health, education and nature. Through privatization, liberalization, deregulation and austerity, public alternatives have been eroded and the social and ecological monetized. Assetization builds on commodification but pushes it further.

This shift erodes use value in favour of exchange value, privileging what can be priced over what truly matters: modern economics, shaped by marginalist thinking, conflates utility with price, essentially stripping unpriced goods such as ecological ecosystems of their intrinsic worth (Barnes 1988; Dymski 2014). The expansion of commodification is thus both functional and ideological, displacing alternative value systems while reinforcing capital accumulation. This dynamic, akin to Dörre's (2015) concept of internal colonization, reveals capitalism's paradoxical dependence on non-capitalist spaces for its continued reproduction (see Luxemburg 2003 [1913]). Assetization, then, is a mode of socio-economic reorganization that reshapes social relations, redistributes power and reconfigures the terrain of politics. In the context of climate change, its implications are especially stark. Nature is no longer to be preserved, restored or valued for its own sake, but managed as an economic portfolio of risk-adjusted revenue streams. Resisting this paradigm demands not only policy reform but a fundamental rethinking of what we value – and whose interests are served by the infrastructures that define value itself. This process intersects with fictitious capital, that is, capital representing the present valuation of anticipated future income.

The outcome is a structural tension between the demands of financial accumulation and the requirements of ecological sustainability. Legal fictions, such as the firm's duty to maximize shareholder value, enshrine the externalization of social and environmental costs (Stern 2008). ESG criteria and taxonomies, although promising, remain politically contested and operationally weak (Dumrose *et al.* 2022; Larcker *et al.* 2022; Parfitt 2024). This fundamental transformation is not an incidental side effect, but the very condition for contemporary wealth accumulation, in which financialization has become the dominant mode of economic organization. As financial institutions seek ever-more sites for investment, entire domains of life – housing (Aalbers 2016), education (Farmer & Weber 2022), healthcare (Hunter & Murray 2019), care work (Horton 2019) and daily life (Martin 2002), statecraft (Karwowski & Stockhammer 2017), land (Ward 2022) and nature (Christophers 2018) – are being reimagined and reproduced as asset classes. Even climate risk is being priced, securitized and traded. Finance is hence no longer a subsystem; it is the system. Yet, in displacing production, deepening the divide between poverty and extreme wealth, and accelerating ecological breakdown, it is a system riven with contradiction.

A further dimension of this political economy lies in the redefinition of economic performance through GDP. Long regarded as a neutral indicator of output, GDP has been progressively restructured to include financial activity – once excluded as non-productive (and even extractive). The 1993 and 2008 revisions to the System of National Accounts (European Commission *et al.* 2009) reclassified speculative and intermediary financial services as productive, enabling especially economies with large financial sectors to report robust growth despite stagnation in real investment (Assa 2017).[8] This reclassification has morphed GDP from a mere metric into a rhetorical device – one that legitimizes austerity, deregulation and financial expansion under the banner of national interest (Christophers 2011). Although GDP is mathematically precise and relatively straightforward to compute, it remains a poor proxy for human wellbeing, the ostensible aim of economic activity (Felber 2021). Furthermore, the financialization of GDP reinforces the *illusion* that financial activity constitutes economic

progress. Yet beneath rising GDP figures, the real economy continues to stag-
nate: asset bubbles inflate, wages remain flat and ecological costs are routinely
externalized. The result is a model of jobless growth and financial accumulation
increasingly detached from material production, a dynamic emblematic of what
Susan Strange (1997 [1986]) termed *Casino Capitalism*. This hollowing out of
productive investment is also evident in patterns of credit allocation. In advanced
economies, an estimated 60–80 per cent of new credit now flows into real estate
and financial asset purchases rather than productive enterprise (Bezemer 2014).

This disconnect was laid bare during the 2007/08 global financial crisis, when
excessive financial activity – particularly speculative investment – inflicted severe
damage on real economies worldwide (Tooze 2018). In its aftermath, a significant proportion of global debt remained non-productive, with capital diverted
into asset purchases and consumption rather than productive investment and
sustainable growth. This reality directly contradicts orthodox economic narratives, which claim that banks channel savings into productive enterprise, thereby
optimizing capital allocation and supporting economic development for all
(Lerner & Tufano 2011). Instead, credit creation has increasingly fuelled asset
price inflation, potentially exacerbating financial instability. In many advanced
economies, household mortgages now constitute a dominant share of total credit.
In Canada, for instance, mortgage debt accounted for approximately 66 per cent
of household debt in 2016, with similar patterns observed across the OECD
(IMF 2017: chapter 2). As Schumpeter (1934) observed, the distinction between
finance that supports production and finance driven primarily by speculative
expectations is critical. In its speculative form, credit is increasingly predicated
on anticipated returns, whether from future income or asset appreciation. This
shift threatens to erode productive capacity while amplifying systemic risk.

Financial fragility and the rise of money manager capitalism

The dynamics of financialization and assetization, as previously outlined, are not
recent phenomena. As early as the 1980s, Hyman Minsky articulated a foundational paradox in capitalist finance: that apparent stability begets instability.
What appears to be equilibrium often masks speculative excess, burgeoning debt
and mounting systemic fragility (Minsky 1986). This insight, long disregarded
in mainstream economic discourse, has proven prescient in understanding
the architecture of contemporary global finance. Minsky's *financial instability
hypothesis* posits a cyclical evolution of financial systems: from hedge finance
(where debt obligations are covered by income), through speculative finance
(where interest is paid but principal is rolled over) to Ponzi finance (where both

principal and interest rely on new borrowing or rising asset prices). Essentially, periods of calm breed euphoria, leverage expands, risk tolerance grows and the system becomes increasingly susceptible to disruption. By the 1990s, Minsky had identified the emergence of a new financial regime: *money manager capitalism.* Here, institutional investors – such as pension funds, mutual funds, insurance firms and, increasingly, private equity and asset managers – displaced traditional banks as the dominant allocators of capital. These actors, driven by the imperative to outperform market benchmarks rather than support productive investment, facilitated a shift toward speculative valuation, financial asset inflation and a growing detachment from material production. This was further amplified by the rise of derivatives and the growth of secondary markets, which enabled the trading of risk and the continuous revaluation of assets without reference to underlying economic activity. The result is an economy governed by more by the performance of financial portfolios than by the generation of goods or services. Importantly, Minsky anticipated the internationalization of financial fragility, as these dynamics extended across borders and integrated global markets.

While productive investment has historically underpinned innovation and economic development, financial innovation – increasingly endogenous to finance itself – represents a departure. As Ülgen (2014) argues, innovation in *finance to finance* differs fundamentally from finance to production. Only the latter aligns with Schumpeter's ideal of creative destruction, whereby innovation enhances societal welfare. Schumpeter (2017 [1912]) viewed profit as arising from entrepreneurial initiative tied to technological progress. Keynes (1937, 1971 [1930]), however, highlighted that money is not a neutral asset: its demand is shaped by speculation, and its accumulation can generate instability (see Knell 2015). Building on this insight, Minsky demonstrated how the pursuit of liquidity and short-term yield heightens financial fragility. In such conditions, credit no longer functions as a productive input but becomes a means of "profiting without producing" (Lapavitsas 2013). This signals a decisive shift: the financial sector no longer merely supports the real economy – it dominates it (Helleiner 1993). This transformation has fuelled a burgeoning asset economy, underpinned by a global financial system. Minsky's (1993) typology of capitalism captures this shift, tracing how changes in what is financed – and by whom – reflect broader historical logics, as echoed in related disciplinary frameworks (Table 1.1).

The 1980s and 1990s witnessed the consolidation of money manager capitalism. Institutional investors increasingly prioritized shareholder value through mergers, leveraged buyouts and stock buybacks. Minsky (1995) warned of a globally integrated financial order characterized by speculative accumulation and systemic vulnerability. This also marked the shift from *managerial capitalism,* in which corporate managers held sway, to a stage where *asset managers*

Table 1.1 Minsky's periodization of capitalism in "financially advanced" countries

	Merchant capitalism (up to the 1860s)	Financial capitalism (1870s–1920s)	Managerial capitalism (1920s–60s)	Money-manager capitalism (1970s–2008)	Global finance capitalism (after 2010)
Characteristic other (or intermediary stages/ monikers)	Classic capitalism/ industrial capitalism/banker capitalism	Classic capitalism/ industrial capitalism/banker capitalism	State finance capitalism	Pension fund capitalism, Asset manager capitalism	Global financial integration as the next era of expansive capitalism
Economic activity	Trade	Production	Aggregate demand Corporate managers as "masters of the private economy"	Asset-value, funded pension schemes: Money managers as the masters	Asset-value, ETFs
Object financed	Merchants, owner-managed enterprises; mercantile activity	Corporation	Managerial corporation (M&A)	International Corporation; Securities; Positions	Assets rather than commodities; Securities
Pivotal source (s) of financing; including the State	Commercial bank (+ internal financing); State secures money value for exchange	Investment bank, capital market financing (stock exchanges), financial securities; Reserves provision for banking system	Central bank (+ internal financing), "state organization" of the capital market (facilitation of the functioning of the capital market)	Managed-money funds (e.g. pension funds, mutual funds); Rise of Euromarkets (eroding state-managed markets); Expansion of pension schemes (passive suppliers of long-term capital for corporations); Quantitative easing (QE)	De-risking States; PE/VC; Commercial banks via shadow banking

Source: author, based on Minsky 1995, Toporowski 2020, Whalen 2001.

became the driving force of expansive capitalism. Minsky (1995: 93) linked this shift to a cautionary view, warning that

> The world is becoming universally capitalist. Because of today's communications, record keeping, and computational capabilities, global financial integration is likely to characterize the next era of expansive capitalism. The problem of finance that will emerge is whether the financial and fiscal control and support institutions of national governments can contain both the consequences of global financial fragility and an international debt deflation.

This realization came too late to influence the course set by new realities that had been decades in the making and took root primarily in the Anglo-American core, although to varying degrees in other Western states as well. After the collapse of the Bretton Woods system in the early 1970s, financial market activity surged. Minsky's prediction of the internationalization of economic integration held sway in finance. By 1979, the Euromarkets[9] had matured significantly. With deregulation and the erosion of capital controls, financial globalization accelerated. This was particularly evident in London's resurgence as a financial centre. Despite the UK's economic decline, the City of London retained its dominance through the rise of Euromarkets, deregulation and capital liberalization (Norfield 2017). The 1979 removal of exchange controls and the 1986 Big Bang reforms transformed London's role in global finance (Augar 2000). By the end of the 1980s, major capitalist economies – the UK, the US and Japan – had dismantled capital controls, aligning with Minsky's vision of globally integrated but fragile financial capitalism. This expansion was not without consequence. It entrenched fictitious capital, which has become institutionalized: enshrined in law, normalized through accounting standards and stabilized via financial intermediation. In essence, asset managers do not only govern productive enterprise, but rather the circulation of expectations.

This speculative logic underpins the volatility and inequality that characterize the contemporary global economy. Crucially, it also shapes the political economy of *climate inaction* (Doganova 2024). Discounting – a technique used to convert future income into present value – has evolved from a seemingly neutral financial calculation into a political technology, one that translates climate uncertainty into numerical form, foregrounding investor priorities while marginalizing long-term ecological risks (Stern 2008). In doing so, it perpetuates inaction by subordinating environmental urgency to financial calculus: the future becomes governable only insofar as it is profitable. Complex questions of ownership, risk and sustainability are thus reframed as matters of valuation, transferring control over uncertain futures to private investors and undermining collective governance (Doganova 2024).

This dynamic is linked to the rise of asset managers as a new ruling class (Braun 2021), whose dominance is sustained not only by financial power, but also by legal frameworks, valuation norms and professional practices (Braun & Koddenbrock 2023; Clark 2000). This ascendancy renders money managers not stewards of economic stability, but, as Minsky (1993) warned, as architects of systemic volatility. In this context, the analytical shift from institutional forms to institutional processes underscores that institutions are not static containers of social life; rather, they are dynamic constructions shaped through social and spatial practices (cf. Beer *et al.* 2005; Boschma & Frenken 2009; Blyth *et al.* 2011). Although embedded in broader economic networks, institutions are continually redefined by geographies of contestation and adaptation (Wood & Valler 2001).

This dynamic is particularly evident in the ongoing economization of law and the expansion of legal territoriality – especially in finance, where jurisdiction extends beyond physical borders to encompass epistemic authority and regulatory reach. Essentially, territoriality is about how space becomes territory through practices of power, identity and control – whether by a nation-state, an economic actor, or a community. It's both material and symbolic, and always political (Storey 2020). Against this backdrop, taking the financial centre as a unit of analysis offers a valuable lens through which to examine these evolving dynamics. Legal innovations are not merely enabling but instrumental: they are strategically deployed and commercialized to generate financial and parafinancial economic opportunity. This transformation of law into an economic resource reflects both the commercialization of professional legal systems and the mobilization of state-backed legal infrastructures to support financial accumulation, especially in and through financial centres. This interplay remains underexplored, and this book seeks to address that gap.

Financial centres as assemblages of authority

Given that financialization shapes the logic of capitalism and assetization redefines value, financial centres serve as the spatial and institutional assemblages through which these dynamics are enacted and consolidated. Far from being passive sites of exchange, they serve as hubs of infrastructural, legal and epistemic power – command nodes in the architecture of global financial capitalism. Indeed, cities such as London, New York, Singapore and Luxembourg are not merely agglomerations of capital; they can also be understood as *legal laboratories* where jurisdictional engineering, regulatory arbitrage and elite professional services converge under the auspices of the state. Within these spaces, financial and legal professionals operate through the broader FABS economy – mainly finance, accountancy, business and legal services – constructing the frameworks that facilitate financial expansion while remaining largely insulated from accountability.

Indeed, these powerful economic clusters of FABS within IFCs are central to the territorial extension of financial capitalism. Embedded in cities, they enable global value transfers and allow specific actors to reshape the global economy to their advantage. Thus, uneven development is not only reproduced within cities but *through* them. The appropriation of global surplus by core regions depends on the agency exercised through these urban nodes (Hadjimichalis 1984). As Braudel (1984) noted, cities act as engines of accumulation – and sites where mechanisms of domination are forged. The unique socio-material infrastructures of cities, that is, the "genius of cities" (Storper 2013: 9), can create spaces for innovation, extraction and contestation. Whether this agency yields climate-neutral technologies or exploitative financial instruments depends, however, on the direction of social and institutional forces (see Parnreiter 2024).

Harnessing this urban genius, financial centres – backed by sovereign states – have, over time, actively expanded their territorial and legal reach. They have leveraged state authority and regulatory capacity to cultivate environments conducive to capital accumulation, often through legal pluralism, regulatory arbitrage and offshoring. Yet, a comprehensive theoretical account of how legal strategies stabilize an otherwise volatile financial architecture remains underdeveloped. Minsky's (1986) insight that financial stability breeds instability over time remains particularly pertinent for assessing the systemic risks embedded in the globally expanding interconnected IFCs.

The expansion of financial territory has been accompanied by the rise of epistemic authority among professional groups – lawyers, accountants, financial analysts – whose knowledge systems underpin the ongoing reproduction of financialization. Inter-urban competition, propelled by neoliberal performance metrics, has further intensified this dynamic (Kay 2016). Financial centres, for example, compete for global status, regulatory advantage, and capital inflows and throughputs (Budd 1995; Musschoot *et al.* 2023; Pan *et al.* 2017; Sigler *et al.* 2023; Storme *et al.* 2019). Other, smaller IFCs such as Dublin, Singapore and Luxembourg have strategically leveraged these particular dynamics to exert disproportionate influence in a globalized financial and economic system (Wójcik *et al.* 2022), particularly when considered in relation to their relatively modest size, contributing to a reconfigured architecture of power.[10] While financial centres are widely acknowledged as strategic nodes of global finance, the interaction between their institutional architectures and expanding jurisdictions has received limited theoretical attention.

Given this book's focus on legal innovation, it also challenges the broad, often uncritical definition of institutions. Social scientists have often reduced institutions to merely the "rules of the game" (North 1990: 3), providing stability to social and economic activity while simultaneously reflecting historically contingent and relational dynamics. The institutional turn in the social sciences – particularly within economic geography (see Cumbers *et al.* 2003; Gertler 2018; Wood & Valler 2001) – has since shifted emphasis towards institutionalization as a process: how institutions are constructed, negotiated and reconfigured through social practice (MacKinnon 2009). This book foregrounds the evolving construction of institutions as central to its analysis.

Such a lens reveals that financial institutions and centres do not merely mirror market logic; they actively produce and institutionalize it, shaping both the spatial and moral economies of our time. Financial centres thus thrive on yet another paradox: they render capital mobile while securing its returns. Through flexible legal instruments, transnational corporate structures and cross-border ownership chains, they facilitate the frictionless movement of capital while anchoring profits within favourable tax and regulatory regimes. This territorial duality – fluid capital, fixed authority – places financial centres at the heart of the asset economy. Moreover, these centres compete not only for investment flows but for epistemic legitimacy. Rankings, indices and global benchmarks fuel inter-urban rivalry, prompting states to recalibrate legal and regulatory regimes to attract capital – often at the expense of transparency, environmental protections and public accountability. This has led to what might be termed the financialization of jurisdiction: the *strategic* manipulation of legal space to accommodate and accelerate financial flows under the guise of economization. Yet economization is not the economy.

Critically, the power of financial centres is not merely economic, but institutional and symbolic. They project an image of efficiency, inevitability and global integration, reinforcing the narrative that finance is the engine of economic growth. Yet behind this veneer lies a deeply uneven geography – one that concentrates wealth in (some parts of) global cities while offloading volatility, risk and ecological cost onto peripheral regions. Understanding financial centres as assemblages of authority allows us to see that finance is not only produced through practices and metrics, but through space: via legal architectures, built environments and professional jurisdictions. IFCs are thus not simply facilitators of capital; they are its institutional manifestations – both cause and consequence of an economic order in which capital is sovereign and climate breakdown becomes collateral damage.

Addressing the financial roots of ecological crisis requires confronting the spatial architectures that sustain them. While financial centres have traditionally been viewed as drivers of national prosperity through finance-led growth, this perspective overlooks their embeddedness in a global financial system that accelerates environmental degradation and breaches planetary boundaries, threatening long-term sustainability. As financialization deepened, regulation and law, rather than acting as neutral infrastructure, have been steadily recalibrated to favour elite actors – chief among them, finance. To adapt meaningfully to climate change requires more than ecological policy. Finance can no longer be treated as a passive tool simply to be mobilized; it must also be re-politicized. Wealth accumulation has become increasingly detached from productive output, yielding a system grounded in long-term asset appreciation and rent extraction, rather than genuine economic growth (Adkins *et al.* 2020). In this reconfiguration of capitalism, assets become both the measure and the vehicle of wealth, reinforcing a reductive conception of *economic* value with significant implications for inequality, resilience and ecological sustainability.

This dynamic aligns with the foundational logic of neoclassical economics, to which – motivated by a financialized understanding of GDP and the accompanying presumption that any transaction is economically inherently valuable – most financial institutions, financial centres and financial policy continue, misleadingly, to subscribe: no price, no value.

Methodology and structure

This chapter has laid the foundation for a critical reappraisal of contemporary finance – one that begins not with markets, but with questions of power; not with scarcity, but with structure. The five thematic pillars introduced here – financialization and assetization, legal innovation, economic value, the asset management industry and the spatial and epistemic/epistemological expansion of financial authority – offer a conceptual scaffold for understanding how these interwoven dynamics co-produce the systemic inertia that continues to obstruct not only meaningful climate action but also the possibility of a more sustainable and productive reorientation of economic activity. Finance, in this sense, is not merely a resource to be mobilized in service of sustainability. The persistent failure to align financial markets with sustainability imperatives – both ecological and social – cannot be attributed to technical deficiencies alone. Rather, it reflects the structural entrenchment of rentier logics, speculative valuation and jurisdictional arbitrage, revealing finance not only as a facilitator, but increasingly as a constraint.

At the heart of this book lies a central contention: that the climate crisis cannot be adequately understood – let alone addressed – without interrogating the legal and spatial infrastructures that underwrite the durability of financialization. From property rights and limited liability to financial centres and offshore jurisdictions, the reproduction of financial power is *inseparable* from legal form and territorial strategy. The chapters that follow build upon this foundational claim by turning to the asset management industry, financial professionals and the shifting geographies of global financial governance. They approach finance not as an abstract economic process, but as a legally constituted, spatially embedded and professionally mediated phenomenon. In doing so, they challenge the prevailing orthodoxy that treats finance as a mere adjunct to the "real economy", and instead reframe it as a central – and contested – organizing logic of the contemporary world.

This book examines the evolving geographies of finance through a relational and spatial ontology, understanding finance as an assemblage of institutions, actors, infrastructures and ideologies. It draws from economic geography, political economy and socio-legal studies to trace how global circuits of capital are materialized in specific places, professional practices and legal forms. Central to this analysis is the concept of *legal geographies* – the dynamic interplay between law and space (Blomley *et al.* 2001) – through which financial centres are reconfigured as strategic sites of (economic) value creation and governance. The book focuses particularly on the asset economy, where the processes of assetization and asset management are reshaping economic structures, with IFCs at the core.

The aim is to develop a refined analytical lens for understanding how legal innovation – a mechanism ostensibly designed to foster stability – paradoxically contributes to systemic volatility under the expansionist logic of financial capitalism. Given the emergent nature of this field, the book prioritizes empirical substantiation over definitive conclusions, while addressing the misalignment between existing legal-economic structures and the imperative for sustainable social and ecological futures. In doing so, it also reveals the diminishing explanatory power of conventional theories in economics and economic geography, laying the foundation for a broader research agenda and future empirical in-depth explorations.

To fully grasp the complexity of financial centres, their global networks and their evolving dynamics, the book adopts a methodology that bridges macrostructural analysis with micro-level practice. Here, Sassen's (2006) assemblage theory proves a particularly valuable lens, emphasizing interconnectedness, fluidity and the contingent nature of power, meaning and social order. This perspective challenges rigid structuralist accounts by demonstrating how financial instruments, governance mechanisms and legal innovations interact dynamically across spatial and institutional scales. This approach highlights the perceived stability of financial capitalism, which may obscure underlying structural instabilities, a concern that becomes especially relevant in the context of addressing the challenges posed by risks related to climate change. By systematically linking diverse data sources[11] through this approach, the book foregrounds processes of institutionalization and spatial reconfiguration – both deeply embedded in, and facilitative of, broader processes of economization (Çalışkan & Callon 2009). Avoiding the framing of financialization as an "empty signifier" – stretched too broadly to retain analytical clarity – this analysis follows Engelen's (2008) call to examine concrete cases in order to uncover its driving forces *and* causes.

One emblematic case is the staggering rise of paper wealth, now approaching $300 trillion (McKinsey Global Institute 2023), encapsulated in *The Asset Economy* (Adkins *et al.* 2020). The interplay between assets, assetization and asset management is not merely descriptive, but appears to influence broader shifts in the socio-economic order. IFCs play a significant role in this process, with implications for socio-ecological systems – particularly in the context of climate change.

The book unfolds across five analytical chapters, beginning with an introductory study of the asset economy and culminating in a spatial analysis of law and financial centres. Chapter 2 examines the global asset management industry, tracing its concentration in the Anglo-American core and its dependence on supporting financial infrastructures. It explores the emergence of what Marxist theory refers to as fictitious capital and the speculative volatility characteristic of asset-backed markets, underpinned by what Weeks (2024) terms "financial plumbers": the ecosystems within IFCs that facilitate and reinforce processes of financialization, particularly in the context of the Americanization of finance. Chapter 3 introduces the concept of global production networks (GPNs) of finance, revisiting, for example, the conventional view of the firm as a legal fiction. It argues that law and legal personhood – not merely business strategy – play a constitutive role in shaping economic and spatial outcomes. IFCs, understood as complex assemblages of authority, emerge as critical intersections of legal innovation and the ongoing processes of financialization.

Chapter 4 focuses on the FABS professions – finance, accounting and law – and their role in shaping contemporary economic transformations. It explores how these professions align financial engineering with epistemological authority, extending jurisdictional control while embedding financial logics within regulatory structures. The interplay between firms, professionals and the state reveals how national monopolies of epistemological authority can simultaneously constrain and facilitate the global expansion of professional authority. Chapter 5 analyses financial centres as strategic sites for capital attraction and legal arbitrage. It examines their role in the proliferation of legal structures, such as limited partnerships and financial corporations, and the tension between economic growth, including fee-based incorporation services, and the potential for regulatory dilution as jurisdictions compete to attract business. While IFCs contribute significantly to financial economic activity, the societal benefits derived from these activities may not be widely distributed. Chapter 6 turns to the socio-ecological costs associated with financial centres, along with the enabling role of the state. It critiques the design of climate policies that prioritize economic metrics, such as cost-efficiency and market-based mechanisms, while giving comparatively less attention to social dimensions, an imbalance that may contribute to socio-spatial inequalities. The chapter calls for a rethinking of regulatory approaches capable of responding to the interconnected challenges of finance and socio-ecological sustainability.

In *Future Finance*, financialization is understood not as a mere extension of finance, but as a deeper process by which financial investment reorganizes society, reshapes power relations and redefines value. It is not just a trend but a systemic transformation. The creation of paper wealth hinges on global capital markets, distinct from national credit and banking systems.

This book develops the argument that financial centres and law, though distinct, function together as infrastructures of global finance. Both serve as sites of legal-financial innovation, shaping access and control, from which IFCs emerge as assemblages of power: institutional spaces where legal and spatial mechanisms are deployed to reshape the global financial order. Analysing global finance through the lens of IFCs reveals how the financial architecture is maintained, and the trade-offs it entails for socio-ecological sustainability.

This approach offers a forensic, interdisciplinary perspective on the contradictions between finance as a proposed solution to climate and inequality, and finance as a structural driver of those crises. It introduces a novel framework for analysing the limits of sustainable finance in the asset economy. By advancing a legal-geographical lens, *Future Finance* argues that addressing the climate crisis requires not only rethinking financial flows but transforming the legal infrastructures that underpin them as strategic economic resources. It interrogates assetization as a technique through which social and ecological systems are subordinated to financial imperatives, revealing how financialization proceeds under the guise of asset creation. As IFCs become integral to national economic growth strategies, they deepen integration with volatile global markets while consolidating socio-spatial control. By unpacking the interplay between law and finance, *Future Finance* offers a structural critique of legal-financial expansionism.

2

DYNAMIC ARCHITECTURES OF THE ASSET ECONOMY

Private equity: a (re)emerging money manager

In *The Finance Curse* (2018), Nicholas Shaxson argues that the excessive influence of global finance undermines overall prosperity, transforming finance into a self-serving system. Arcand *et al.* (2012) assert that having "too much finance" in the financial system can be perilous, and the 2007/08 financial crisis highlighted how certain countries had developed disproportionately large financial systems as compared to their domestic economies. In essence, finance has re-engineered large parts of the global economic order not to generate wealth but to extract it from the underlying economy. In recent decades, financial companies have shifted from revenue models centred on interest from lending to those based on fees, premiums, spreads and commissions, driven by the creation and sale of increasingly complex financial products. This evolution has significantly increased both the volume and complexity of financial instruments traded and introduced a proliferation of financial companies. Among the most contentious players are PE firms.

In a nutshell, PE firms raise funds from institutional and accredited investors to acquire, manage and ultimately sell companies for profit (Chen 2024). PE firms typically purchase entire private or public companies, often through buyouts, but generally refrain from holding shares in publicly traded firms. Unlike venture capital (VC) firms, which focus on start-ups, most PE firms and funds invest in more mature companies. In the context of financing Europe's sustainability transition, proponents of PE highlight its role as a key financier and challenge the common "misconception" of PE firms acting like "locusts" on the economy (*Der Spiegel* 2006).[1] Critics, however, argue that PE funds acquire companies using high leverage, strip them of assets, cut jobs and provide little economic or consumer benefit (Feldman & Kenney 2024). However, as Adveq (2013: 4), a consultancy firm, points out, PE contributes significantly to the economy, both directly and indirectly, a stance that has since been adopted by the European

Commission in its efforts to finance (parts of) the Green Deal.[2] In the specific context of financing Europe's sustainability and net-zero transition, proponents firmly maintain that PE

> is a highly active and long-term oriented ownership model. As such, it is able to make significant, sizable and rapid changes to companies. Therefore, the private equity industry offers one of the most effective approaches for responsible investors to push the implementation of ESG principles in companies. [...] The long term perspective of private equity investments allows full implementation of ESG measures and to return a profit to investors through the resulting increase in enterprise value. [...] The comparatively high ownership fragmentation of public companies makes it much more difficult for their investors to push through the necessary change. Private equity has grasped ESG as an opportunity both to reduce the risk of investments and to increase returns from them. The asset class drives the implementation of ESG principles on all levels from investors, through fund managers, and into portfolio companies. (Adveq 2013: 12)

Often underestimated in its broader influence beyond its strategic control over acquired assets, PE is, among other things, a hallmark of money manager capitalism (Minsky 1993; Table 1.1). PE firms are critical to study as they now serve not only as key vehicles for green investments – such as by acquiring small and medium-sized enterprises in Europe, often hidden champions in their own global market niches, as well as large-scale green and digital infrastructure – but also as important investment intermediaries for institutional investors, such as pension funds and endowments. PE exemplifies how financial motives and strategies can significantly shift both the economic and corporate landscapes. Traditionally, PE firms have focused on key performance indicators such as the size of their asset portfolios, income streams and profits realized upon exiting investments. These indicators have, in turn, shaped PE industry rankings (see Table 2.1). Yet, they fall far short of capturing the materiality – or the concrete, on-the-ground impacts – of their investments.

Appelbaum and Batt (2014) effectively demonstrate how PE firms emerged from a complex blend of overlapping policies and regulations beginning in the late 1970s, soon evolving into pivotal players in the US. This shift led to a transition from a managerial to a finance-centred business model, accompanied by the promotion of the shareholder value-maximization principle. PE firms wield significant influence owing to their use of high levels of debt (leverage) to acquire ownership and control of their portfolio companies, with the primary aim of increasing company value and delivering high returns on investment

(ROI) for both the PE firm (acting as the general partner, GP) and its investors (limited partners, LPs). The latter typically comprise institutional investors such as pension funds, endowments, insurance companies and ultra-high-net-worth individuals (UHNWI, including family offices), from whom PE firms raise substantial pools of capital (see Table 2.1). In the leverage economy[3] of recent decades, characterized by readily accessible and inexpensive debt,[4] PE firms have long flourished by leveraging "other people's money" (Kay 2016), thereby facing minimal downside risk themselves. Unlike VC or hedge funds, the reliance on external debt is a distinctive feature of PE. As major financial investors today, PE firms offer a lens through which to view the dynamics of a fusion of legal and commercial ecosystems in modern financial economies; processes that predominantly unfold in and through financial centres.

The concentration of PE in the US as its primary backbone, compared to other countries, is striking. Equally notable is the sheer volume of investment capital raised to be channelled through PE funds (see Table 2.1). However, to fully grasp their far-reaching implications for the real economy and society, it is useful first to examine the commercial emergence of PE strategies, their geographic reach and organizational models. The rise of PE firms, rooted in the shareholder-value revolution and leveraged buyout (LBO) movements of the 1970s, has transformed corporate structures and management practices. Beginning in the 1950s, a series of institutional shifts in the US, both within and beyond industrial corporations, began to erode the managerial capitalism that had shaped the preceding 50 years. Key institutional transformations included modifications to corporate, tax and pension laws that enabled financial institutions to amass and direct large pools of capital towards productive innovation.

This shift reduced companies' reliance on traditional equity and bond offerings initiated by corporations. In tandem with these legal changes, a new epistemological framework emerged in academia: agency theory (Jensen & Meckling 1979). The agency theory of the firm provided the theoretical foundation for replacing corporate managers with investor-managers, thereby spurring the LBO movement in the 1980s and facilitating the rapid growth of PE firms in the 2000s (Appelbaum & Batt 2014; see also Figure 6.1). Together, these legal and theoretical shifts entrenched PE firms' role in reshaping corporate governance and the broader economy. In the pivotal 1980s, a new generation of financiers invaded the management-controlled corporation through LBOs, embedding financial engineering models at the heart of finance-based management practices. By the 1990s, Wall Street had thoroughly institutionalized the shareholder-value model of corporate management and diffused it across non-financial sectors of the economy.

While the law classifies PE firms and their funds as investors, in practice, PE firms act as managers of the companies they acquire and sell, as well as de

Table 2.1 Largest PE firms globally, comparison 2023 and 2024

2024 rank*	Fund manager	Headquarters	5-year fundraising total ($ million)	Year founded
▶ 1	Blackstone Inc.	New York City, US	123,993** 125,612***	1985
▶ 2	KKR	New York City, US	103,241 103,713	1976
▶ 3	EQT Partners	Stockholm, SE	99,123 101,660	1994
▲ 4	CVC Capital Partners	Luxembourg, LU	77,570 41,750	1981
▲ 5	TPG Inc.	Fort Worth, US	61,934 54,965	1992
▼ 6	The Carlyle Groupe	Washington DC, US	60,178 69,681	1987
▼ 7	Thoma Bravo	Chicago, US	59,060 74,093	2008
▼ 8	Advent International	Boston, US	52,939 52,939	1984
▲ 9	Warburg Pincus	New York City, US	51,730 48,534	1966
▼ 10	Hg	London, UK	51,365 51,046	2000
▲ 11	Clayton, Dubilier & Rice	New York City, US	50,039 41,082	1978
▼ 12	Silver Lake	Menlo Park, US	49,121 48,281	1999
▲ 13	Hellman & Friedman	San Francisco, US	46,715 40,925	1984
▲ 14	Vista Equity Partners	Austin, US	45,262 41,500	2000
▼ 15	General Atlantic	New York City, US	43,482 48,696	1980
▼ 16	Clearlake Capital Group	Los Angeles, US	42,941 43,697	2006
▼ 17	Goldman Sachs Asset Management	New York City, US	42,432 45,358	1986
▲ 18	Leonard Green & Partners	Los Angeles, US	40,870 39,465	1989
19	TA Associates	Boston, US	40,000 /	1968
20	Permira Advisers	London, UK	37,322 /	1985
/	Bain Capital	Boston, US	/ 44,347	1984
/	Insight Partner	New York City, US	/ 40,166	1995

* As compared with 2023.
** January 2019–December 2023.
*** January 2018–December 2022.

Source: Private Equity International 2024b, 1 June 2023 and 31 December 2023.

facto employers of those companies' workers (Appelbaum & Batt 2014). This legacy warrants close scrutiny: general partners (GPs) in PE firms typically face less shareholder and investor pressure, public scrutiny and regulatory oversight than publicly traded corporations. Limited partners (LPs), usually institutional investors, commit capital, often up to a decade, which can reduce transparency and weaken GP accountability. This regulatory gap enables PE firms to take on substantial debt, pursue high-risk strategies and engage in financial engineering, including the use of junk bonds, asset stripping and dividend recapitalizations. Structured as limited partnerships,[5] PE firms also benefit from favourable tax treatment, paying lower capital gains rates compared to standard corporate tax rates.

As the managerial model gradually gave way to the financial model, the original separation of ownership and control was effectively dismantled. This separation was first articulated by Berle and Means in their 1932 classic, *The Modern Corporation and Private Property*. Prior to their analysis, ownership and control had generally been assumed to go hand in hand. Initially, this divide enabled managers to oversee capital accumulation and reinvest retained earnings in technology, machinery, skills, research and development, or strategic acquisitions. In this arrangement, Wall Street served Main Street: shareholders received steady dividends, while workers benefited from rising wages that underpinned mass consumption (see Minsky 1992, 1996). Despite its shortcomings, the managerial model allowed both employees and consumers to share in the gains of rising productivity. During this period, core sectors such as banking, telecommunications, airlines, healthcare and education were heavily regulated, ensuring broad and affordable access to essential services. Service labour markets remained largely local, shielding them from global competition and sustaining the commercial resilience of local communities. However, the low profitability of US conglomerates – exacerbated by the recession and stagflation of the 1970s – sparked shareholder discontent, criticisms of corporate management and widespread dissatisfaction with the managerial model. This discontent ultimately catalysed a shift towards improving shareholder returns, leading to the dismantling of the managerial model in the late 1970s (Appelbaum & Batt 2014).

Milton Friedman's influential 1970 article, alongside the works of other Chicago School economists, argued that maximizing profits is the sole purpose of corporations, providing academic legitimacy for the emerging financial model that quickly gained traction. This perspective encouraged economists to apply economic theory to corporate law, culminating in the development of agency theory (Jensen & Meckling 1979). Agency theory (misleadingly) posits that shareholders are the principals – and thus the residual claimants – of the corporation, while directors and corporate managers act as agents tasked with maximizing shareholder profits. In this regard, "[a]gency theory turned corporate law on its head" (Appelbaum & Batt 2014: 19). While this framework has become embedded in economic orthodoxy, public policy and business practice, legal scholars argue that, in law and precedent, corporations are recognized legal persons, distinct from their shareholders (Robé 2011): upon incorporation, founders appoint a board of directors to act on behalf of the corporation itself, which may subsequently issue shares. From this legal standpoint, directors are the true principals, while shareholders are merely one class of contractual agents – akin to bondholders, suppliers or employees – who hold stock under a contract.

Crucially, legal theory maintains that corporations are required to act lawfully, and that shareholder value represents only one among several legitimate purposes. This interpretation carries significant implications for corporate accountability and liability, particularly in instances where *obligations to society* are breached (Robé 2020). This legal interpretation stands in stark contrast to prevailing economic theory and corporate practice, which, since the 1980s, have largely embraced shareholder-value maximization as the corporation's primary objective. The rise of agency theory has entrenched a focus on maximizing share price, reshaping both the practice and perception of corporate responsibility, while reinforcing the (misleading) doctrine: no price, no value.

The immediate impact of agency theory was profound, compelling managers, particularly in low-growth industries, to return excess cash flow to shareholders, the (perceived) principals. This approach encouraged the use of debt (rather than equity) to finance new investments. Mature companies, with accumulated assets that can be used as collateral, often generate substantial free cash flow – enabling them to service debt without incurring significant financial distress. However, as Jensen (1986: 324) articulated in his concept of the "control function of debt", the imperative to repay debt kept managers "focused" on cost reduction. This pressure to deliver short-term shareholder returns paved the way for the core-competency model central to competitive-advantage discourse, which encouraged firms to concentrate on primary operations by outsourcing or divesting non-core activities – freeing up cash flow for shareholders. This financial logic reduced the autonomy of top managers and fuelled the rise of a new consultancy industry (Mazzucato & Collington 2023).

Indeed, in earlier eras, companies could mitigate financial distress by cross-subsidizing across divisions, buying time for internal reorganization or new product development. That buffering capacity, however, was largely dismantled. As a result, employees often bear the brunt of restructuring – through layoffs or intensified workloads – a pattern that persists today (Appelbaum & Batt 2014). This environment has created fertile ground for the expansion and enduring success of PE firms, which have thrived on precisely these (extractive) dynamics (cf. Kaplan & Stromberg 2009).

Asset manager capitalism

However, PE firms represent only a fraction of the long-evolving asset management industry, which itself is a spin-off of dynamics that have been developing over several decades. The roots of asset management can be traced back to the post-Second World War era, when economic growth and rising wealth levels spurred the creation of various investment vehicles. Initially focused on traditional investments such as stocks and bonds, asset managers expanded into a wide array of financial products, including hedge funds, mutual funds and, later, real estate investment trusts (REITs). The rise of institutional investors, such as pension funds, endowments and insurance companies, in the latter part of the twentieth century further catalysed the growth of asset management, driving the demand for more sophisticated strategies for portfolio diversification and risk management. This evolution led to the development of new investment approaches. As a result, asset management increasingly integrated *alternative* investment strategies, including PE, VC and hedge funds. PE firms, in particular, have capitalized on these trends by leveraging high levels of debt to acquire companies, streamline operations and ultimately enhance returns for their investors. As such, while PE plays a prominent role within the broader asset management landscape, it is just one component of an intricate and multifaceted financial ecosystem shaped by historical developments, regulatory frameworks and shifting market conditions over time (see Table 1.1). This evolution has been accompanied by significant regulatory changes, advancements in technology and shifts in market dynamics, all of which have contributed to the complexity and scale of the asset management industry today.

However, the global financial crisis of 2007/08 highlighted the risks associated with excessive financial innovation, particularly speculation and arbitrage, as well as the proliferation of complex instruments like asset-backed securities, and practices such as securitization and market risk assessment employed by both banks and non-bank financial institutions. This situation was further exacerbated by relatively lenient regulatory oversight, which facilitated a significant shift from traditional investment banking to shadow banking.[6] In this context, non-bank financial institutions such as BlackRock, Allianz and Amundi emerged as major players (Wójcik *et al.* 2018). Unlike traditional banks, asset managers primarily manage other people's money, often with little skin of their own in the game. This enables them to operate within the shadow banking system, largely escaping the scrutiny of established banking regulations (see Thiemann 2018). To illustrate this development with current figures, as of 2023, global assets in regulated open-ended funds alone reached approximately $60.1 trillion (Figure 2.1). To highlight the sheer volume and scale of the industry, these assets are distributed

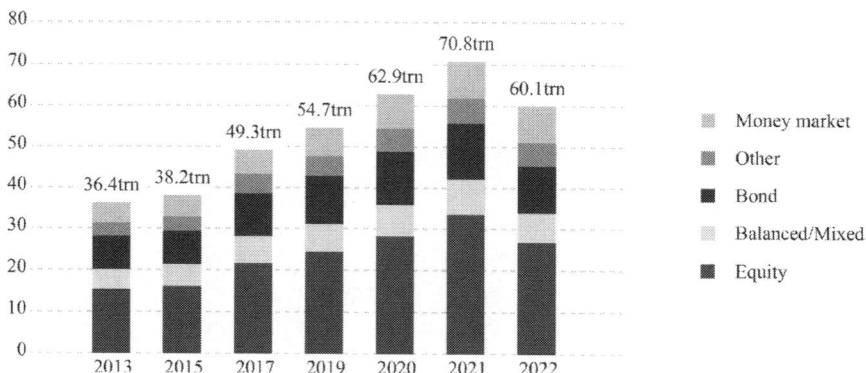

Figure 2.1 Total net assets of worldwide regulated open-end funds, in trillion dollars by type of funds, year-end[7]

Source: International Investment Funds Association 2024.

as follows: $28.6 trillion in the US, $19.1 trillion in Europe, $9.1 trillion in Asia-Pacific and $3.4 trillion in other regions (Investment Company Institute 2024). It is important to note that these assets are often financed through borrowed funds, making the financing highly leveraged and interconnected. This "art of leverage" (Sgambati 2019) extends to banks that provide funding to shadow banks, illustrating the intricate links within the financial system.

Furthermore, despite recurring financial crises and scandals – such as the Enron case, which exposed the extensive use of offshore jurisdictions such as the Cayman Islands to conceal debt, and was brought to public attention by US Senator Carl Levin during a 2002 Senate subcommittee investigation[8] – financial centres have continued to evolve into economic powerhouses and significant regional growth poles. This trajectory, consistent with orthodox economic thinking, ostensibly suggests that financial innovation – driven by collaboration among accountants, lawyers and financial professionals – is functioning at its finest. And perhaps it is – at least for them. However, the cities that host these financial centres do not always reap the income benefits typically associated with innovation-led growth and societal wellbeing. In reality, the gains from finance-driven development are highly unequally distributed. Cities with prominent financial hubs such as London, New York and Hong Kong have seen surging property prices and escalating living costs, making them increasingly unaffordable; even for dual-income middle-class households. These adverse social and urban outcomes are, in part, a direct consequence of financial innovation itself.

Financial innovation broadly involves creating new financial products, services and processes that enable firms to raise capital more effectively and at lower costs than was previously possible (Lerner & Tufano 2011). It aims to overcome inefficiencies in capital allocation that could otherwise hinder real economic innovation. Such financing activities, which include lending, investment management and the circulation of money, are thought to enhance the capacity to foster social, economic and environmental change by transforming ideas into technologies, industries and jobs (Allen & Yago 2010). This conventional narrative holds that financial innovation encompasses products, practices and instruments from various financial sub-industries. Examples include innovations in payments, such as credit cards and mobile payment apps, and in retail banking, such as ATMs, mobile banking and lending platforms, where innovation – hailed by consumers – mainly manifests as (technology-driven) efficiency gains, including organizational innovations like crowdfunding platforms.[9] Innovation in investment banking, encompassing derivatives, mortgage-backed securities and more recent techniques like supply-chain financing (such as the securitization methods employed by the now-defunct Greensill Bank), is increasingly met with ambivalence. The rapid expansion in the scale and complexity of financial products, alongside practices like large-scale securitization and "advanced" valuation methods, combined with relatively lax regulatory oversight, played a significant role in the global financial crisis of 2007/08. Each financial innovation, from the creation of junk bonds to the trading and pricing of risk through new insurance contracts, reveals its own unique micro-history and micro-geography. These innovations have empowered asset managers and banks, while increasing demand for legal and accounting services to support sophisticated financial engineering.

Indeed, asset management is a substantial and growing sector within global finance, entrusted with investing funds from individuals and various institutions, including banks, insurance companies, pension funds, family offices, university endowment funds and sovereign wealth funds (SWFs), among others. The scope of the industry encompasses the diversification of investments across various asset classes, such as equity and debt securities, along with alternative assets like real estate, infrastructure and nature. The management of assets plays a pivotal role in investment chains, connecting savers to companies that are issuing securities.

Investment funds (IFs) serve as the primary vehicle for pooling investors' resources to invest in a well-defined set of assets and adhere to a clearly outlined strategy, enabling investors to access investment opportunities without direct ownership. These funds are tailored for the management of assets and securities across various asset classes and categories (Figure 2.2).[10] The surge in demand for asset management services over the past 40–50 years can be attributed to factors such as the decline of the welfare state in advanced economies, rising wealth accumulation in emerging economies and the individualization of risk, particularly in private pension provision (see Langley 2006; Adkins *et al.* 2020).

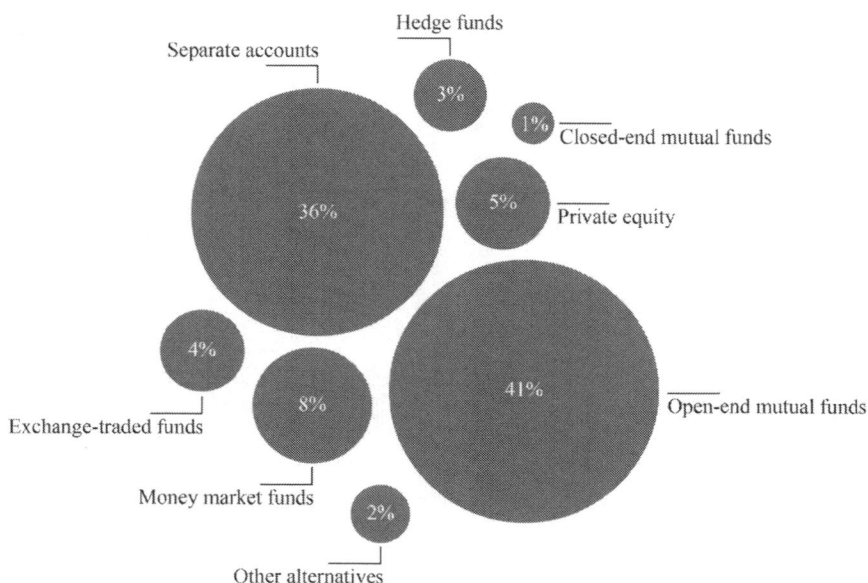

Figure 2.2 Investment vehicles according to sub-industry

Source: author, based on International Investment Funds Association 2023.

An asset manager is an individual or a firm responsible for overseeing investments on behalf of clients, which may include individuals, companies, institutions and governments. Their primary role is to manage these investments to achieve specific financial objectives, such as increasing returns, preserving capital or reducing risk. BlackRock, headquartered in New York City, stands as the largest private asset manager globally, managing a massive portfolio exceeding $11.5 trillion as of 2024 (Reuters 2025) (see Table 2.1). With 70 offices in 30 countries and clients across the world, BlackRock controls substantial amounts of capital. Investments are made using clients' capital and are typically governed by mandates set by those clients, for instance, a focus on European or North American equity markets. Asset managers usually levy a fee calculated as a percentage of assets under management (AUM), regardless of investment performance, which may at times be negative. These fees are frames as remuneration for the expertise and services rendered to capital owners. Although they invest on behalf of others, asset managers wield considerable social and economic influence due to the discretionary authority they exercise over investment decisions. For example, within the parameters of a mandate, such as investing in European equities or US corporate bonds, the asset manager determines which specific companies or issues to select. By contrast, hedge funds and PE firms often claim a share of the profits they generate. Crucially, pension funds and insurance companies – among the most prominent clients in the PE space – are increasingly in conflict with GPs over fee structures, particularly when returns fall short of expectations.[11]

Asset managers operate across a range of institutions, including investment banks, mutual funds, pension funds, insurance companies and independent asset management firms. These entities form intricate sub-economies that interact in complex ways, collectively the global financial landscape.

Institutional investors – such as insurance companies, pension funds, SWFs and endowments – allocate capital across a variety of asset classes, including PE and VC, depending on their strategies and risk appetites. Pension funds represent the largest group of LPs in PE, with major players including Singapore's Temasek Holdings and Sweden's Sixth National Pension Fund (AP Fonden 6) (Private Equity International 2024a). SWFs and endowments similarly channel capital to PE in pursuit of higher returns.[12] Insurance companies, too, are increasingly turning to PE to diversify portfolios and improve long-term performance, although their participation varies by regulatory context and internal policy. Table 2.2 illustrates the significant capital flows from leading SWFs into PE by the end of 2023.

Understanding the roles and relationships among funds, fund managers and investors (who may themselves be funds) is essential for grasping the incentives and underlying economics of the asset management industry. Funds, which pool capital from multiple investors, are established to invest in securities or other assets and exist in various forms – mutual funds, exchange-traded funds (ETFs),

Table 2.2 Top ten largest PE investors

2024 rank	Institution name	Headquarters	Allocation (%)	Allocation ($ million)
1	Temasek Holdings	Singapore	52	153,428
2	CPP Investments	Toronto	32	141,885
3	GIC Private Limited	Singapore	17	130,900
4	Mubadala Investment Company	Abu Dhabi	34	101,957
5	Abu Dhabi Investment Authority (ADIA)	Abu Dhabi	10	98,400
6	California Public Employees' Retirement System	Sacramento	14	67,882
7	China Life Insurance Company	Beijing	8	65,158
8	Caisse de dépôt et placement du Québec (CDPQ)	Montréal	18	60,318
9	APG Asset Management	Amsterdam	9	57,182
10	Hong Kong Monetary Authority	Hong Kong	10	52,749

Source: Global Investor 150.

hedge funds, pension funds and more. These are managed by fund or portfolio managers, who allocate assets in line with defined investment objectives such as growth, income generation or capital preservation. Acting under mandates often outlined in the fund's prospectus, fund managers bring expertise in financial analysis, market dynamics, risk management and asset allocation.

Investors – whether individuals, institutions (such as pension funds) or high-net-worth clients – allocate capital to these funds with the expectation of returns. Given their diversity, investor objectives vary widely. In some cases, however, funds themselves act as investors (such as funds managed by pension managers), allocating capital into other funds or asset classes as part of broader portfolio strategies. Technically speaking, a notable example is the fund of funds (FoF), which invests exclusively in other funds (Hudson 2014).

Thus, the following section delves into the spatial economics of investment funds and explores how the legal design of complex fund structures contributes to processes of economization. Building on Çalışkan and Callon's (2009) view that the "economic" is constructed through social and material practices, this analysis highlights how legal personhood and fund architecture – far from being neutral – allocate property rights and responsibilities. These complex legal-institutional arrangements are routinely overlooked by economic orthodoxy, yet, as Robé (2020: 31) argues, this "World Wide Web of Contracts" reveals the concentration of property rights within financial firms.

Investment funds and their economics

Both FoFs and umbrella funds are collective investment vehicles, although they serve different purposes and operate under distinct structural frameworks (see Hudson 2014 for a technical overview). FoFs invest in a portfolio of other funds, such as mutual funds, hedge funds or PE funds, rather than directly in securities, enabling diversification across managers, strategies and asset classes. Their legal structure varies and may include regulated vehicles like Undertakings for Collective Investment in Transferable Securities (UCITS) within the European Union. By contrast, umbrella funds (also known as multi-compartment funds) consolidate multiple sub-funds under a single legal structure. Each sub-fund operates independently, with its own investment strategy, objectives and management team, while benefiting from shared administrative infrastructure. Whereas FoFs represent a second layer of investment by allocating capital into other funds, umbrella sub-funds typically invest directly in securities – representing the first layer.

Exchange-traded funds (ETFs), often (although not always) passively managed, are predominantly direct investment vehicles. Typically designed to track specific indices or benchmarks, they offer efficient and transparent market exposure. Unlike FoFs, ETFs do not add a second investment layer; they hold the underlying assets directly – be it stocks, bonds or commodities. The ETF market is largely dominated by the "Big Three": BlackRock, Vanguard and State Street (Fichtner *et al.* 2017).

PE funds differ fundamentally in structure and strategy. Rather than operating as umbrella funds, PE firms invest directly in private companies – or acquire public firms with the intent to take them private through LBOs. Typically structured as limited partnerships, PE funds are capitalized by LPs and managed by a GP, who controls the investment strategy. PE firms pursue returns through operational improvements, financial engineering and strategic exits such as secondary sales or IPO (Appelbaum & Batt 2014). Despite a currently "challenging" fundraising environment, the PE sector remains robust. As of December 2023, the top 100 investors had committed approximately $2.3 trillion to PE – an 8.5 per cent increase from the previous year. Average allocations have also risen, indicating sustained LPs' interest despite caution.[13]

Insurance companies are central institutional players in the asset management ecosystem. By collecting premiums from individuals and businesses in exchange for risk coverage, they accumulate substantial investable capital. These funds are deployed into financial markets to generate returns sufficient to cover claims and ensure profitability. Berkshire Hathaway, under Warren Buffett, is the world's largest insurer by market value. Insurers diversify across asset classes, including fixed income, real estate and increasingly PE, to outperform traditional bond-based returns, subject to regulatory constraints and internal policy. For companies, insurance functions as a redistribution of profits, while for individuals, it constitutes a household expense, with pay-outs compensating for loss or death.[14] Pension funds, established by employers, unions or states, pool long-term savings to finance retirement incomes (Clark 2000). Contributions from employees and/or employers are invested to generate sustained returns. Notably, large insurers such as Aviva also operate as pension funds.[15] ABP, the Netherlands' largest public pension fund, ranks fifth globally, despite its base in a relatively small economy.[16] Pension funds leverage consistent inflows to build diversified portfolios, investing across equities, bonds, and increasingly alternative assets such PE, infrastructure and commodities. As Braun (2022) notes, workers' savings are literally transformed into capital by these institutional investors, who play a growing role in shaping financial markets. Since the early 2000s, pension funds have entered commodity markets via futures, contributing to price dynamics shaped by global demand, supply shocks and speculative activity.[17]

Figure 2.3 illustrates the significant concentration of American firms across these investment sectors, reflecting broader patterns of financial dominance and capital centralization.

Figure 2.3 highlights the uneven global distribution of the top 100 institutional investors, segmented into three key categories: public pension funds, which

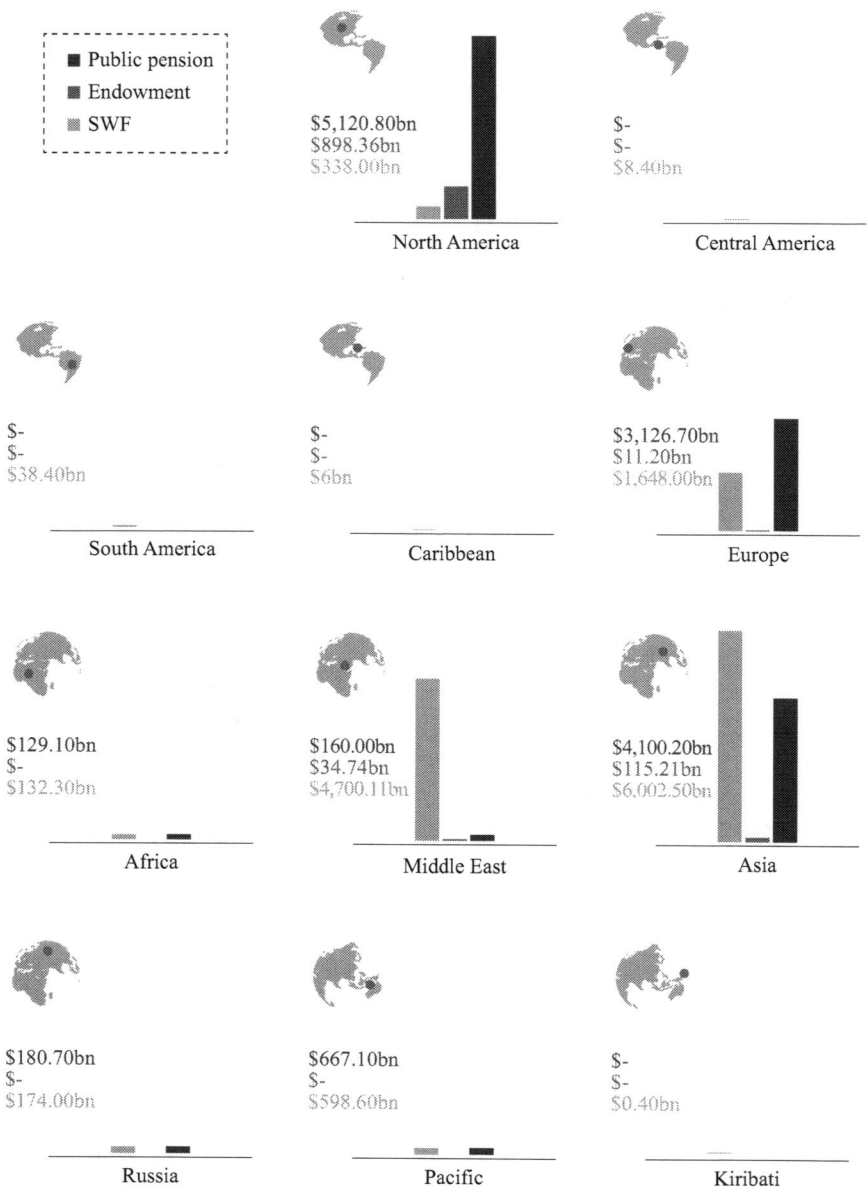

Public pension
Endowment
SWF

North America
$5,120.80bn
$898.36bn
$338.00bn

Central America
$-
$-
$8.40bn

South America
$-
$-
$38.40bn

Caribbean
$-
$-
$6bn

Europe
$3,126.70bn
$11.20bn
$1,648.00bn

Africa
$129.10bn
$-
$132.30bn

Middle East
$160.00bn
$34.74bn
$4,700.11bn

Asia
$4,100.20bn
$115.21bn
$6,002.50bn

Russia
$180.70bn
$-
$174.00bn

Pacific
$667.10bn
$-
$598.60bn

Kiribati
$-
$-
$0.40bn

Figure 2.3 Distribution of SWFs, endowment and public pension funds by region, by December 2021 (in billion dollars, different sources)[18]

are particularly concentrated in North America, Europe and Asia; endowment funds, largely associated with US universities; and SWFs, with notable hubs in Asia and the Middle East. Public SWFs alone account for approximately $12.05 trillion in AUM. These funds are managed on behalf of a wide range of sovereign entities, including countries such as Norway, China, Austria, Greece, Israel (including Palestine), as well as subnational units such as Abu Dhabi and US states such as Utah and Alabama.

SWFs are defined as "state-sponsored institutional investors that are liable only to the state and invested in accordance with a mandate defined by the interest of the state" (Dixon *et al.* 2022: 2). With long-term investment horizons, they frequently engage with global economic challenges (Alami & Dixon 2024). Established to promote fiscal stability and future growth, SWFs vary in design and purpose, rendering their macroeconomic impacts difficult to generalize. Typically, they channel revenue from natural resource exports or foreign exchange surpluses into independent investment vehicles. SWFs are commonly classified into three categories based on their strategic objectives: (1) stabilization funds to buffer national economies; (2) savings funds to preserve wealth for future generations and diversify portfolios; and (3) development or strategic funds aligned with national economic priorities (Dixon *et al.* 2022). While the largest SWFs are concentrated in Asia and the Middle East, the global centre of public pension fund activity remains in the United States, with strong representation in Asia and Europe (including the UK). This geographic pattern of institutional dominance is mirrored in the distribution of the world's leading law and other financial services firms, which play an integral role in servicing the private asset management industry.

Figure 2.4 ranks countries by the size of their SWFs, illustrating that several smaller nations manage substantial assets and that some states operate multiple funds. Notably, China and Norway are home to two of the world's largest SWFs – China Investment Corporation and Norway's Government Pension Fund Global. Singapore, despite its relatively small size, operates two major SWFs: Temasek Holdings (established in 1974) and the Government of Singapore Investment Corporation (GIC, founded in 1981). This reflects the country's fiscal discipline, strategic investment objectives and efforts to grow and diversify foreign reserves – as well as its outsized role in global finance.

To offer a striking point of comparison, the AUM of the world's largest private asset managers, such as BlackRock and Vanguard, each exceed the GDP of major national economies. In 2021, Germany's GDP was approximately $3.6 trillion, while India and the UK each recorded around $2.7 trillion. Even when combined, the total economic output of these three nations fell short of BlackRock's colossal AUM. The scale and power of BlackRock are extraordinary – and warrant careful scrutiny: It is the largest shareholder in several of the world's leading banks, including J.P. Morgan, Bank of America, Citigroup, Deutsche Bank and India's

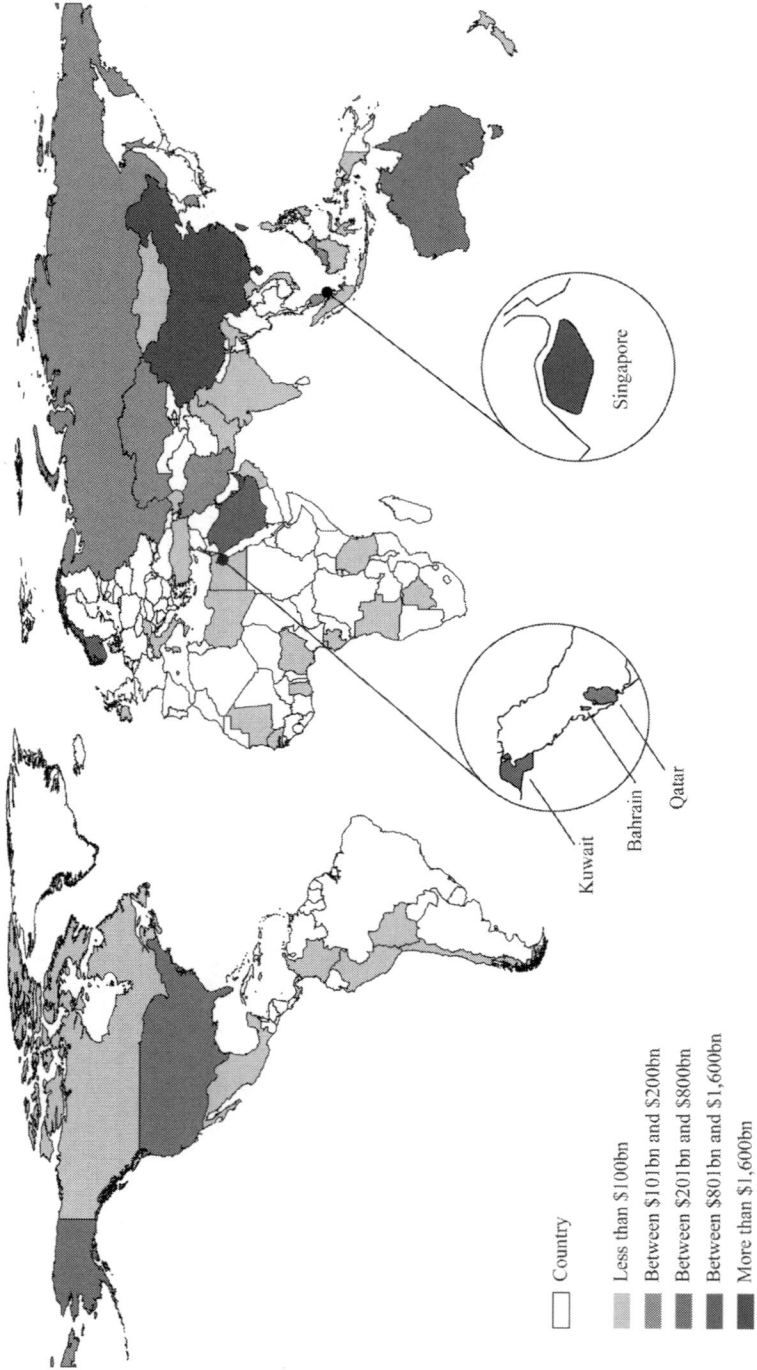

Figure 2.4 Countries hosting the 53 largest SWFs[19]

Legend:
- Country
- Less than $100bn
- Between $101bn and $200bn
- Between $201bn and $800bn
- Between $801bn and $1,600bn
- More than $1,600bn

Singapore

Kuwait
Bahrain
Qatar

HDFC Bank (Marketfeed 2021) and a major shareholder in companies such as Apple, Microsoft, NVidia, Amazon and Meta.

Lastly, it is important to distinguish between asset managers and fund providers (Figure 2.5), as they serve distinct – although occasionally overlapping – roles within the investment ecosystem. Asset managers are primarily responsible for making investment decisions on behalf of clients. They actively manage portfolios, selecting and trading assets to meet defined objectives, tailored to each client's goals, risk tolerance and time horizon. Prominent asset managers include BlackRock, Vanguard and Fidelity, all of which are engaged in active investment decision-making. In contrast, fund providers – also known as fund sponsors or fund companies – create and offer investment funds (IFs), such as mutual funds, ETFs and hedge funds. Fund providers are responsible for designing a fund's structure (delegated to a lawyer), determining its investment strategy, setting fees and managing operational aspects such as regulatory compliance, reporting and distribution. Funds act as legal persons for channelling capital into underlying investments. Notable fund providers include T. Rowe Price, Charles Schwab and State Street Global Advisors.

Confusion can arise because some firms, including BlackRock and Vanguard, operate in both capacities – managing their own funds while also making investment decisions. The core distinction lies in their primary function: asset managers focus on managing investments on behalf of clients, while fund providers oversee the creation, structuring and administration of investment funds, often employing multiple asset managers.

Law firms in flux

While fund providers are responsible for the design and operational management of investment funds – including compliance, reporting and customer service – law firms play a pivotal role in establishing the legal fund structures that enable these strategic and operational functions on behalf of fund providers. Two notable trends are shaping the evolution of the legal sector.[20] First, large corporate law firms are reassessing their previously aggressive international expansion strategies, shifting their focus towards identifying new growth markets. This recalibration has led them to follow PE firms and other asset managers into emerging regions and markets.

Second, in response to an increasingly dynamic investment landscape, PE firms have embarked on an investment spree in major law firms themselves. This trend is not driven solely by the pursuit of financial returns but by a broader strategic objective: to enhance the profitability and competitiveness of law firms, often through the implementation of cost-cutting measures and lean management

The 50 largest law firms, by revenue (US$ billion)

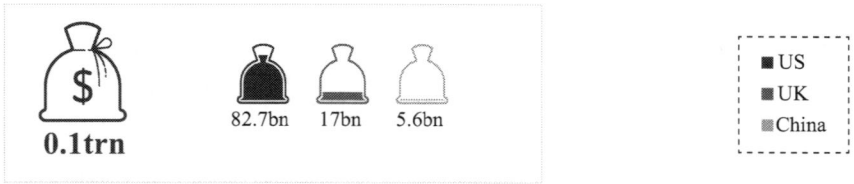

$ 0.1trn   82.7bn   17bn   5.6bn

US
UK
China

The 10 largest fund providers, by net assets (US$ trillion)

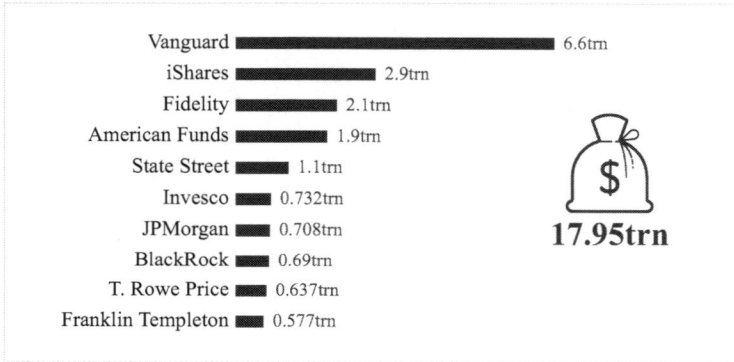

Vanguard	6.6trn
iShares	2.9trn
Fidelity	2.1trn
American Funds	1.9trn
State Street	1.1trn
Invesco	0.732trn
JPMorgan	0.708trn
BlackRock	0.69trn
T. Rowe Price	0.637trn
Franklin Templeton	0.577trn

$ 17.95trn

The 10 largest asset managers, by AUM (US$ trillion)

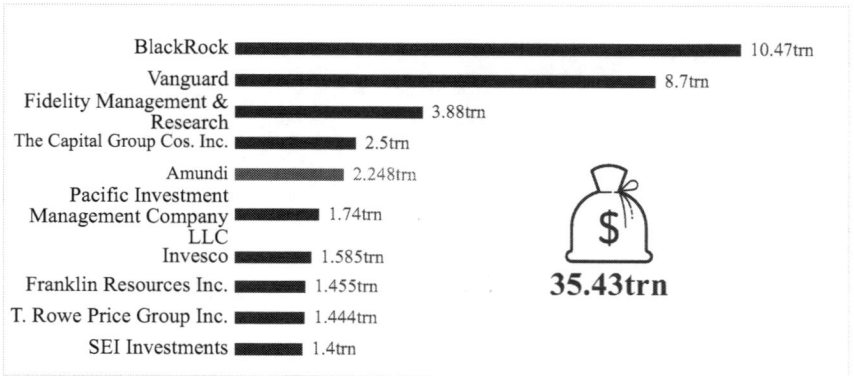

BlackRock	10.47trn
Vanguard	8.7trn
Fidelity Management & Research	3.88trn
The Capital Group Cos. Inc.	2.5trn
Amundi	2.248trn
Pacific Investment Management Company LLC	1.74trn
Invesco	1.585trn
Franklin Resources Inc.	1.455trn
T. Rowe Price Group Inc.	1.444trn
SEI Investments	1.4trn

$ 35.43trn

Figure 2.5 Revenue and geographical distribution of the world's largest law firms, compared to assets by fund providers and asset managers

Source: author, different sources.[21]

practices tailored to the rapidly evolving legal economy. Notably, between 2019 and 2024, UK law firms received approximately £1.2 billion in PE investment (Hyde 2025). Together, these trends point to a profound transformation in the growth strategies, competitive positioning and private investment dynamics of the legal industry.

On the first issue, the rapid global expansion of US law firms – particularly into markets such as China and South Africa – may be approaching its peak, or at the very least entering a phase of cautious reassessment. In the 1980s, amid China's rise as a destination for offshoring, US and UK law firms seized the opportunity to establish offices catering to both inbound and outbound investment. Firms such as Paul Weiss and Clifford Chance capitalized on this trend, setting up offices in Beijing and Hong Kong. However, recent economic and geopolitical developments have prompted strategic reconsideration. China's economic slow-down, compounded by post-pandemic challenges and a faltering property market, alongside mounting national security concerns, has made it increasingly difficult for firms to justify their continued presence. Paul Weiss and Milbank were the latest US firms to close their Beijing offices, reflecting a broader trend of withdrawal from the region. This shift signals a growing industry-wide emphasis on evaluating whether a particular office materially contributes to revenue, yields short-term gains or constitutes a key strategic market.

By contrast, Luxembourg has emerged as a priority destination. Law firms frequently cite the country's favourable tax environment, its flourishing private capital (mainly PE) sector, and the rising demand for elite legal expertise in fund structuring as central to their expansion strategies. As Luxembourg evolves into a core hub for PE firms, it has simultaneously attracted law firms aiming to strengthen their European foothold. For firms such as Herbert Smith Freehills and Simpson Thacher & Bartlett, establishing a Luxembourg presence was a clear business decision – one that contrasts with less strategic expansions into regions with more uncertain financial returns. Meanwhile, firms with a constitutionally global presence, such as DLA Piper and Baker McKenzie, are less likely to exit more volatile regions like South Africa, where longstanding international strategies necessitate sustained commitment.

What we are witnessing is a curious transition: the once-unchecked global growth of US law firms is now being tempered by a more discerning, strategically focused approach. In response to shifting geopolitical and geoeconomic realities, firms appear to have entered a new era of expansion – essentially one in which locations are assessed primarily through the lens of long-term alignment with core business objectives.

The second issue is more intricate and reveals deeper structural changes. While law firms have long operated as commercial businesses, intensifying competition, evolving market dynamics and shifting geopolitical pressures are prompting law firms to seek private investment to enhance both their financial standing and long-term strategic viability. A handful of firms have experimented with listing on public stock exchanges, although such moves remain relatively uncommon. The primary obstacle is the traditional partnership model, in which equity is collectively held by partners. However, the rise of alternative business structures (ABSs) in jurisdictions such as the UK and Australia is reshaping this landscape.[22] ABSs allow for external investment without requiring a public listing, enabling firms to attract capital while preserving elements of conventional legal practice. As a result, PE firms and other institutional investors are gaining traction in the legal sector, circumventing traditional ownership barriers. This trend draws notable parallels with the erosion of the traditional partnership model within the Big Four accountancy firms – a transformation fuelled by the vast financial resources and strategic influence of these firms. Their operations, often routed through offshore financial centres and micro- or small states, have significantly reshaped the state-capital nexus under globalization. Notable examples include the restructuring of auditor liability laws in the UK – a powerful reminder of the state's enduring role in facilitating capital accumulation and shaping global economic relations (Sikka 2008).

The legal sector continues to demonstrate robust financial performance. According to the Thomson Reuters Institute's Law Firm Financial Index, law firms recorded near-record profits in Q3 2024 – an 11.2 per cent year-on-year increase – although this growth is not limited to corporate law alone (Sloan 2025). While initial EU rulings appeared to obstruct PE investment in law firms, capital is now flowing through alternative legal and jurisdictional routes. Investors are leveraging jurisdictions such as the US, UK and Spain to bypass regulatory restrictions, subtly redrawing the boundaries of law firm financing.[23]

In parallel, many firms are exploring capitalization methods beyond ABSs. A notable strategy is service bifurcation – separating the core legal practice from a service company that manages operations, technology and human resources. This structure enables capital inflow while avoiding the regulatory burdens associated with formal ABS conversion, and is a perfect environment for PE investment. Although these firms have yet to enter the elite *AmLaw 25*, several already generate over $100 million in annual revenue, operate with minimal debt and frame their market narratives around innovation – particularly in artificial intelligence. These characteristics have caught the attention of financial investors who anticipate that momentum will extend to larger firms.

Given the estimated size of the US legal services market ($600 billion and $700 billion) and the global market's approach to the $1 trillion mark, law firms remain one of the last untapped "gold mines" for PE. As one investor put it, market participants who fail to act early may soon find themselves at a competitive disadvantage.

At the core of this analysis is the argument that the legal industry has embarked on a path toward financialization itself, aligning increasingly with the imperatives of standardization, measurability and conformity – as dictated by financial institutions, particularly PE firms. These actors' profit expectations are now instrumental in shaping the business models and practices of law firms. While these developments merit deeper exploration, this chapter focuses on a related insight: that the primary beneficiaries of these trends are the growth-driven economies of IFCs.

These jurisdictions – having positioned themselves as key hubs of financial opportunity – actively reinforce a mutually beneficial dynamic with legal and financial firms. This *firm–region nexus*, which links a financial centre's regional assets to its ability to attract global economic activity, has been explored in economic geography under the concept of strategic coupling (Hendrikse *et al.* 2020; Horner 2014; MacKinnon 2012; Yeung 2016). Although originally applied to production and innovation, this literature often presents economic development as a largely positive, growth-generating process, traditionally equating economic growth with social wellbeing.

Yet, as this chapter argues, the strategic alignment of law firms and PE capital with favourable regulatory regimes reveals implicitly a more ambivalent reality, in which regulatory arbitrage and financial extraction are not by-products, but central objectives. Drawing on the concept of economization – the process by which domains are actively made "economic" through calculative practices, devices and institutional arrangements – it is increasingly evident that the legal industry is undergoing full-scale economization. The infusion of nearly £1.2 billion into the UK legal sector by PE stresses how law is being restructured through market logics. As larger PE firms move decisively into this space, the legal field is no longer merely a professional domain but a site of strategic *financial* investment, shaped by the metrics, expectations and machinery of financial capital.

Indeed, the profit-maximizing expansion of law firms be critically examined. Law, after all, is both written and rewritten by the very firms now competing within an increasingly financialized landscape – yet it remains ultimately backed by the authority of the nation-state. What is more, PE firms are poised to invest in the very law firms that design the fund structures instrumental to PE's return optimization – complete with the occasional, strategically placed loophole. In certain domains, law appears to have become a booming marketplace in its own right. Whether this expansion of the legal sector is organic – driven by rising demand from productive industries – or synthetic – fuelled by the artificial growth of legal-financial services – remains an open question. In this regard, the currently shifting geopolitical landscape may offer little comfort to some of the largest firms, whether within or beyond the borders of the United States.

The finance and para-finance industries are in a state of flux, reshaping power hierarchies among investors, asset managers and professional service firms. These developments have further consolidated the US as the core of global finance and para-finance – encompassing sectors such as law and accountancy. While the mechanisms for signalling and attracting footloose global businesses are well established, and the economic entanglement between place and business follows familiar patterns, the implications of the *finance-led growth regime* (Boyer 2000), as realized through IFCs, extend beyond the scope of traditional regional development theory (Kitson *et al.* 2004; Pike *et al.* 2017). Rather than simply fostering economic development through productive business services, this process entrenches financial power structures, deepens economic interdependencies and sharpens the global competitiveness of a select group of financial centres. The role of IFCs in these evolving dynamics is the subject of the next chapter.

3

ASSEMBLAGES OF GLOBAL AUTHORITY

Financial centres as strategic nodes

As stated at the outset, financial centres, backed by their sovereigns, have expanded their territorial reach over recent decades, benefiting from various legal strategies at the intersection of the state and the law. However, financial centres have seldom been employed as a central analytical framework for examining financial expansion and its material impacts. Consequently, they remain a methodologically challenging object of study, in part due to the lack of sustained conceptual development around them. Sassen's (2006) assemblage methodology offers a valuable heuristic for unpacking the evolving and increasingly diffuse power dynamics within contemporary financial economies – especially when linked with the concept of economization. The key principle of economization (Çalışkan & Callon 2009) is that the "economic" is not a pre-existing domain, but is actively constructed through social and material processes. Understood as the assembly and qualification of actions, devices and practices as "economic", this perspective shifts the analytical focus from treating the economy as a given, self-contained system to examining the processes and practices through which certain – here, financial – activities and behaviours are *made* "economic".

Adopting the perspective of financial centres as assemblages of power and authority, and drawing on Doreen Massey's (2008) insight that the global is produced in the local, this chapter explores how intersecting systems – financial professions, legal frameworks, spatial configurations and the state – overlap and reinforce dominant power structures while marginalizing others. Unavoidably, the empirical analysis is selective and has its limitations. However, this chapter seeks to elucidate the finance-driven expansion mechanisms that direct our analytical focus towards an intersection that has, until now, remained in the shadows: the geographies of law and legal practice. To this end, the chapter integrates the assemblage lens with a forensic analysis of the micro-geographies and micro-histories underpinning asset-related mechanisms, which collectively stabilize a capitalist macro-regime – one that accommodates change to ensure its own per-petuation, yet remains fundamentally exposed to, and accountable for, disruption and crises. This perspective mitigates the risk of falling into the endogeneity trap inherent in the study of large-scale phenomena such as financialization, by exam-ining the causalities that have engendered the complexity and systemic nature of the asset economy (see Engelen 2008). It treats financial processes, institutions and places not as static entities but as *relational* constructs shaped by their geographies.

A global economy invariably centres on urban economies, with cities function-ing as the logistical epicentres of its operation (Braudel 1984). Finance, particu-larly asset management, is no exception. Financial centres, often characterized as the production sites of finance, host dense clusters of financial corporations, encompassing banks and non-bank financial institutions, alongside auxiliary services such as financial brokers, dealers, insurers, and law and accounting firms. These companies fall under the broader conceptual umbrella of FABS, as recently explored in a themed journal issue on "updating the advanced producer services complex" (Bassens *et al.* 2024). Collectively, they forge dynamic busi-ness ecosystems, embedded within global financial networks (Coe *et al.* 2014).

Crucially, financial expansion has long been associated with innovation (Lerner & Tufano 2011). However, as demonstrated, innovation *in finance for finance* has reshaped the financial landscape, redirecting the purpose – although not necessarily the processes – of innovation away from its textbook definition. Rather than enhancing societal welfare through improvements in production, financial innovation is increasingly geared towards an unending manipulation of global super-profits. It does so by leveraging national legal frameworks to generate continuous business opportunities for finance – a practice referred to as "legal bricolage" (see Engelen *et al.* 2010; Fourcade & Savelsberg 2006). Bricolage refers to the practice of addressing immediate social challenges by creatively repurposing available, often limited, resources. It is individuals who perform this improvisational – or bricolage – work (see Preface to this book; Iida 2023; Lévi-Strauss 1966). In this context, financial centres emerge as pivotal sites where demand for, and supply of, legal bricolage converge. They are spaces where knowledge and epistemic authority – preconditions for legal bricolage – are concentrated, and where the interface between law, geography and the state functions both as a boundary and a conduit through which capital, legal forms and ideas circulate (see Zhang & Morris 2023). These characteristics are central to the processes of economization and capitalization, enabled through arbitrage and speculation, wherein difference itself becomes a resource.

For example, the conditions for arbitrage are not merely discovered or natur-ally occurring – they are actively produced. One way is through practices such as the strategic creation of synthetic differences between places (in terms of price, time or institutional variation) and the deliberate use of legal bricolage to exploit these constructed asymmetries. As such, the multiple interfaces of financial centres can be understood as assemblages in their own right (Galloway 2012; Rose 2016). At the spatial interface – where finance intersects with urban and regional geographies – financial centres act as laboratories of innovation, spawning new business ecosystems tailored to evolving financial imperatives. At the politico-spatial interface, they may function as strategic nodes from which the geography of finance is "remapped" through expansion. Across both, novel configurations of legal territoriality and epistemic authority are forged.

Moreover, the interlacing of these interfaces further amplifies the scope for economization – what may be termed a process of hyper-economization – which unfolds in and through financial centres, often via legal and regulatory practice. Legal bricolage, in this sense, helps to underpin the spatialized and enduring power of financial centres. However, access to law and legal bricolage as economic resources – and to the creation of difference itself as a resource – remains highly selective. These privileges are tightly controlled by gatekeepers within the FABS industry and the state, who actively compete for this control – a dynamic that is reshaping the balance of gatekeeping power both within the FABS complex and in its relationship with the state.

Together, these intertwined dynamics have sustained the ongoing manipulation of global geographies of super-profits. Geographers have offered valuable insights into these processes (see Beaverstock *et al.* 2000, 2002; Faulconbridge *et al.* 2007). Bassens and Van Meeteren (2015), for instance, illustrate the deep interconnections between the FABS economy and world cities/financial centres, conceptualizing them as co-constitutive infrastructures for global super-profit generation. They demonstrate how cities such as London act as centres of financial accumulation, while peripheral spaces, including offshore jurisdictions, play structurally significant roles within core–periphery dynamics. Offshore financial jurisdictions such as Luxembourg, the Cayman Islands and the City of London extend to non-residents a legal architecture that rigorously safeguards property rights while remaining permissive in matters of taxation and oversight. Offshore finance, in its broader conceptualization, comprises a constellation of financial services intentionally inscribed in legal codes to bypass domestic regulatory regimes, often operating beneath the threshold of visibility. Indeed, far from being solely instruments of tax minimization or regulatory evasion, these structures are strategically employed by global ultra-high-net-worth individuals (UHNWIs) and corporations as mechanisms for wealth generation and capital accumulation. It is this lawful yet opaque capacity to fabricate financial value beyond the purview of the state that most profoundly undermines, for example, sovereign fiscal power (Binder 2023; Clark *et al.* 2015).

These core–periphery dynamics operate both within the "world city archipelago" and in relation to its external territories (Van Meeteren & Bassens 2016).

This underscores the role of financial centres, which often blend offshore and onshore characteristics (Haberly & Wójcik 2015a, 2015b), in sustaining the concentration of economic power in major urban centres (Leffel *et al.* 2023). More broadly, scholarship has drawn attention to the arbitrage-driven architecture of world city networks, which enables the many financial industries to capitalize on its inherent logic of spatial arbitrage – including its capacity to "do the business it wants, where it wants, despite regulators putting lines on the maps" (*Economist* 2020: 27). Yet, despite this extensive body of literature, the practices that bridge, connect and facilitate the smooth functioning of the boundary-like and conduit-like interfaces of finance remain only partially explored. Political economists traditionally conceptualize financial centres as the nerve centres of the global economic system, focusing on how corporations and states utilize financial operations to control global resources. For example, in *The City: London and the Global Power of Finance*, Norfield (2017) illustrates in meticulous detail how the City of London generates substantial revenues for the UK economy through its financial industries' massive amount of global transactions, thereby also elevating the UK's position as a political force on the global stage. As Lenin famously observed, "politics is a concentrated expression of economics".[1]

Indeed, by capitalizing on the City's exceptional role, the UK utilizes its financial system to literally extract (economic, social, ecological and other forms of) value from other countries – under the noble guise of providing services (see the financialization of the GDP, Assa 2017). The significance of UK finance can be illustrated in multiple ways. For instance, in 2013, the assets held by UK-based banks exceeded four times the country's GDP, underscoring the vast scale of their financial operations. In Europe, only smaller nation-states such as Switzerland, Luxembourg and Ireland possess larger financial sectors relative to their domestic economies, largely because of their specialized niches in global financial markets. Financial privilege, therefore, serves as a manifestation of economic power. This also explains why the Anglo-American financial system should not be seen merely as an extension of US markets (Norfield 2017; Wójcik 2013). Figure 3.1 illustrates the high concentration of the world's leading financial centres (represented by the number of circles), predominantly in the Northern Hemisphere. While Asian financial centres have risen in the global rankings over the past decade, the dominance of wealthy countries hosting the most significant IFCs remains firmly entrenched. Indeed, financial services export revenues are highly concentrated in a small number of countries. The size of the circle corresponds to financial centres' positions in one of the latest Z/Yen rankings, reflecting not only the current geographical concentration of financial power in North America, Europe, East Asia and Australia, but also a discernible shift towards Asian and Middle Eastern IFCs.[2]

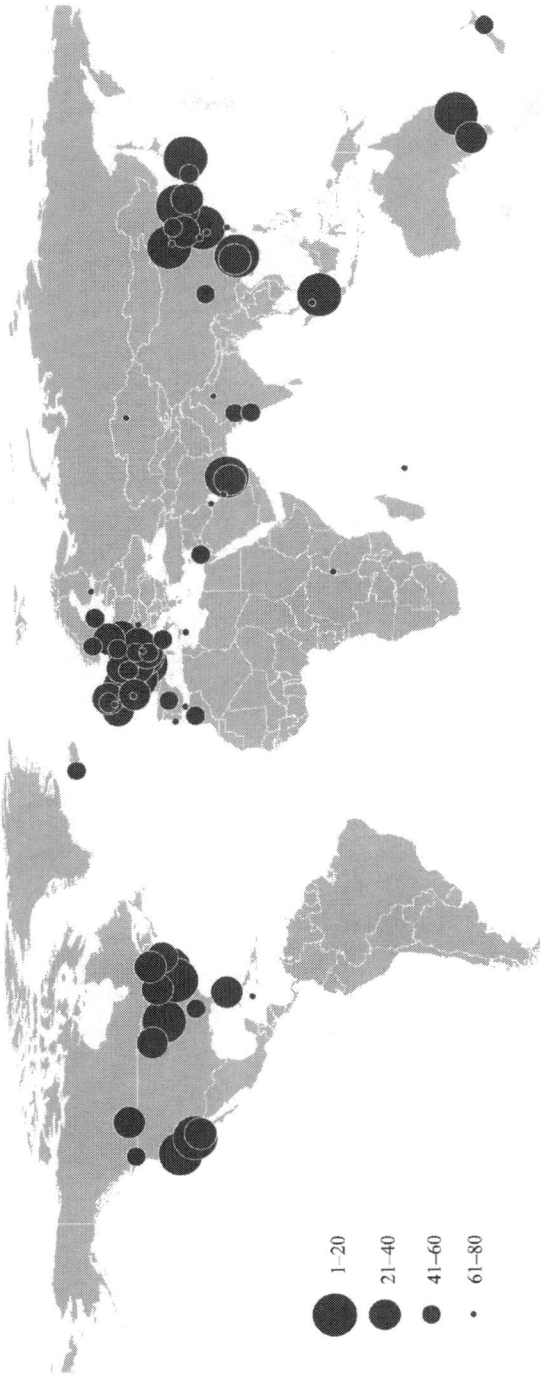

Figure 3.1 Concentration of the 80 leading financial centres in the world[3]

Source: Z/Yen 2024b.

Legend:
- 1–20
- 21–40
- 41–60
- 61–80

While the specialization and performance of financial centres – as reflected in global rankings – offer some insights, they reveal little about underlying organizational shifts or innovations in financial instruments, both of which are crucial to enhancing the competitiveness of financial firms in alignment with their respective IFCs. Importantly, rather than engaging in direct competition, as such rankings often suggest, financial centres are deeply interconnected. They operate within carefully balanced ecosystems and participate in a broader global division of labour that underpins the "production" of finance. This includes, for example, multi-centre arrangements that enable tax optimization and fiscal advantages for global clients.

Thus, while ranking exercises (see Figure 3.1) primarily assess the *perceived* strength and efficiency of IFCs' local business ecosystems, they exert *real* and disciplining pressure on policymakers within IFC jurisdictions. These pressures drive continuous efforts to enhance "competitiveness" – particularly in legal and regulatory frameworks – thereby pushing financial centres to strengthen, renew and reposition themselves as regional assets. Although scholars have been highly critical of the flaws and distortions inherent in such ranking exercises – highlighting their role in polarization and flawed incentive-setting (see Derudder *et al.* 2012) – policymakers nonetheless continue to rely on them. The Z/Yen financial centre indices, for example, are but one prominent case.[4]

The divergent historical trajectories underpinning the rise of European financial centres help to illuminate the distinct offshoring–onshoring strategies adopted by their respective nation-states. Unlike smaller jurisdictions, major financial centres with expansive economic hinterlands – such as the US, UK, France and Germany – cultivated robust banking infrastructures and established enduring credit networks with a broad spectrum of domestic industries and corporate actors. These deeply embedded financial ecosystems shaped not only the institutional character of their financial centres but also their strategic orientation towards offshore finance. Well into the 1990s in Europe, prior to the liberalization of national financial markets, key financial functions and systems were often duplicated across jurisdictions, a defining feature of historically and culturally distinct national markets. However, the development of the Euro(dollar) markets – arguably the first true and enduring global financial markets, operating initially without supervision or regulation – created new opportunities for financial centres to extend their spatial reach by servicing these rapidly expanding offshore markets from the 1950s onwards (see Burn 2006; Dörry 2016). In essence, the itinerant US dollar, while geographically "touching down" in Europe, remained offshore, as no national regulator had the legal authority to supervise these markets, that is, US dollars circulating outside the United States. As a result, the Eurodollar currency and bond markets expanded rapidly and have thrived ever since.

The following example – focusing on the co-development of the financial centres of Dublin, London and Luxembourg – illustrates how path dependency and historical contingency enabled some IFCs to evolve and capitalize on these Euromarkets. In 2013, nearly 60 per cent of Europe's financial services export revenues originated from just three countries – the US, the UK and Luxembourg – according to data available since 2000 (Wójcik *et al.* 2022). For example, Luxembourg's profitable niche as an investment fund (IF) management centre remains significant. However, in recent years, France and Ireland have increasingly challenged its longstanding, uncontested position as Europe's leading IF hub. As suggested earlier, prior to financial globalization, national systems shaped financial markets in ways that left limited room for manoeuvre by small states lacking a substantial economic hinterland requiring financing. Nevertheless, small financial centres now play a critical role in the global financial system, as exemplified by Luxembourg, Ireland and Singapore, or Dubai, Jersey, Guernsey and the Cayman Islands. The financial geographies of these centres are complex and interwoven, as extensively documented by economic geographers (for example, Wojcik *et al.* 2024). For instance, Switzerland maintains strong historico-economic ties with Luxembourg and today serves as a feeder hub for Luxembourg's asset management sector through elite-tier private wealth management services and their investments in funds. Simultaneously, Luxembourg functions as Switzerland's gateway to the EU asset management market – a market from which it remains excluded, due to its non-EU status. Switzerland's consistently high ranking in global financial centre league tables – long sustained by its banking, insurance and wealth management sectors – is largely underpinned by tax engineering by the world's wealthy elites, a practice from which the Swiss financial system and broader economy have historically benefited (see also Zucman 2015). Similarly, Hong Kong and Singapore, both former British colonies, have flourished as international banking and broader financial hubs. Singapore, in particular, solidified its position through the early establishment of its powerful sovereign wealth funds in 1974 and 1981, respectively.

Ireland's economic boom began in the 1980s, when it positioned itself as a low-tax jurisdiction to attract (primarily US) corporations to Europe. It soon replicated Luxembourg's successful industrial IF management model (Wójcik *et al.* 2022). Both Ireland and Luxembourg highlight the dependence of their small nation-states on the global positioning of their financial centres within international financial markets. Between 2003 and 2019, AUM of IFs domiciled within the European Single Market (ESM) grew from $4.8 trillion to $12.5 trillion. In 2003, the UK was the leading domicile, followed by Luxembourg, France, Italy, Germany and Ireland. Relative to GDP, however, Ireland – and particularly Luxembourg – had already established themselves as specialized IF domiciles with financial sectors vastly outgrowing the scale of their domestic economies.

A key factor in the early growth of both Luxembourg and Ireland as IF hubs was their swift adoption of the pioneering 1985 UCITS Directive, introduced by the European Economic Community (EEC), the EU's predecessor. Before 1985, cross-border asset management in Europe was relatively limited, focused primarily on private wealth management centred in London, Switzerland and Luxembourg. The management of retail investors' assets, however, remained largely domestic, with IFs and associated functions typically located in the same jurisdiction as their investors (Merki 2005). At this stage, the asset management industry was still in its infancy.

Luxembourg's pioneering role in European economic integration has deep historical roots, including a monetary and economic union with Belgium dating back to the 1920s. The country has a long tradition of attracting international business through favourable regulatory and tax regimes, including the 1929 Holding Company Regime and a wide network of double taxation treaties, facilitated by its OECD membership (Calabrese & Majerus 2023). In the post-Second World War decades, Luxembourg established itself as a key centre for private wealth management, Eurobond issuance and listing, and the clearing and settlement of cross-border financial transactions.

Ireland, which joined the EEC in 1973, had by 1985 emerged as a major foreign direct investment (FDI) destination. This was enabled by several structural advantages: its English-speaking environment, common law legal system, the Irish diaspora in the United States (a key source of FDI), its geographical position between the US and UK, and an expanding network of bilateral double taxation agreements designed to eliminate or minimize cross-border tax burdens (Donaghy & Clarke 2003; OECD 1998; Trautman 2016). Ireland's growing access to European markets via the EEC further enhanced its attractiveness for international investment. A major draw of Dublin's newly created International Financial Services Centre (IFSC) in the Docklands area was its preferential 10 per cent corporate income tax (CIT) rate – well below the prevailing rates across Europe and far lower than the 40 per cent rate applicable in the rest of Ireland at the time. The IFSC initially focused on three sectors: IFs, cross-border banking and insurance.

In regulatory and tax terms, Luxembourg became the primary model for Ireland's IF industry. Knowledge transfer was facilitated by FABS firms – particularly PricewaterhouseCoopers (PwC) – which emerged as the dominant auditor and consultancy provider for both IFs and the IFSC more broadly. Seeking to compete directly with Luxembourg, Ireland aggressively promoted itself as an alternative IF domicile, including for hedge funds, private equity and later REITs. While Ireland implemented the UCITS framework, Luxembourg responded by enhancing its own tax incentives for IFs, including lowering CIT from 34 to 30 per cent and abolishing trade capital tax. Both countries continued "refining" their legal frameworks to expand the range of available IF structures. Ireland, for example, introduced a new Companies Act and Unit Trust Act in 1990.

Several factors contributed to the rapid growth of IFs from the early 2000s onwards, from which both Luxembourg and Ireland benefited. The creation of the Eurozone accelerated industry integration and made the region more attractive for cross-border investment. Meanwhile, widespread securitization introduced new financial instruments that could be structured within IFs. Regulatory developments, however, were equally – if not more – significant. The UCITS III Directive (2001) expanded the investment scope of IFs, allowing them to hold a broader array of financial instruments, including derivatives. Crucially, the UCITS IV Directive (2011) introduced the management company passport, removing the requirement for fund management companies (FMCs) to be domiciled in the same jurisdiction as the investment fund (IF) – a regulatory shift that further accelerated integration. Indeed, both Luxembourg and Ireland were strategically well positioned to capitalize on these favourable regulatory and economic tailwinds (Wójcik *et al.* 2022).

To stay with the example of the evolving asset management industry, the UK is home to Europe's largest institutional investors, including pension funds, which drive demand for IF products. These forces create strong incentives to retain key activities such as investment advice and fund distribution within the UK, thereby encouraging the localization of other critical functions, including domiciliation. More broadly, however, the geography of European IF networks is shaped predominantly by major US asset management firms, which establish and manage funds in Luxembourg and Ireland, while routing investments through London. This pattern exemplifies European financial integration through *Americanization* (Bonizzi & Kaltenbrunner 2024; Kipping & Bjarnar 1998). Although the Luxembourg and Irish IF industries are based in Europe, they are primarily connected to London and New York, functioning as satellites of the NY–LON financial axis (Wójcik 2013). This dynamic highlights how analysing the differentiated roles of financial centres can reveal deeper insights into the nature of financial globalization and integration (Wójcik *et al.* 2022). To reiterate, economics is one factor, but purposeful legal bricolage – often aimed at increasing a place's attractiveness for incorporation and enhancing its business ecosystem for financial arbitrage and other finance-to-finance activities – has played a more powerful role in shaping the preconditions underpinning the complex and dynamic development of IFCs.

A spatial analysis of investment funds

Asset management is a truly global business, dominated by a few powerful firms operating out of a select group of IFCs. These centres are not just financial silos – they are deeply enmeshed in the real economy, managing capital linked to infrastructure, energy, housing and more, while drawing on specialized expertise.

Acting as high-level control centres within the global financial system, they also channel investment into tangible, real-world products and projects. But their tight interconnectedness – coupled with an increasing reliance on complex, often speculative products – makes them inherently vulnerable. This fragility was starkly exposed during the 2007/08 financial crisis, when shocks in one corner of the system reverberated across the globe.

In an effort to unpack the underlying economics and business models of financial products, including their input–output structures, the specific geographies into which each value-generating step is embedded, and the governance arrangements shaping the overall "production process" of core instruments such as IFs, scholars, particularly economic geographers, have drawn on established heuristics from global value chain (GVC) analysis, while also engaging with broader analytical perspectives from globalization theory. Originally developed to map the spatio-organizational configurations of globalizing manufacturing industries since the early 1990s, frameworks such as global production networks (GPNs) and their GVC antecedents have increasingly been repurposed to interrogate the shifting geographies and governance architectures of financial services and their specific territorialities (Coe *et al.* 2014). At their core, GVC approaches were originally developed to illuminate the socio-spatial dynamics of economic development, focusing on where value-adding activity touches down (and why), and particularly on how value is created, captured and distributed across places and actors within an increasingly interconnected global economy.

Although globalization was once heralded as a pathway to broad-based prosperity, its outcomes have often been uneven. Rather than fostering inclusive growth, the integration of regions into financial GPNs has frequently exacerbated spatial inequalities and entrenched socio-economic marginalization (Diemer *et al.* 2022; Evenhuis *et al.* 2021). The analytical apparatus developed through GVC and GPN research – particularly its focus on spatial interdependencies, governance structures and the concept of strategic coupling – has nonetheless proven valuable in exposing the place-based foundations of global financial architectures, especially how regional endowments are transformed into investable assets. This is all the more important given that the global is *always* materially and institutionally constituted in the local.

However, much of this scholarship remains anchored in a growth-centric, neoliberal paradigm that privileges inter-urban competitiveness and the relentless expansion of financial activity, a logic traditionally underpinned by the *legal fiction* of the firm. Yet, despite this conceptual tension, the versatility of the GVC/GPN frameworks as analytical tools – and the normative assumptions embedded within them – warrants a brief conceptual genealogy, including that of their key offshoots. This is useful for unpacking the evolving relationship between financial centres and the production of core financial products such as IFs. This involves not only the co-evolution of IFCs with key forms of financial activity, but also the gradual, strategically managed integration of financial regimes into local economies, framed to maximize perceived benefits such as employment, income generation and tax revenue for host jurisdictions, much of which has proven illusory.

Indeed, inter-urban competition has rendered many places economically marginalized, left grappling with the persistent reality of being "left behind" (Rodríguez-Pose 2018; Rodríguez-Pose *et al.* 2024), a condition for which, curiously, the role of financial activity remains strikingly under-analysed. Against this background, the following section introduces the key conceptual lineages underpinning these frameworks.

The GVC and GPN frameworks originated in efforts to understand how globalization reshaped economic organization and spatial structures. Early studies of newly industrializing countries in East Asia and Latin America (Gereffi 1983, 1989) highlighted the growing role of core and peripheral capital in commodity chains and export networks, which became central to analysing the emerging global manufacturing system. The Global Commodity Chains (GCCs) approach (Gereffi & Korzeniewicz 1994) aimed to capture the spatial logic of these shifts, emphasizing the concentration of production and control within a few dominant nation-states in the global North, from which "multinational corporations" – that is, economic terminology for firms' internationalization strategies that obscures the legal structures enabling economic activity – asserted control over global economic flows. This reorganization produced new socio-economic relationships, linking distant regions through an international division of labour while reinforcing spatial inequalities due to uneven access to markets and resources. Informed by World-Systems Theory (Hopkins & Wallerstein 1982), GCC analysis challenged the idea of globalization as a uniform process, foregrounding the differentiated spatial and temporal dynamics of competition (Talani 2019) and the essential, yet changing role of states amid global capitalist restructuring (Cerny 2010).

As GCCs evolved into *trans*national networks, growing institutional complexity progressively eroded the regulatory power of nation-states. The removal of capital controls enabled unprecedented financial mobility, leading to the concentration of capital – increasingly financial as well as industrial – in key global clusters. Global cities, and increasingly international financial centres, shaped by intensifying neoliberal competition, emerged as critical nodes mediating the interface between global capital and local economies.

A defining feature of the original GCC approach, grounded in a materialist "follow the thing" perspective (Bair & Dussel Peters 2006; Bair & Gereffi 2002), was its critical focus on labour conditions and power asymmetries along commodity chains. This stands in contrast to the later GVC approach, which placed greater emphasis on governance structures and policy applications, and the GPN framework, which emerged from a more managerial and relational economic tradition. While all three frameworks have offered valuable insights into global economic integration, their distinct intellectual lineages have shaped their analytical orientations and policy relevance in different ways.

Since the late 1970s, capitalism has been increasingly organized around financial infrastructures and technocratic expert systems that underpin a globalizing knowledge economy (Amin & Cohendet 2004; Mazzucato & Collington 2023; Esmark 2020). A parallel feature of this transformation, conceptualized by Harvey (1996) as time–space compression, has been the impact of new technologies in reducing transport and communication costs, enabling the rapid expansion of transnational business operations. These developments not only reconfigured global production and manufacturing networks but also spurred new research into GVCs. This scholarship called for more nuanced, meso-level analyses of sectoral dynamics (see Bair 2005), moving beyond the macro-historical lens of World-Systems Theory.

The GVC approach enabled closer scrutiny of the institutional and structural contexts in which value chains operate, particularly in shaping regional and national development trajectories – or upgrading and downgrading – in less advanced economies. Scholars have examined governance mechanisms within globalizing economic architectures (Gereffi *et al.* 2005), exploring how dependence on lead firms – powerful coordinators of value chains and gatekeepers to key markets – can offer both opportunities for, and constraints on, regional development. In doing so, this body of work has contributed to a more critical and context-sensitive understanding of how globalization interacts with local development dynamics (Bair 2005).

Rooted in two key intellectual influences – Peter Dicken's seminal *Global Shift* (1986) and Gary Gereffi's early work on GCCs from the late 1980s – the GPN approach began to crystallize in the early 2000s (Dicken *et al.* 2001; Dicken & Malmberg 2001; Dicken & Thrift 1992; Henderson *et al.* 2002). It gained traction partly due to the growing influence of international business scholarship and reached its peak in the mid-2000s, coinciding with the high tide of globalization. During this period, trade liberalization, technological innovation and economic integration reinforced a firm-centred perspective, situated at the global–local interface, where regional income generation (value creation) was increasingly seen as contingent on favourable cost structures and place-specific skills – attributes actively sought by globally mobile firms.

Aligned with the neoliberal logic permeating much of the business literature as well (Kogut 1985), a new strand of GPN research emerged that promoted regional asset-building as a strategy for gaining competitive advantage in attracting long-term capital investment, development opportunities and income generation. Despite its stated analytical ambition to unpack the dynamics of value creation, capture and enhancement – broadly summarized as *value-driven policies* – GPN scholarship has faced growing critique for its narrow conceptualization of economic value and its insufficient engagement with the processes of value appropriation (Guthman 2009). Yet, the field has largely refrained from substantively addressing these concerns.

Meanwhile, early efforts were made to apply GVC and GPN frameworks to the study of financial centres (Grote *et al.* 2002), although these initial explorations remained peripheral within the broader literature and had limited disciplinary impact.

The subsequent GPN 2.0 framework (Coe & Yeung 2015) aligns even more explicitly with an *economic* conception of value, focusing on the key drivers shaping regional value capture trajectories. These include firm agency and strategic decision-making, particularly amid intensifying competition structured by cost–capability ratios, market dynamics and financial disciplining, all of which influence regional development outcomes. The causal mechanisms behind GPN formation and operation are understood to reflect the strategic investment choices of global firms, shaped by shifting risk environments and competitive pressures.

In this respect, GPN 2.0 challenges earlier assumptions embedded in the GPN 1.0 framework, where regional development was primarily conceived through inward investment by multinational firms. Instead, it promotes an "active" regional development model, encouraging regions to reach out and enhance their appeal as business environments to attract global investment, a view firmly rooted in mainstream economic orthodoxy. The intensified portrayal of regions as "assets" for multinational firms illustrates the growing subordination of regional economies and communities to the logic of foreign direct investment (FDI). Yet while difficult to trace statistically, the nature of FDI itself has significantly shifted. Financial capital increasingly assumes a transgressive and opaque role, often operating under the guise of FDI, while in reality functioning as little more than financial throughput (Balmas & Dörry 2023). This conceptual reframing of FDI-related financial transactions as economically valuable aligns closely with the methodologies used to construct IFC rankings (see Figure 3.1).

Until recently, the conceptual frameworks of GPNs and GVCs have remained relatively agnostic about the role of capital in globalization and regional development. This began to shift with the rise of financialization and the emergence of a new conceptual offshoot: global financial networks (GFNs) (Coe *et al.* 2014). GFNs aimed to revitalize the dialogue between production and finance by examining how financial flows permeate and reshape global manufacturing operations and their geographic sites. Crucially, they also opened up analytical space for interrogating the offshore–onshore dichotomy within this context. While this represents a valuable development, the precise nature of finance – particularly as an increasingly self-referential industry – remains conceptually ambiguous.

Despite increasing recognition of the need to explore the evolving relationship between industrial and financial capital (Hampton 1996b), GFN frameworks have yet to fully integrate critical insights concerning the displacement of traditional money's fiduciary function by credit money and *fictitious capital* as dominant international commodities. GFN scholarship has compellingly demonstrated the deep entanglements between GPNs and GFNs, suggesting that financial networks may be even more globalized and interconnected than their production-based counterparts. These contributions have significantly advanced our understanding of the finance–production interface, particularly in relation to the offshore–onshore nexus. Nonetheless, a key omission persists: financial "multinationals" – despite their centrality to these dynamics – remain analytically underexplored within the GFN literature. These institutions are deeply embedded within their production sites, namely IFCs, yet have received insufficient scholarly attention. This gap has prompted calls for a conceptual shift towards studying the GPNs *of* finance itself (Dörry 2015), highlighting a broader limitation within economic geography – particularly its continued reliance on the firm as the core unit of analysis, albeit one that is a legal fiction. This conceptual oversight carries important implications for both the analytical scope and the conclusions drawn from this body of research.

Before engaging further with this evolving approach, it is essential to critically interrogate the largely unchallenged notion of economic value embedded within GPN frameworks. Understanding how asset worth is defined and calculated is crucial – not least in the context of policy strategies such as the European Green Deal, where unaccounted-for negative externalities continue to challenge conventional paradigms of value creation, distribution and aspirations for sustainable regional development.

What value – and for whom?

Emerging critiques of how value is analytically treated have gained renewed prominence, particularly in light of the geopolitically sensitive formation of green-tech supply chains. These critiques draw attention to the continuity – and in many cases intensification – of extractive practices in the global South, driven by the North's decarbonization agenda (Hercelin & Dörry 2024). A growing body of literature on green extractivism (Acosta 2013; Dorn *et al.* 2022) questions the foundational assumptions of value creation in sustainability transitions, profoundly challenging the notion that these necessarily lead to more equitable global economic arrangements. Relatedly, and exemplified by the complex business models of private equity (PE), the securitization of financial debt (mortgages, car loans, student loans, credit card debt, etc.) into tradable financial instruments has detached abstract assets from their productive base through financial and accounting engineering (Mian & Sufi 2014). In this context, the economic performance of financial assets and asset management strategies increasingly hinges on value extraction from underlying tangible activities, rather than on productive investment itself. Whereas the reinvestment of profits was once the norm, financial investors now largely channel profits back to their own investors, rather than reinvesting in productive assets.

These financial abstractions have inspired a growing strand of research into how assets are governed and controlled (Seabrooke & Wigan 2018). The global wealth chains (GWCs) framework marks a shift from spatial and developmental concerns to the agency of key financial actors – particularly FABS professionals and firms – as central units of analysis. Rather than focusing on conventional notions of value production, GWC analysis interrogates strategies of *wealth* creation and protection, which operate through legal jurisdictions, legal structuring and the governance of assets across diverse sectors such as utilities, food, pharmaceuticals and art. Crucially, the *governance of asset control* – further enabled by legal and accounting instruments such as transfer pricing arrangements, double tax agreements and intellectual property regimes – plays a central role in explaining how GWCs function and, to a significant extent, extend financialization (Leaver & Martin 2018, 2021). These mechanisms highlight how financial and legal architectures are not only used to facilitate wealth accumulation but also to insulate assets from regulatory oversight, thereby reinforcing the structural logics of financial capitalism.

Intriguingly, while analyses of the nexus between firms and location have yielded valuable insights into economic relationships, spatial and social inequalities, labour conditions, and the developmental trajectories of regional upgrading and downgrading – both in terms of places (local economies) and economic actors (businesses) – these approaches continue to exhibit traces of orthodox economic thinking (Coase 1937, 1992). A key limitation lies in the persistent conceptualization of the firm as the fundamental unit of analysis in economic geography, and the state as the core analytical category in political and social scholarship – both typically examined through the lens of economic performance and value creation, yet with little attention to their specific legal status as *legal persons* (see Figure 3.3). Rather than acknowledging firms and states for what they are – distinct legal structures endowed with specific rights, responsibilities and protections – academic discourse has often reduced them to *legal fictions* (for an insightful critical reflections, see Picciotto 1999; Sani 2020; Watson 2019; Worthington 2022) or treated them as evolving *fictitious species* (see Pagano 2010). This tendency reflects a longstanding bias toward conceptualizing the firm primarily as an economic actor, rather than a legal construct that ought to be held accountable beyond its privileged capacities to "own" property, generate profits and maximize shareholder value. Likewise, the state is frequently understood through governance and power structures, rather than in terms of its legal obligations – and even constraints. In practice, however, these dimensions – legal, economic and political – are inseparable.

Yet studies in regional development have traditionally failed to fully account for the material implications of legal personhood when assessing value creation and value capture (Coe & Yeung 2015). This analytical oversight contributes to the entrenchment of neoliberal assumptions within regional development discourse, reinforcing an uncritical acceptance of state- and company-led economic expansion while neglecting its socio-ecological consequences. As Robé (2020) persuasively argues in *Property, Power and Politics*, such legal abstraction has profound consequences – particularly in obscuring accountability. This is especially troubling given that both business corporations and nation-states frequently cause significant socio-ecological harm (Castree & Henderson 2014), yet routinely evade legal and moral responsibility, not least due to the conceptual privileging of their economic function. This reflects a notable gap in regional studies, rooted in a limited theoretical perspective that warrants critical reconsideration. The failure to interrogate these legal dimensions calls for a fundamental reassessment of the frameworks used to study firms, states and their roles in economic development. Without such scrutiny, the structural conditions enabling harm – and shielding it from accountability – remain hidden in plain sight.

Extending this critical perspective to the study of the GPNs of finance – and, by way of example, to the analysis of investment funds (IFs) as businesses operating across sites of incorporation, administration and wider production sites (IFCs) – highlights the need to examine how IFs intersect with legal personhood and accountability. While existing approaches provide valuable insights into the spatio-organizational dynamics of value creation, they often overlook the legal infrastructures that underpin financial strategies. This omission limits our understanding of how financial structures operate and obscures their broader socio-ecological consequences – an increasingly urgent concern in the context of accelerating climate change. The following example, drawn from Wójcik *et al.* (2022), illustrates this gap, even while offering important insights into the economic logics structuring the exclusive web of IFCs.

An IF sells shares – also referred to as "units" – to investors and uses the proceeds, primarily to invest in securities, in pursuit of its stated investment objectives. The net asset value (NAV), representing the current economic value per share, is calculated at least daily, after deducting all applicable fees and costs. The NAV determines the price at which existing investors may redeem their shares and new investors may purchase them. As illustrated in Figure 3.2, a wide

Figure 3.2 Structuring an investment fund

array of firms and services are involved in the operation of an IF. A fund management company (FMC) serves as the legal structure responsible for establishing the fund (business entity), applying for its registration, and overseeing its legal and financial affairs, including the appointment of service providers. The fund's assets are entrusted to a custodian bank, which ensures safekeeping and verifies that unit transactions and NAV calculations comply with the fund's rules and regulatory standards.

Fund administrators maintain the unit-holder register, process subscriptions and redemptions, handle client relations, and oversee accounting and compliance. An investment advisor manages the fund's portfolio, while a promoter markets the fund to potential investors. Each fund also requires legal counsel and must undergo an independent audit to ensure that the financial statements prepared by the administrator offer a true and fair view of the fund's financial position. Beyond these core roles, IFs depend on a wide range of FABS services, including audit, tax, IT, legal and HR advisory. Figure 3.2 presents a stylized IF structure; however, actual configurations vary by jurisdiction and fund type. Importantly, specialist law firms, the Big Four accountancy firms and global custody banks – originally support actors in the IF sector – have grown into global industries in their own right, and generating continuous demand for their services is imperative to their business model.

The IF industry exhibits substantial economies of scale and scope. Given the inherent uncertainty of investment returns – and the well-documented difficulty of consistently outperforming market benchmarks – cost minimization becomes essential. Many operational costs, such as IT infrastructure and regulatory compliance, are fixed, meaning that larger AUM reduce average costs. This is especially true in custody and administration – high-volume, low-value activities where scale delivers considerable cost efficiency. Consequently, the industry has become dominated by large asset management firms, which often integrate multiple functions through specialized subsidiaries. However, regulatory frameworks prohibit certain combinations of responsibilities – for example, a FMC may not also serve as custodian.

Economies of scale also extend to advisory functions. The Big Four, in particular, offer integrated service packages that span audit, tax, legal structuring and regulatory compliance. While IFs are subject to EU-wide directives set by the European Securities and Markets Authority (ESMA), they must also comply with national laws in their country of domicile. These national regulations vary in both interpretation and implementation – from liberal approaches to so-called "gold-plating", where additional domestic rules increase compliance costs.

Among the many actors involved, transfer agents play a vital role in managing investor registrations and processing subscriptions and redemptions. In the hedge fund sector, prime brokers are particularly central. These intermediaries support complex trading activities and offer a suite of services, including securities lending, cash and collateral management, trade execution, custodial services and leverage provision. In doing so, they form essential infrastructure for highly sophisticated financial operations (cf. Wójcik *et al.* 2022).

Indeed, all of these "entities" and firm strategies in this example are underpinned by their legal personalities, enabling them to contract and trade with one another. While this is widely acknowledged as a legal and institutional fact, its economic, theoretical and policy implications are often overlooked. The fictitious dimensions of legal personality – long embedded in both economic theory and policymaking – have contributed to persistent blind spots. These gaps are further exacerbated by large-scale, data-driven analyses, where abstract modelling risks reproducing additional layers of legal fiction and institutional opacity. As a result, misleading theoretical assumptions become embedded within policy frameworks, reinforcing flawed conclusions, perpetuating conceptual misunderstandings, and often overlooking the social interests and dynamics that challenge assumptions such as rationality and other untenable orthodoxies.

What further emerges from this study is the deep economic entrenchment of a complex array of FABS firms, which not only capitalize on existing market opportunities but also actively create new ones – a process that can be described as hyper-economization. This dynamic reflects a persistent economic orthodoxy that assumes all economic *transactions* inherently produce growth (see Assa 2017), and that financial transactions are therefore beneficial simply because growth is presumed to be desirable. This circular logic often escapes critical scrutiny, yet it underpins the expansion of financial economies in and through international financial centres.

This is deeply problematic. On the one hand, it reduces legal personhood to a mere instrument for conducting business and maximizing profit, overlooking its foundational role in establishing corporate accountability and delineating the responsibilities that firms are expected to uphold towards society and the environment. After all, the right to use property does not equate to possession, and it also carries obligations. On the other hand, legal personhood itself – originally conceived to define the scope of a firm's legitimate actions – has undergone a process of implicit economization. Law and legal status have increasingly been repurposed as "sites" of financial innovation, not in pursuit of socio-economic stability, but as mechanisms for rent extraction and regulatory arbitrage – processes that unfold within practices' and mechanisms' distinct micro-geographies and micro-histories. This evolution illustrates how legal frameworks, far from merely regulating economic activity, are increasingly instrumentalized to engineer financial opportunity within and across the production sites of finance. In doing so, they reinforce the logic of financialization and align both the production site (IFC) and process (creation and operation of IFs) with neoliberal market imperatives.

This analysis resonates with a broader tendency to conceptualize institutions – often simplistically – as fixed "rules of the game", reducing them to testable hypotheses or normative abstractions (Amin 2001). In contrast, Amin's (2001: 1237) conception of institutions as "processes of institutionalisation of socio-economic practices" remains highly relevant, particularly for understanding financial economies as fluid, evolving formations that continually reshape social orders. At its core, law defines social order. A more productive analytical approach therefore views institutions as dynamic, mobile entities – fragile socio-geographical accomplishments rather than static regulatory structures. This shifts the analytical focus towards the unfolding processes of organizing and instituting, and their broader socio-spatial ramifications (see Philo & Parr 2000).

Studying financial centres through this lens allows for a deeper interrogation of how local contexts function as crucibles of institutional formation, shaping economic financial activity through specific geographical instantiations. Crucially, a still underexplored dimension within economic geography is the role of law and legal practices – not only in their co-evolution with economic forms, but as sites of institutional innovation, through what might be termed *legal bricolage*. When subject to such bricolage, law becomes an active contributor to the emergence of financial formations imbued with power and privilege. This alternative perspective – grounded in empirical evidence – is further elaborated in the following section.

Expanding finance's reach: jurisdictions and territorial claims

Law can be understood, in a somewhat naïve sense, as constitutive of social reality – in that its operation directly causes events to unfold. Yet beyond this instrumental view, law also shapes social relations and, by extension, the institutional frameworks within which individuals and organizations act. As a force of change, domination, resistance and a mechanism for the realization of justice, law has, in countless ways – albeit often provisionally – influenced the fundamental terms and lived experiences of social life. If social reality is shaped through legal structures, it is equally produced through spatial relations. As Blomley *et al.* (2001) argue in *The Legal Geographies Reader*, space and place are not passive backdrops but active dimensions through which legal and social relations unfold. Consider the flows of people, commodities, information and imagery across local, national and global scales – their intersections generate dynamic contexts from which both individual agency and institutional practices emerge.

Social space, then, is actively produced – with spatialities unfolding in relation to broader socio-economic structures, including capital accumulation and shifting relations of production. Yet in much social theory beyond geography, the spatial dimension remains under-theorized, despite its role as a powerful "enabling technology" (Massey 1995, 2007). Boaventura de Sousa Santos's (1987) concept of *interlegality* – the overlapping and interaction of multiple legal orders – highlights the complex ways in which legal spaces can intertwine. These are not static domains, but dynamic and relational fields of practice. To grasp them fully, we *must* move beyond economistic reasoning and attend to the multiple, uneven ways legal codes operate across spatial scales and institutional contexts (Klabbers & Palombella 2019; Walker 2022).

If we accept that law is not merely regulatory but constitutive – shaping social, economic and spatial realities – it becomes essential to engage more directly with key legal-geographic concepts. One such concept is *jurisdiction*: a socially constructed framework that defines both legal authority and territorial boundaries, while also projecting legal power across time. As Ford (2001) argues, the legal and institutional decisions made today actively shape the jurisdictional landscapes of tomorrow. To overlook the spatial and temporal politics of jurisdiction in the context of financial centres is, therefore, to neglect how financial capitalism continually reconfigures legal geographies and the social spheres entangled within them.

Grasping the transformative power of contemporary finance requires close attention to the entanglement of national legal systems, firms, governments and citizens within global financial processes. These relationships are enacted through everyday legal and financial practices that help construct and redefine the asset economy. Innovation – whether legal, technical or organizational – is central to this ongoing transformation. Financial centres are pivotal in driving these shifts.[5] They formalize new institutional arrangements and frameworks, often in ways that are partial, opaque and highly specific. Although these changes may not always amount to systemic overhaul, they represent critical micro-transformations that accumulate significance over time. To render such transformations visible, it is necessary to examine how institutions are reconfigured through practice – a form of legal and institutional *bricolage* – in the ongoing institutionalization of specific socio-economic dynamics. Again, global structures are not pre-given or fixed; they are actively produced through interconnected practices and legal-organizational forms. These practices, such as contracting, governing, producing and innovating, are embedded in social, material and legal contexts. They evolve over time, are shaped by power relations, and interact in complex ways across spatial scales and jurisdictional boundaries. The global patterns emerge from these interwoven systems of practice, legal arrangements and institutional constructs, rather than existing independently of them. Hence, a focus on practices themselves seems a valuable exercise.

The practices and organizational forms through which global dynamics operate are themselves constitutive of what is typically understood as "global". At their core, practices with bricolage-like characteristics can be seen as purpose-driven innovations embedded in social and material contexts, continuously evolving and prioritizing particular interests (Hui *et al.* 2017). Aligning with Esmark's (2020) view of professions as social engineers, Ong and Collier (2005) highlight the global diffusion of technologies, resulting in complex systems that entangle technology, politics and actors beyond predefined scales or political categories. Similarly, Sassen (2006) reminds us that territory, sovereignty, authority, ownership and property rights are not fixed attributes, but institutionally constructed through conflict and negotiation. While these elements are interdependent, they remain analytically distinct. Boltanski and colleagues (2006, 2020) further suggest that practices are marked by multi-positionality, power asymmetries and competing perspectives, making them inherently *unstable*. Far from producing stability through habituation alone, practices also generate diversity and contestation – indeed, a pertinent foundation for innovation. This stresses the relational and processual nature of social order *construction*, including that of contemporary financial economies.

Nicolini's (2017) concept of "connected situationalism" complements the GPN/GVC heuristic and resonates with empirical observations: large-scale structures emerge from interconnected webs of practice – including webs of contracts (Robé 2020; Figure 3.3), which act as legal-institutional scaffolding. Such practices are bundled and interlinked through *shared* actions, material entities or chains of activity (Schatzki 2017), overlapping and referencing places and trajectories. "Matters of practice" (Shove 2017) offer a way to connect seemingly disparate domains of producing, making and doing. Yet these *connections* – the mediating devices between discourses and actual practices – are often subject to *manipulation* in the global choreography of resources. This illustrates how the interplay between practice and legal-organizational form shapes on the

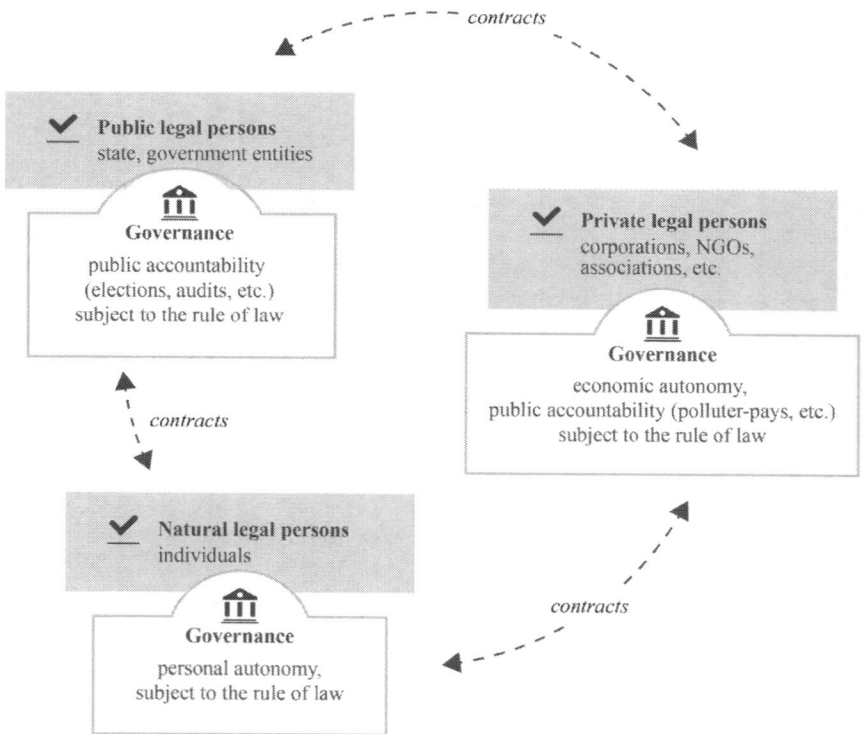

Figure 3.3 Webs of contracts between legal persons

micro-scale – including its many micro-geographies and micro-histories – what is conventionally perceived as the global scale.

In a nutshell, law is a central – yet often somewhat "invisible" – infrastructure of financialization and financial economies, enabling the economization of social life through legal manipulation, discretion and the strategic construction of jurisdictions. In fact, legal artefacts serve as crucial devices through which manipulation can be enacted and articulated. Far from passive instruments, they not only reflect insights from legal geographies but actively shape them – an often-overlooked dimension in spatial analysis. In common law-based systems, legal action is not bound by rigid rules but remains responsive to circumstance. This flexibility affords legal actors discretion – a quality that is both enabling and constraining. A closer examination of how discretion is exercised, limited and maintained is vital (see Silbey 2001).

Law is not merely a practical tool; it also encompasses conceptual frameworks that shape the categories through which social interactions are understood and organized. These frameworks – rooted in legal artefacts – are frequently instrumentalized to serve commercial imperatives, more often than not subordinating broader social and ecological considerations to the logic of economization. Given law's dual role – both shaping and being shaped by social action – its entanglement with markets merits closer and more critical examination. While the presumed autonomy of legal and market domains may serve analytical convenience, this distinction arguably warrants rethinking. Despite law's apparent ubiquity, socio-legal scholars remind us that its power is neither absolute nor unbounded: *law alone cannot claim ultimate authority* (Silbey 2001). Economic and legal practices are deeply interwoven, forming bricolage-like configurations with distinct micro-histories and micro-geographies. The overlapping of legal spaces – or "interlegalities" (Klabbers & Palombella 2019) – has itself become a terrain of economic strategy, particularly in financial centres where (indirect) legal authority and finance-commercial interests intersect.

Understanding the interplay between law, socio-political relations and economic power is therefore essential. Indeed, financialization can be understood as operating through socio-legal strategies that reshape and expand both its territorial and epistemological jurisdictions. One interviewee wryly captured this dynamic: "Law is like sausage-making; you don't want to know what goes into it" (tax lawyer, May 2024). The remark reflects the often-opaque processes through which legal practice generates new liberties, constructs regulatory boundaries and extends sovereignty – frequently in the service of economic gain. In this sense, law – a curiously "unquestioned" infrastructure – underpins processes such as global business operations and the commodification of state sovereignty. The creation of synthetic or artificial legal linkages and disconnections, which economic theory and policy frequently take for granted, regularly lacks

substantive legal grounding (Robé 2020), which, in turn, reinforces the disconnection between economic activity and its wider social context – including
accountability.

At the heart of contemporary financial economies lies the interplay between
legal bricolage, global financial networks, jurisdictional engineering and the
many legal fictions, among them of the firm, capital and the state. Financial
innovation has shifted from enabling productive growth to strategically manipu-
lating legal frameworks. The demand for financial services now rests not on
economic output but on the exploitation of legal asymmetries – a process that
has led to a hyper-economization of law. Finance becomes self-referential, with
legal ingenuity supplanting productive activity as the primary driver of economic
value. Within this system of multiple overlapping practices resting on numerous
distinct micro-geographies and histories, financial centres operate not merely as
competitors but as *interdependent* nodes in global financial networks. Through
a multi-centre division of labour, cities such as London, New York, Dublin,
Singapore, Dubai and Luxembourg function as *jurisdictional conduits* for arbi-
traging legal and regulatory differences, that is, exploiting (synthetically created)
differences to make a profit. However, despite the illusion of market rivalry presented by numerous ranking indices (Z/Yen, several years), financial centres are
tightly interwoven. Their interdependence does not curb regulatory arbitrage –
it exacerbates it, enabling financial capital to bypass oversight via legal differentials across jurisdictions. Asset management and its many sub-industries serve
as an apt case in point.

Crucially, and consequently, a jurisdiction is not a fixed legal structure but
a flexible construct, continually redefined by financial centres to expand their
influence. The remaking of legal geographies through finance allows states to
both commodify and extend their sovereignty, transforming regulation into an
asset tradable on global markets. The resulting *interlegalities* foster, for example, opaque environments where financial operations occur in the gaps between
national oversight, deepening inequality and entrenching advantage. Beneath
this architecture lies a deeper abstraction: the legal fictions in economic orthodoxy. Many of the world's largest financial institutions and corporations – despite
wielding immense economic power – retain the privileges of ownership without
proportional responsibility and accountability, as illustrated by the fossil combustion industry. Law, in this context, no longer constrains; it enables: through
legal bricolage, jurisdictional manipulation and the economic growth logics that
foster and push the expansion of global financial networks, financial centres
maintain their dominance – not by competing, but by mastering the legal infrastructures that ostensibly regulate them.

IFCs are not just hubs of economic activity; they are powerfully engineered
spaces where legal, financial and political authority converge. Their influence

stems from the ability to shape and stretch legal boundaries, using tools like jurisdictional flexibility and legal bricolage to attract capital and bypass regulation. IFCs do not simply respond to global finance; they actively make it – by designing the legal infrastructures that allow financial markets to operate across borders through the entrenched interlinkages between core FABS professions, professionals/firms and the state. It is not in vain that the most powerful IFCs generate disproportionately high volumes of legal work and demand for law firms. Chapters 4 and 5 will elaborate further.

4
EXPANDING EPISTEMOLOGIES

Embedded epistemologies

The asset economy not only underpins but actively constructs the social and institutional infrastructure necessary for the perpetual generation and accumulation of capital. This inescapable, organizing logic of the asset economy – driven by the necessity to sustain economic growth and stave off stagnation – has engendered an increasing reliance on performance indicators as the dominant means of managing both resources and people. Individuals and entities alike are increasingly conceptualized and evaluated as assets, often at the expense of more humane or socially oriented practices (Esmark 2020). Since the 1980s, this shift has facilitated the emergence of new social structures and trust systems that have normalized and legitimized the ascendancy of financial markets and their underlying logics. These mechanisms have engendered a broad societal acquiescence to financialized models of governance, where the promise of prosperity for the many masks the reality of wealth concentration among the few. Central to this transformation has been the state's abdication of its traditional regulatory and welfare responsibilities in favour of an unfettered free market ideology, effectively ceding control of public goods and services to private financial actors. Through privatization and the systematic withdrawal of the state, critical infrastructure, such as social welfare, pensions, education, healthcare, public housing and essential utilities, have been repurposed as financial instruments, prioritizing shareholder returns over public interest (Peck 2010). As a result, municipalities and public authorities have been compelled to renegotiate their relationship with financial markets (Pike 2023), navigating a landscape where debt, speculative investment and financial engineering dictate the provision of essential public services.

As suggested in Chapter 3, the global architecture of (super)profit generation is not an organic outcome of economic forces alone but is instead carefully orchestrated through the intersection of legal frameworks, spatial arrangements and financial practice. The manipulation of regulatory environments, territorial jurisdiction and legal instruments sustains the profitability of financial markets while shaping the material and social geographies within which these mechanisms operate. Crucially, these structures are embedded in micro-histories and micro-geographies, where financial techniques – such as accounting – are not neutral tools but practices deeply contingent on specific spatial and institutional contexts (Leaver 2024; Leaver & Martin 2021). This entanglement of finance, law and geography reveals the extent to which the modern economic order is not merely sustained by markets but actively constituted through legal and spatial practices. It reinforces a system that prioritizes economic growth over social welfare, while equating the two in theory – a logic that fails in practice and perpetuates financial hegemony.

The FABS industry, introduced in Chapter 2, has been instrumental in shaping the financial economy by establishing powerful economic ecosystems within IFCs. These ecosystems are sustained by major consulting firms, such as McKinsey & Company, Boston Consulting Group and Bain & Company, which have evolved into dominant global players. However, as Mazzucato and Collington (2023) argue, these firms frequently embody competing interests, simultaneously advising governments and companies in ways that undermine the very institutions they are meant to serve. Their extensive networks across industries blur the distinction between impartial expertise and self-serving agendas, particularly when public sector policy advice intersects with corporate strategies that benefit private sector clients. This conflict of interest raises fundamental concerns about the integrity and objectivity of their recommendations, particularly in policy domains where regulatory decisions can directly shape market structures. FABS professionals wield significant influence, not only through their advisory functions but also because of their embedded role within political, economic and financial institutions. As Folkman *et al.* (2007: 557) delineate, these professionals operate as either "responsive functionaries" or "proactive initiators". The former group, which includes, for example, audit partners, corporate lawyers, compliance consultants, pension fund managers and stock market analysts, ensures adherence to governance frameworks and facilitates capital market transactions. Their function is primarily one of sustaining and legitimizing the financial order, providing essential expertise that reinforces existing corporate structures.

By contrast, proactive initiators – including investment bankers, hedge fund managers, traders and activist investors – drive market-making activities, corporate restructuring and investment arbitrage. Characterized as agents of change, they thrive on non-routine transactions that generate new market opportunities, often engaging in speculative strategies that prioritize short-term financial gains over long-term stability. The ascendance of activist investors has further entrenched this dynamic, as corporate strategies increasingly cater to demands for enhanced economic value extraction rather than productive reinvestment. Both categories of professionals remain deeply integrated within major financial businesses, reinforcing the dominance of large corporate clients. This has led to what critics term a technocracy (Esmark 2020), a global consultocracy (Ylönen & Kuusela 2019) or simply a Big Con (Mazzucato & Collington 2023) – an expansive, consultancy-driven economic model in which *expertise* is commodified, reinforcing economic and financial hegemony under the guise of advisory neutrality. The previous chapter established the link between expanding legal jurisdictions and financial territorialities, demonstrating how IFCs serve as key sites of governance and orchestration. To deepen this analysis, the present chapter explores the role of professional expertise as a gatekeeping mechanism, demonstrating how financial industries justify and perpetuate their dominance through exclusive yet expanding epistemological frameworks.

Professions are key sites through which continuity and change are negotiated. Building on the previous chapter's argument that *practice* connects complexes and complexity (Hui *et al.* 2017), this chapter explores how professional actors carry, shape and embed these practices – (re)defining and (re)legitimising systemic and institutional power within the financial economy. The concept of institutionalization – understood as the process by which abstract rules are transformed into the constitutive elements of recurring interactions (Jepperson 1991) – offers a critical lens for analysing how professions influence industry standards, innovation capacity and the spatial organization of financial economies.

Professions do not merely adhere to established regulatory and industry norms; rather, they actively shape and expand the very boundaries of their expertise, that is, their epistemological authority, reinforcing their authority over financial, legal and economic practices while simultaneously redefining their limits. Decades ago, Andrew Abbott (1988) drew attention to the pivotal – yet largely underappreciated – role of the professions in the dynamics of capitalism, challenging the academic tendency to prioritize those concerned with life and death over those engaged in matters of loss and profit: his observation that "accounting is today far more socially important than medicine" (Abbott 1988: 325) highlights the fundamental influence of FABS professionals and technical expertise in shaping and controlling economic systems, regulatory landscapes and companies' decision-making. As *gatekeepers* of knowledge and *enforcers* of industry norms, these professions define (at least to a high degree) not only how financial markets operate but also who holds (epistemological) authority within them. Their institutionalized expertise legitimizes financial expansion, dictating regulatory interpretations, risk assessments and governance frameworks that shape the behaviour of both private and public economic actors. Through this lens, professions emerge not merely as service providers but as *architects* of financialization, constructing the epistemic, epistemological and institutional foundations that sustain the contemporary financial order.

The evolving role of the FABS professions is particularly evident in their response to shifting regimes of risk and regulation, especially from the late twentieth century onward. Since the 1980s, financial risk has emerged as a central organizing principle of economic activity (Germain 1997), prompting the creation of new governance frameworks and regulatory mechanisms (Thiemann 2018). In tandem, the expansion of the FABS industry has become a defining feature to the economization of risk, commonly framed as risk management, and of broader financialization.[1] Operating globally, these firms serve as intermediaries between finance and business, bridging core–periphery hierarchies and facilitating the commodification of specialized knowledge. This reliance on professional expertise has transformed it into a lucrative asset class, fuelling the rapid growth of the FABS sector. Their influence is particularly pronounced in public–private financial dependencies, where they have played a central role in structuring financialized policy shifts. As Mazzucato and Collington (2023) argue, these firms embed themselves deeply within both government and corporate infrastructures, enabling tax engineering, regulatory arbitrage and capital mobility strategies that frequently circumvent state oversight (Haberly & Wójcik 2022; Palan *et al.* 2010).

As an interconnected complex, the near-hegemonic role of FABS firms and professionals not only generates commercial value but also shapes national institutions, exporting ostensibly universal economic principles and codifying "best practices" as global standards. Their influence thus extends well beyond economic metrics, permeating legal architectures, governance reforms and the institutionalization of calculative norms (Harrington 2016). Beyond their economic and regulatory reach, FABS firms leverage collective knowledge resources, extract class-monopoly rents and craft strategic narratives that entrench neoliberal orthodoxy (Cahill & Konings 2017). In short, the very actors who codify financial practices and standardize governance mechanisms – lawyers and accountants – function as *nomospheric technicians* (Delaney 2010), shaping the *nomosphere*: the way law organizes space and influences behaviour and relationships through the dynamic interplay between law and geography. Lawyers, who "write the law", and accountants, who "define what the prescribed numbers mean" (Abbott 1988: 30), wield a unique capacity to institutionalize financial logics (Cutler 2003), entrench regulatory asymmetries and consolidate global financial hegemony. This, in turn, affords them strategic power to circumvent, reshape or compete for dominance over regulatory frameworks (Miller 1986).

Operating through the languages of risk management, performance metrics and connective governance, these professions embed themselves within policy infrastructures by projecting their expertise as neutral, apolitical and techno-cratic. This rhetorical positioning serves not only to deflect public scrutiny but also to obscure the vested interests that underpin professional authority. Technocracy, conceptualized as an "art of government" (Esmark 2020: 7), legiti-mizes decision-making through ostensibly objective expertise, institutionalized via councils, committees and independent – often consultancy-driven – agencies.

Yet this transformation is far from procedural. It signals a deeper *economiza-tion of knowledge*, a process that has accelerated over the past four decades. In post-industrial economies – where intangible assets and knowledge imprints constitute core sources of value – professions function as gatekeepers, orches-trating specialized knowledge circuits that underpin financial and managerial decision-making. Crucially, they do not merely mediate flows of expertise; they commodify and capitalise on them, reinforcing their own centrality within gov-ernance frameworks. FABS firms, in particular, have positioned themselves as *arbiters* of economic value, rendering expertise both a commodity and a cur-rency within contemporary governance. This is a crucial aspect of how financial-ized societies institutionalize specialized, often technocratic forms of expertise that underpin and legitimize complex financial systems.

Further, and as engineers of institutional knowledge, they strategically con-struct and inhabit what may be termed *epistemological jurisdictions* – territo-rialized domains of expertise in which knowledge is produced, contested and weaponized to uphold professional authority. Legal knowledge, in particular, is recognized not only as a social construct but as a potent source of strategic power (Dingwall & Lewis 2014 [1983]). In this context, technocratic legitimacy operates less as a neutral expression of truth and more as a mechanism of insti-tutional dominance. Through FABS professions' cultivation of epistemological jurisdictions, FABS professionals/firms align the logics of expertise with the structural imperatives of financial capitalism, ensuring that knowledge remains both a tradable asset and a tool for maintaining control.

The co-constitution of FABS professions and their affiliated professionals and firms emerges as a defining feature of financialization, wherein standards are articulated through distinct epistemologies of expertise. These standards have not only reconfigured economic theory and policy frameworks but have also played a pivotal role in legitimizing and entrenching dominant forms of pro-fessional authority and conduct. Nation-states – once primarily tasked with governing the global financial system – have increasingly assumed the role of commodifying agents (see also Cerny 1993), endorsing and institutionalizing the highly specialized forms of technical knowledge required to establish and maintain these evolving norms. Nowhere is this dynamic more apparent than in the fields of law, legal practice and accounting, where regulatory regimes have become both products and instruments of financial expansion. Far from acting as neutral arbiters, states have facilitated the *juridification* of financial epistemology, reinforcing the authority of select professions whose expertise is central to the legitimization and governance of markets – that is, to the construction of financial truths.

Two less-explored insights further illuminate this argument. First, although professions are defined and legitimized through national legal and political structures, they increasingly operate transnationally – exporting and importing specialized knowledge regimes that, while formally anchored to specific jurisdictions, in practice transcend them. This mobility of legal and financial expertise gives rise to a globalized professional economy (e.g. Ryngaert 2013), in which regulatory convergence is increasingly driven by industry-defined standards rather than sovereign prerogatives (for a historical perspective on this shift, see Molt 2006).

Second, in a world predicated on the unfettered circulation of capital, individuals and goods, the professions of law and accountancy have become central to global governance systems that regulate and facilitate these flows. Their influence now extends well beyond clearly demarcated sovereign borders, shaping the logics of jurisdictional expansion and territorialization that underpin contemporary financial capitalism. As epistemic authorities, these professions do not simply respond to regulatory change; rather, they actively define, interpret and enforce the legal and technical parameters that structure financial markets.[2] In doing so, the state, FABS professions and financial firms have collectively reconfigured regulatory authority, shifting the locus of power from sovereign control towards professional standards as the dominant arbiters of global economic governance – a transformation that continues to reshape territorialities, jurisdictions and the architecture of financial regulation itself.

The rising demand for specialized financial expertise – manifest in both professional bodies and firms – has further entrenched the dominance of FABS professions over other occupational domains. Notably, FABS remain among the UK's most successful export sectors, particularly in the management of financial assets (Kay 2016). Under persistent shareholder and investor pressure to maximize value, and guided by financial metrics, the private sector has become increasingly financialized, expanding in scope, scale and global reach, while embedding market-disciplinary logics into everyday governance. Across these shifting terrains, FABS professions function as potent mechanisms of social control, reproducing standards of expertise and professional practice across multiple scales (Evetts 2003). Within this landscape, financial risk analysis and risk management have become indispensable instruments – analytical techniques that do not merely assess uncertainty but actively shape how institutions perceive, prioritize and govern it (Jarvis & Griffiths 2007).

Alluding to Golka (2025: 77), we have established that assets function as *boundary objects*, accommodating the diverse "information needs" of different social contexts. For instance, accountants may interpret assets on corporate balance sheets as "resources available for business operations", while portfolio managers evaluate them through risk–return profiles (Chiapello 2024). These interpretations are not necessarily aligned. The process of *narrative transformation* can serve to reconcile these divergent professional perspectives – accountants, investors, lawyers, business developers – by illustrating that assetization is, at its core, a *relational transformation*: it dislocates objects from their original contexts or claimants and reassembles them as financial assets (Tellmann 2022).

Because various social groups participate in the valuation of objects, the asset form increasingly enables the colonization of this process by investors – whose primary concern lies with anticipated future cash flows. Financial valuation tools, particularly discounting, play a pivotal role in this shift by translating those future cash flows into present value. Discounting thus operates as a political technology (Doganova 2024), one that shapes how expectations about the future are quantified, valued and ultimately acted upon. By reducing future costs and benefits to their present equivalents, discounting embeds itself within financial markets and policy frameworks, exerting a profound influence over contemporary decision-making – and the futures these decisions bring into being.

For asset managers and investors, discounting is indispensable: it enables the calculation of an asset's present value based on projected profitability, aligning valuations with prevailing interest rates. This translation of future potential into current worth serves to mitigate investor uncertainty and incentivize investment, despite inherent risk. Yet this process is far from neutral. While discounting ostensibly quantifies the "time cost of money" (Doganova 2024: 11), it is in fact a situated and contested practice, embedded within specific historical, social and economic imaginaries. Crucially, discounting shifts attention away from long-term value creation and toward short-term financial returns – with far-reaching implications. Nowhere is this more apparent than in the context of climate change, where discounting effectively diminishes the urgency of addressing long-term systemic risks. By prioritizing investments that yield high present value, the practice of discounting marginalizes broader socio-ecological concerns. The underlying assumptions of discounting paradoxically centre the future while simultaneously devaluing it, erasing the past and present as meaningful coordinates for decision-making.

Ultimately, discounting transforms complex questions of property, value and ownership into seemingly objective matters of financial calculation. In doing so, it grants investors disproportionate influence over uncertain futures – futures that are governed not by collective deliberation, but by private expectations.

This redistribution of authority raises critical questions about which temporal and institutional perspective – governmental or investor-led – should prevail in shaping decisions across divergent discount rates and time horizons (Doganova 2024).

Sassen (2010) underscores the fragmented architecture of financial services, a condition that produces knowledge asymmetries which FABS firms and professionals – armed with specialized expertise – are well-positioned to exploit. As financial networks mirror a global hierarchy of knowledge intensity and epistemic embeddedness (Knorr Cetina & Preda 2005), FABS' epistemic labour becomes not only foundational to the construction of financial products, but also essential to grasping the situated practices of financial agents and intermediaries. These actors include analysts, strategists, technical specialists and other knowledge workers embedded across a diverse array of institutions: banks, asset managers, credit rating agencies, investment firms, law and accountancy firms, consultancies and adjacent finance-related domains. One particularly revealing case is that of credit intermediation via the shadow banking system, which underscores the profound entanglement of financial transactions with knowledge production. Far from being a peripheral phenomenon, shadow banking comprises a dense web of non-bank financial entities – such as private equity firms, special investment vehicles (SIVs), hedge funds and money market funds – operating through opaque, highly bespoke contractual arrangements (Ban & Gabor 2016). These transactions are anything but mechanical; they hinge on specialized expertise, tacit knowledge and finely tuned coordination among financial professionals who effectively act as the architects of these complex structures.

A second illustrative example lies in the knowledge-intensive passporting process for investment funds across the European Union. These schemes hinge on intricate reciprocal arrangements between jurisdictions, whereby regulatory approval granted in one member state enables the cross-border distribution of financial services with minimal additional oversight. Designed specifically for federal or quasi-federal polities such as the EU, passporting mechanisms rest not merely on legal harmonization but on an implicit trust in the regulatory competence and institutional credibility of counterpart regimes. In this sense, financial integration is as much a function of epistemic confidence as it is of formal compliance.

A third illustrative example is the burgeoning practice of fractional ownership, which enables multiple investors to hold shared equity stakes in high-value assets – be it real estate, fine art or infrastructure (Dörry & Hesse 2022). Departing from traditional co-ownership models, fractional ownership platforms reconfigure property rights by converting tangible assets into tradeable financial units. This transformation is increasingly mediated through tokenization, whereby blockchain technology encodes fractional shares as digital tokens, facilitating their exchange with enhanced liquidity and reduced transaction costs. By financializing property rights to create more liquid markets under the guise of "democratization", new financial platforms extend market access to assets that were once the preserve of institutional or UHNWI investors. Yet this shift also unsettles conventional notions of governance, as ownership becomes progressively abstracted from use, stewardship or spatial proximity. Revenue is generated not through the productive use of the asset, but through transaction fees, platform levies and intricate legal-financial structuring. In this sense, tokenized fractional ownership exemplifies the deepening financialization of real assets, reshaping both investment logics and the ontology of ownership itself.

These examples stress the significant reliance of financial practices on networks of knowledge and expertise, although the relevance and efficacy of specialized knowledge within these networks vary depending on context. The implementation of new financial regulations has increased demand for specialized expertise, often embodied in consultancy services, positioning them as essential *organizational commodities* (Mazzucato & Collington 2023). In asset management, FABS professionals/firms play an indispensable role in fund design, restructuring and liquidation, while also providing critical legal certification and auditing services for fund-related transactions. Their influence is further reinforced by their ability to leverage diverse forms of knowledge and exercise financial-functional power *ad positionem* – allowing them to propose policy solutions that not only serve regulatory compliance but also create new markets for their services.

As key knowledge providers to a broad spectrum of stakeholders, FABS firms operate as powerful *epistemic arbiters*, actively shaping both the regulatory and operational contours of financial markets. This role is particularly pronounced within the legal profession, where international lawyers and law firms play a formative role in constructing the global legal architecture. Indeed, international legal practices do not merely navigate existing rules – they actively shape the institutional and legal frameworks that underpin global finance and trade, managing complex interstate conflicts and facilitating cross-border negotiations (Riles 2011). To perform this function, they must mediate between localized legal regimes and global normative structures, effectively assuming a quasi-sovereign role in transnational legal affairs.

Having established the centrality of embedded epistemologies in financial expansion, it becomes essential to recognize the role of *professionalization* in consolidating and safeguarding these epistemological jurisdictions. As a complementary social technology, professionalization reinforces the authority, legitimacy and economic privilege of professionals vis-à-vis other expert communities. In doing so, legal and accountancy professionals not only secure their dominance within financial governance but also enhance their capacity to influence the evolution of regulatory and market structures.

Indeed, for Abbott (1988), for example, *jurisdiction* is a critical analytical concept for understanding the division of expert labour – both in its historical reproduction and its ongoing evolution in modern societies' institutionalization of expertise. Jurisdictions refer to the categorization of social problems around which expert tasks are organized. These categories encompass not only the (re) framing of problems themselves but also the tools, technologies and material facts that shape professional practice. Jurisdictions – conceived as the abstract organization of expert labour – are fundamental to the structuring, reproduction and transformation of financial and economic life. They act as the connective tissue linking complexes of practices, while moments of professional performance serve to reproduce these practice complexes as outcomes of the interplay between jurisdictional logics and temporal, material and spatial dimensions. Sociologists increasingly recognize the FABS professions as authoritative occupational groups that exert considerable influence over markets, subordinate other professions, and shape regulatory architectures through "regulative bargains", often negotiated to advance their own interests (Evetts 2003). While this perspective may attract criticism for its Anglo-American bias, it remains salient in light of the substantial expansion of FABS professions within the neoliberal Anglo-American capitalist model – preceding and, indeed, facilitating their global diffusion from the late 1970s onwards. Since then, FABS firms and professionals have undergone profound transformations, extending their reach across global financial markets.

Within the broader dynamics of financialization – nuanced, adaptable and uneven though they may be – this transformation reflects the ascendancy of financial institutions and sources of capital over their non-financial counterparts. It has also introduced new complexities to the structure and operation of globalizing financial markets, not least through an intensified focus on financial risk and its management (Germain 1997).

Professions and professionals

A defining characteristic of any profession is its monopoly of expertise, with jurisdiction serving as its constitutive asset. This monopoly grants the profession the power to command society's trust, thereby securing and maintaining a privileged and autonomous position (Rueschemeyer 2014 [1983]). Yet, as Rueschemeyer notes, such monopolization carries the inherent risk of eroding that very trust. The idealistic assumption – voiced by Goode (1957) – that professional exploitation would inevitably lead to diminished prestige and increased lay oversight has been increasingly challenged. This tension is particularly evident in high-profile scandals such as WorldCom, Parmalat and Enron in the early 2000s, and in the aftermath of the 2007/08 financial crisis, all of which highlighted a widening rift between professional values and broader societal expectations.

Nonetheless, a profession's jurisdiction remains closely intertwined with the state, affording it opportunities to extend its influence beyond its immediate domain. Lawyers working within the judiciary, for instance, operate as extensions of state authority, occupying a space at the nexus of public and private governance. Accountants, similarly, have expanded their jurisdiction by monopolizing key accountancy services, such as auditing, while also asserting control over adjacent domains including taxation, management consultancy, insolvency, company flotations, mergers and share issuances (see Macdonald 1995). In doing so, they have, at times, encroached upon the epistemological jurisdiction of law, thereby blurring conventional professional boundaries.

Both the legal and accountancy professions assert comparable levels of institutionalization, marked by the codification of jurisdictional boundaries and their incorporation into a hierarchically structured national professional system – reinforced through state-sanctioned licensing regimes. This process of institutionalization is central to the production and maintenance of epistemic authority, upon which professional legitimacy ultimately rests. Unlike more organizationally fluid occupations such as management consultancy, law and accountancy occupy a more privileged normative position within the professional landscape (see Table 4.1).

The degree of *institutionalization* within a profession significantly shapes its capacity to negotiate, legitimize and defend its jurisdiction against rival occupational groups, thereby influencing its ability to sustain professional authority. Jurisdictional control and epistemic authority are not fixed assets but are instead subject to ongoing contestation – precisely because such authority constitutes a valuable commercial resource within the corporate sphere. Legal and accountancy professions, for example, lay claim to historically protected jurisdictions closely aligned with state-regulated domains and institutional power. In contrast, professions such as management consulting have either struggled to secure similarly advantageous relationships with the state (Muzio *et al.* 2011) or have succeeded only within specific national contexts (Paterson *et al.* 2003).

The ability to defend epistemic authority is readily observable in the professional landscape. A particularly illustrative case is the often covert yet intense competition between professions – most notably between elite law firms and the Big Four accountancy firms – for extended client contracts. This jurisdictional rivalry surfaced more publicly in Luxembourg in 2016, within the world's second-largest asset management centre. The Bar Association there contemplated legal action against the Big Four, alleging persistent encroachment on the legal profession's domain. At the heart of the dispute was what legal professionals

Table 4.1 Characteristics of FABS professions

Examples of ABS professions	Forms of professionalism, degrees of state institutionalism
Accountancy; law; real estate surveying; etc.	*Occupational professionalism ("traditional" professions):* • discourse constructed within professional groups: discretionary decision-making in complex cases, collegial authority, occupational control of the work, based on trust in the practitioner; • operationalized and controlled by practitioners, based on shared education and training, strong socialization process, work culture and occupational identity, codes of ethics monitored and operationalized by professional institutes and associations. *High degree of institutionalization:* • high degree of social constraints such as licensing, mandatory association membership, developed formal interaction and communication; • professionalism constructed "from within" the profession; • state-granted monopoly of jurisdictions.
Management consultancy	*Organizational professionalism:* • discourse of control by managers in work organizations: rational-legal forms of decision-making, hierarchical structures of authority, standardization of work practices, accountability, target-setting and performance review, based on occupational training and certification. *Low degree of institutionalization:* • low degree of social constraints such as licensing, mandatory association membership, developed formal interaction and communication; • professionalism constructed "from the outside" (work organization, firm); • no/low state protection of their jurisdictions.

Source: author, based on Evetts 2006, Greenwood *et al.* 2002.

viewed as a systematic infringement of their jurisdiction – an erosion of professional autonomy. As one interviewee remarked with evident frustration:

> Legally, auditors are obliged to audit investment funds. The trade-off is that they also handle everything for our clients. They provide consulting services, including [...] reporting consultancy and regulatory consultancy. Of course, the auditors claim to have internal procedures in place to prevent conflicts of interest. I will not expand on that issue. [...] The management company or the fund appoints [...] us as their legal adviser. [...] However, auditors frequently engage in both tax advisory services and the preparation of annual accounts for the funds. In other words, they first design a fund's tax structure and then audit it. Any reasonable person would recognize this as a clear conflict of interest.

[...] The most concerning aspect is that auditors gain access to our clients' case files, review tax rulings, and examine the entire structure. [...] Then, during Board of Directors meetings – when presenting the annual report – they say: 'Look, we could also provide regulatory advice for you, as well as this, this, and this ... and it would cost you such and such an amount.

(Partner of a global law firm, May 2014, author's translation)

In the context of financial risk and its management, the accountant's commitment to ensuring security operates as a powerful legitimizing discourse (Jensen *et al.* 2012). This discourse has been instrumental in delineating the operational parameters that have enabled the banking, insurance and fund management industries to exert considerable influence over the global economy. In response, the accountancy profession has strategically reinforced and expanded its approach, placing increased emphasis on the identification, control and management of financial risk – as explored further below.

Beyond intensifying inter-professional competition, another critical transformation gained traction in the late 1990s: the transition to *prudential regulation*, strongly endorsed by the state, marked a shift in regulatory emphasis from public oversight to private-sector governance (Riles 2011; Thiemann 2018).[3] Unlike earlier frameworks designed to facilitate cross-border capital mobility, prudential regulation prioritized global financial stability. This pivot spurred a surge in financial auditing and a growing focus on risk. Simultaneously, the domain of global private law – particularly in areas such as financial derivatives – expanded rapidly, as banks and financial institutions began to reframe themselves as providers of *risk products* (Germain 1997). In this evolving landscape, collateral emerged as a central instrument of private governance, while demand for accountancy, audit and legal services rose sharply.

Amid accelerated financial globalization, this shift towards prudential regulatory practices constituted a critical caesura, during which professions traditionally regarded as custodians of technical knowledge increasingly came to function as societal *brokers of meaning* (Noordegraaf 2007). FABS professionals played a pivotal role in embedding new financialized practices and technologies within regulatory and corporate frameworks. Yet, investing, trading, auditing and accounting are not purely technical activities; they are culturally embedded, iterative and enacted through multi-agent, often transnational interactions. These processes give rise to divergent understandings of financial instruments across professional and institutional communities, each shaped by its own distinctive evaluation culture (MacKenzie 2011). While such pluralism fosters innovation and contributes to the ongoing evolution of financial markets, it also introduces systemic vulnerabilities. Irresponsible practices, misaligned incentives or epistemic disjunctures can generate market distortions, financial crises and scandals – exposing the fragility of the very frameworks intended to ensure stability.

The preceding examples elucidate how shifts in jurisdiction have intensified inter-professional competition, how professions increasingly align with and reinforce the logics of financialization and how the evolving relationship between the state, firms and professional bodies has shaped strategic spaces for capital accumulation and risk management – two core dynamics of both financialization and assetization. Grounded in practice-thinking, these discussions help to "[d]isclos[e] the hows, whys, and so-whats" of the structural fabrics underpinning legal geographies, thereby uncovering their broader socio-political significance (Delaney 2015: 98). Within this analytical frame, the relationships among agents who shape social processes through the deployment of social technologies and artefacts coalesce into a powerful nexus of state, firms and professions.

This state–firm–profession nexus (Figure 4.1) is deeply embedded in contemporary commercial practices, resonating with Sinclair's (2000: 489, emphasis in original) notion of a "*deep infrastructure* of contemporary commercial life". Complex socio-technical arrangements – such as prudential regulation – involve a constellation of informal committees, international organizations (e.g. the G20, the Financial Stability Forum [FSF], the OECD, the IMF and the World Bank) and decentralized professional networks engaged in highly technical regulatory matters (Porter 2005). For example, the FSF was established to coordinate

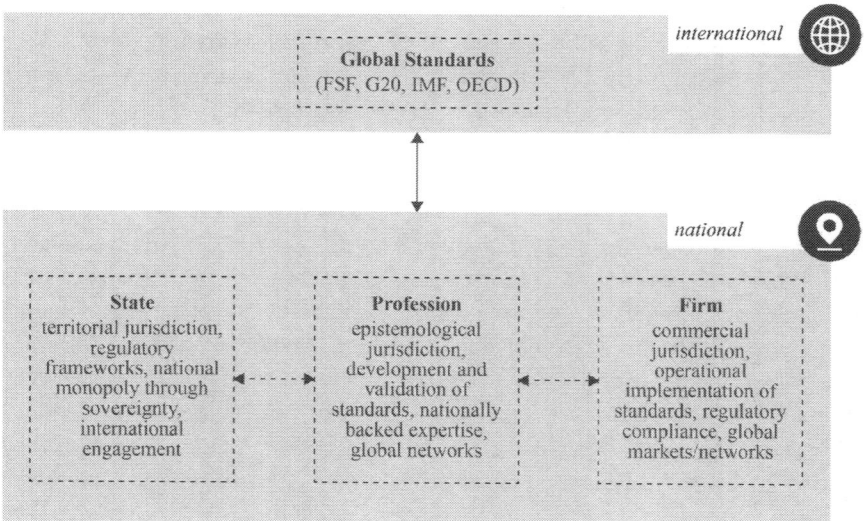

Figure 4.1 The state–firm–profession nexus

the development of global financial standards and codes following the financial crises of the 1990s, which had previously been formulated in a fragmented and uncoordinated manner. These standards were intended to enhance market actors' capacity to manage financial complexity, quantify regulatory compliance and apply mathematically derived risk models.

The work of these practice-oriented networks has centred on shared systems of abstract knowledge as a key mode of social organization – effectively displacing formal legal structures and enabling greater adaptability to global change (Porter 2005). This transformation has significantly increased global demand for financial, legal and regulatory expertise, further entrenching the position of FABS professionals as highly effective institutional agents. Positioned at the intersection of markets, states and transnational organizations, these professionals mediate, coordinate and arbitrage strategic interests, consolidating their role in the governance of global finance (Boussebaa 2015).

However, economic agents do not always adjust their activities to fit existing regulatory frameworks; rather, depending on their power and influence, they may seek to reshape the rules themselves. As Miller (1986: 459) notes, "major impulses to successful financial innovations have come from regulations and taxes", prompting a continuous cycle of action and reaction – a dynamic aptly described as a "regulatory dialectic", and one that is, in effect, subsidized by the state (Brezis & Cariolle 2019; Kane 1986). Within this context, expert knowledge assumes a central role in the governance of prudential regulation, which has increasingly favoured performance-oriented and managerialist approaches. Ultimately, the state–firm– profession nexus operates as a repository of values aligned with neoliberalism and financialization, further entrenching the authority of financial expertise and the imperative of regulatory adaptability within global governance.

For FABS professions, this nexus functions both as a means and an end. It serves as a space for the generation, defence, expansion and institutionalization of specialized knowledge – shaped by the everyday practices of professionals, firms and state actors. Simultaneously, these interlinked spaces orchestrate the strategic knowledge required to manage capital flows and regulatory complexity, operating through what might be termed nexus-thinking. Each dimension of the nexus reinforces alliance-building with external stakeholders, thereby sustaining the professional infrastructure of financial capitalism.

To visualize this interplay between the state, firms and professions, we outline their respective roles:

- The state comprises governmental bodies and regulatory agencies responsible for formulating policies, laws and regulations governing commercial activity. Key actors include formal legislative frameworks and international organizations (e.g. the G20, IMF and World Bank) that shape global financial standards.

- Firms operate within these regulatory frameworks, ensuring compliance while aligning with both state policies and transnational standards.
- Professions refer to specialized bodies of knowledge and expertise (such as financial accounting, auditing and law) essential to the interpretation, implementation and translation of regulation. Although often decentralized, professional networks and associations wield significant influence over both state and business practice.

Arrows connecting these three spheres represent dynamic processes of influence, interaction and collaboration (Figure 4.1). These are enacted through informal committees, transnational standard-setting bodies (e.g. the FSF) and technical-professional networks that translate abstract regulatory norms into applied guidelines and procedures.

Figure 4.1 further illustrates the global character of these interactions, highlighting how international organizations and transnational networks contribute to regulatory harmonization and compliance. This process fosters the *adaptive capacity* of the nexus in response to global economic shifts, while enhancing risk management through the dissemination of standardized practices and regulatory norms. These complex socio-technical arrangements – although formed outside the traditional economic domain – underpin contemporary financial and commercial activity by shaping global epistemologies; that is, the jurisdictions through which they operate.

Over time, such dynamics generate structural transformations within economies and institutions, reinforcing prevailing norms and facilitating legacy-building processes. The practices embedded within the nexus do not simply support existing systems; rather, they actively shape and modify their social significance through "the distinctive practices of naming, classifying, ruling, governing, or ordering associated with law most broadly conceived" (Delaney 2015: 98). In this sense, authority is not only exercised but also enacted and legitimized across multiple scales, with epistemic authority frequently converted into economic capital.

The following three vignettes illustrate how professional practices evolve into institutional forms. Each example draws attention to specific micro-structures and their integration into emerging macro-structures, illuminating the mechanisms through which the state–firm–profession nexus reproduces itself and extends its reach.

Changing epistemological jurisdictions

Chartered accountants: from core tasks to multidisciplinary practices

The creation and expansion of new epistemic authority is not an automatic process, as demonstrated by the evolution of the Canadian profession of chartered accountants (Greenwood *et al.* 2002; Suddaby & Greenwood 2005). Its radical redefinition of occupational membership and values unfolded over more than two decades, beginning in the late 1970s, when the accountancy profession remained largely focused on its traditional core tasks: auditing, accounting and taxation. By 1996, however, it had transformed into a multidisciplinary practice, fully incorporating business advisory services, assurance, risk and management consultancy, corporate finance and legal services.

Technically, accountants, lawyers and management consultants were all equally qualified to transition into multidisciplinary practices, yet accountants were initially more successful in expanding their jurisdiction than their counterparts in other professions (Muzio *et al.* 2011). The underlying process of claiming epistemic authority can be understood as *mediation through theorization.* Professions mediate adjustment for their practitioners and corporate clients, aid in the theorization of change, endorse innovations and facilitate their diffusion (Greenwood *et al.* 2002). Jurisdictional innovations can be far-reaching, often involving the introduction of new standards, which in turn reorganize economic activity. Theorization, a crucial aspect of occupational transformation, serves to justify change and translate new ideas or deviations from prevailing conventions into an accessible, structured form for wider economic adoption. Firms mimic peer firms in anticipation of similar economic gains (Scott 1995); however, in the long term, a profession must align new ideas with normative prescriptions before they can be widely diffused (Greenwood *et al.* 2002).

Professional associations thus play a pivotal role in enforcing pragmatic legitimacy, defending jurisdictional exclusivity and consolidating existing markets while creating new ones. At a transnational level, national accounting associations have sought to align with and promote internationally harmonized standards, reinforcing their global influence. Standardization, a key precursor to global market penetration, ultimately benefited the Big Four accounting firms when national professional accounting divisions transferred this matter to a transnational level. As described by Richard Roberts (2008: 213–14):

> [I]n the early 2000s the International Accounting Standards Board, the leading international accounting body, drew up a set of standard accounting rules known as International Financial Reporting Standards (IFRS). The drive to create a single European market in financial services led to the adoption of an EU directive that required all listed European companies to prepare their accounts in accordance with IFRS from 2005. The EU countries, joined by Australia and South Africa, constituted wave one of what is rapidly becoming a global standard. Wave two consisted of around 70 other countries which by 2007 had undertaken to move towards adoption of IFRS, including Japan, India, South Korea

and Canada. [...] The head of audit at KPMG hailed the IFRS story as "the biggest revolution in financial reporting in living memory".

Fundamentally, the calculative expertise of accountancy functions as a mechanism for addressing the challenges of liberal government. By establishing a realm of specialized, 'private' knowledge, which governments must recognize for their own administrative and regulatory purposes, accounting technologies have secured a critical role in governance. This enables a dual dynamic: while political intervention is limited, the state acknowledges the political significance of private sector activities. Consequently, accountancy has evolved into an instrument for governing the economy, aligning with a governmental approach that recognizes the state's limited power to act as directly related to its limited power to know. It is within this gap between governmental rationalities and economic expertise that accountancy has positioned itself, objectifying and shaping an aspect of economic life central to (neo-)liberal governance (Miller & Power 1995).

Expanding professionals' jurisdictions

The example of commercial real estate financing highlights intensified competition for epistemic authority within evolving professional jurisdictions, particularly in relation to new financial metrics. Financial innovations in real estate have broadened its geographical scope, shifting profit sources across organizations, industries and regions. The Royal Institution of Chartered Surveyors (RICS), for instance, has played a pivotal role in setting global standards and institutionalizing real estate knowledge. In the context of economic globalization, real estate consultancies faced growing competitive pressures, while accountancy firms and UK and US banks emerged as key challengers in cross-border real estate investment financing. However, the RICS successfully consolidated its position as a global epistemic authority, empowering real estate practitioners to regain influence by facilitating the adoption of new services and financing technologies for cross-border property transactions in the 2000s. The case of commercial real estate financing, emblematic of both financial and asset capitalism, illustrates the heightened competition for epistemic authority at the boundaries of evolving professional jurisdictions, particularly in relation to new financial metrics. This competition has fuelled additional finance-related work for FABS professions and practitioners. Financial innovations in commercial real estate have expanded the global geographical scope of the sector, redistributing profit sources across organizations, industries and regions, with professions actively contributing to the (hidden) innovation of new financial techniques.

The RICS, a quasi-monopolistic knowledge authority, operates as a prominent international professional organization with quasi-monopolistic influence, exerting authority in two key areas. First, it establishes professional standards, with RICS certification serving as a crucial credential for international real estate advisory firms seeking to attract business and build client trust. Second, the RICS has institutionalized education, exercising authority over curriculum development. RICS-accredited higher education institutions worldwide facilitate multidirectional knowledge exchanges, reinforcing knowledge institutionalization. However, knowledge is not merely disseminated; rather, it is actively generated, legitimized by professions and made economically viable by professionals. Crucially, this process empowers real estate advisory firms to act as strategic intermediaries and information brokers, thereby shaping and reshaping markets. In this context, the transformation of 'property space' – the assetization of commercial real estate – was not driven solely by legal professionals. Changes in other fields and domains of expertise, particularly surveying, played a crucial role.

Surveying, reimagined as a technical discipline, transitioned from simply documenting use-rights linked to specific locations to conceptualizing land as distinct, bounded parcels of space (Blomley 2022). Chartered surveyors, leveraging their RICS-accredited expertise, assumed a leading role in the late 1970s, coinciding with the privatization initiatives of the Thatcher administration, which created a pressing demand for property valuation skills. As the UK property sector flourished, it became increasingly entwined with complex finance, with the real estate profession acting as a conduit for the adoption of new property performance metrics – soon mimicked by the corporate sector (Lapier 1998).

By the early 1980s, real estate consultancies faced significant challenges owing to their territory-bound organizational structures, particularly in continental Europe, where state-supported professions dominated locally fragmented markets, such as in Germany (Dörry & Heeg 2009). The onset of economic globalization further challenged advisory firms with narrow geographical scopes, yet it also opened opportunities for international accountancy firms, which were seeking to diversify amid downturns in their traditional markets. These firms expanded into real estate taxation, accounting, auditing and financing, facilitated by their ongoing jurisdictional diversification and expansion strategies.

Alongside accountancy firms, the increasing financial expertise of major UK and US banks posed a formidable challenge to nationally oriented real estate advisors. These banks offered a range of complementary services, including international public securities, capital markets services, foreign tax management and investment strategies. However, it was US investment and merchant banks, and later their UK counterparts, that initially met the growing demand for cross-border real estate investment financing. Banks such as Goldman Sachs, Merrill Lynch International and S.G. Warburg leveraged their expertise in developing innovative debt and equity instruments and managing international real estate investments. Although UK banks did not dominate global real estate finance, British financiers played a significant role in financial innovation, largely because of their close ties with leading chartered surveyors (Lapier 1998). Meanwhile, the RICS further entrenched itself as a global epistemic authority, establishing a quasi-monopoly over knowledge standardization and facilitating the institutionalization of real estate expertise. This enabled its members to reclaim epistemic authority, particularly as real estate advisory firms embraced new services and financing technologies for cross-border transactions and refinancing in the 2000s, including risk management.

Managing financial risk: the legal transplant

To appreciate how private legal solutions and financial regulatory technologies have been fostered by the state, we turn to the derivatives market in Japan (Riles 2011). This example underscores the technical dimension of legal and financial regulation as a crucial link between national and global regulatory regimes. Specifically, by examining the collateralization of credit risk, this case illustrates how collateral serves as a prudential regulatory tool, delegated from state authority to private financial institutions, to manage risk in the global swap market.

A key aspect in this regard is the influence of American legal ideology on Japanese commercial law, particularly through the introduction of the American Law of Collateral in 1951, aimed at enhancing the efficiency of commercial transactions. The concept of a legal placeholder is central to this process, functioning as a technique that enables temporary legal transferability between jurisdictions, thereby facilitating standardization and a shared legal understanding across different legal and economic contexts.[4] Additionally, this process highlights the role of epistemic networks and documentation practices in transplanting foreign legal regimes into the Japanese market, ultimately contributing to the standardization and "formatting" of financial markets. In sum, the derivatives market in Japan demonstrates that private legal solutions and technologies for financial regulation have consistently been shaped by state intervention, fostering closely integrated legal ecosystems that enable private regulatory solutions. More broadly, it underscores the importance of the technical dimension of legal and financial regulation as the critical link between national and global regulatory regimes, particularly through the legal technique of collateralization of credit risk.

Collateral, as a component of prudential regulation, represents a set of knowledge practices that bridges the compartmentalized nature of global private law with the transnational character of swap markets, where parties operate across different jurisdictions, transact in multiple currencies, and – particularly in the case of bonds – engage with issuers from different national governments (Riles 2011). The delegation of risk control from state authorities to private financial institutions via collateralization ensures adequate capital holdings, reinforcing financial stability within the global swap market. The elevation of collateral from a national legal framework to a global regulatory tool became necessary to meet the demands of the global swap markets, particularly in New York and London. This legal technique encompasses both material and procedural knowledge practices, alongside documentary and institutional tools that facilitate coordination among market participants while reinforcing social and institutional relationships. Japan's legal framework governing firms, banking and securities, although historically influenced by German and French civil law traditions, was substantially redrafted by American technocrats in the post-Second World War period. The integration of US legal principles aimed to enhance commercial efficiency, aligning Japanese commercial law with American practices. This culminated in the introduction of the US Law of Collateral into Japan in 1951, further embedding American legal structures within the Japanese regulatory framework.

The pressure exerted by foreign banks led Japanese financial institutions to advocate for the adoption of collateral law, prompting Japanese regulators to integrate these principles into domestic legislation. However, the process of incorporating established market practices into the legal framework necessitated collaboration between legal professionals and public technocrats to resolve the technical complexities of legal adaptation. This challenge was ultimately addressed through "the actual intellectual connections [public] technocrats formed with the agents of private governance at the level of the technical legal detail" (Riles 2011: 109).

The creation of legal placeholders enables temporary legal solutions that facilitate the transferability of legal concepts across jurisdictions while accommodating differing interpretations of commercial law. A legal placeholder, although not legally binding, provides a practical and adaptable solution through documentation-based technical legal knowledge, rather than relying on abstract legal theory. In Japan, this technique has been implemented through collaborative efforts between national and international lawmakers, judges, regulators and legal professionals affiliated with organizations such as the International Swaps and Derivatives Association (ISDA). Legal placeholders, particularly through documentation practices, have standardized regulatory processes and fostered a shared legal understanding, leading to extensive collaboration between academics and bureaucrats. These collaborations formed epistemic networks, which produced self-evident legal norms and facilitated the transplantation of foreign legal regimes, particularly those originating in New York, into the

Japanese financial system. Legal artefacts – such as standardized contractual documents – play a critical role in structuring financial markets, transcending cultural, institutional and geographic barriers while reinforcing the global standardization of financial law.

These three vignettes show that innovation, as discussed here, emerges as both a consequence and a driver of expanding and competing professional jurisdictions. Innovation is deeply embedded within local cultural and social contexts (Spigel 2016), a dynamic particularly visible in the jurisdictional migration and expansion of accountancy-related professions (see Greenwood *et al.* 2002). While the empirical cases reflect distinct settings and trajectories, they collectively underscore the pivotal role of *epistemic authority* in enabling professional expansion at the intersection of professions, professionals/firms and the state. Each case illustrates how epistemic jurisdictions have been successfully extended – across geographical spaces, administrative boundaries or in contestation with rival knowledge claims asserted by competing professions. Within this nexus, boundaries remain fluid, enabling the creation, validation and economization of professional knowledge. Crucially, these epistemic resources are often reinforced by the nation-state, securing legitimacy and commercial value.

The continual evolution of knowledge structures within these jurisdictions reflects a process of directed, purposeful innovation – innovation that occurs not randomly, but within institutional frameworks and in response to opportunity spaces created by jurisdictional shifts. These practices unfold within *fields*, understood as structured systems of social relations and hierarchies of power (Bourdieu 1977). Here, innovation is not a merely technical or economic process; rather, it is culturally and socially embedded. Local norms act as institutions, shaping interactions and determining which practices attain legitimacy and success. Innovation thus comprises a constellation of interrelated practices: the development of new knowledge, cross-organizational collaboration and the strategic recombination of insights to generate novel technologies and markets.

The *local field* – the social and institutional environment in which actors are embedded – plays a critical role in shaping these innovation processes. Actors' habitual understandings of their field influence strategic decisions, while their capacity to innovate depends on alignment with prevailing cultural and institutional norms. Moreover, this embeddedness also informs how actors interpret and respond to external practices and global trends (Spigel 2016). Cultural embeddedness, then, becomes a defining feature of professional innovation, particularly within the close-knit communities that characterize financial centres.

Legal actors, in particular, operate with a degree of discretion that is both inevitable and flexible (Silbey 2001). Their actions are not solely dictated by legal rules but are mediated by everyday social interactions. Through typifications – conceptual shortcuts developed via repeated social encounters – legal actors navigate complex legal environments. Law, in this sense, both reflects and reproduces broader social life: it draws on shared cultural norms, institutional practices and collective understandings to frame and legitimize social relationships. Socio-legal scholarship emphasizes that law is neither fully autonomous from nor wholly subordinate to the market. Rather, it functions through an interplay of social and economic forces. Mapping the intersection of law with other social fields reveals that its power does not lie in omnipotence, but in *omnipresence* – in its entanglement with the very practices that shape governance.

Why is a focus on professions and professionals important when analysing the development of IFCs as assemblages of authority? To a certain degree, core professions of law and accounting have morphed from stewards of technical knowledge into commercial growth machines – actively leveraging expertise to shape markets and generate future profits. Their authority now lies not only in what they know, but in how that knowledge is used to capitalize on financial opportunities. Professions and firms construct the markets they operate in, influence regulation and legitimize financial logics. Understanding their expanding epistemological reach is key to understanding how IFCs develop and maintain influence.

IFCs promote a model of financial economies often framed as a catalyst for regional development – with London being a prominent example. In practice, however, profit is siphoned off rather than reinvested. With decreasing corporate tax rates, less revenue remains for public infrastructure or welfare. Although FABS firms generate jobs and pay high salaries, they also exacerbate inequality – especially through access to housing in the cities hosting IFCs. To sustain these specialized financial economies, cities aspiring to become or expand as IFCs have invested heavily in cultivating "talent": professionals and firms who carry, refine and expand the epistemologies of finance, law and accounting. Talent itself becomes a strategic asset – mobile, competitive and indispensable to IFC performance. Professions not only supply this talent but also shape the standards by which it is valued.

Law and accountancy play especially central roles. Their jurisdictional competition – often over who can offer the most authoritative knowledge – has spilled over into academia, especially business schools and universities' economics departments, many of which are physically and intellectually embedded within IFCs. This has helped fuel a globalized education industry, producing students whose debt has itself become a valuable asset class, investable by the very financial firms they hope to join. Simultaneously, these institutions work to legitimise and elevate the status of the professions they serve. Thus, professional knowledge is no longer solely about service provision but has become a foundation for future business. This embeds each profession's legitimacy in its capacity to perform: to generate value, attract clients and command influence. While professions and professionals may compete for clients, markets and prestige, they also cooperate to expand the reach of financial industries – growing the metaphorical cake together before dividing it. They help construct regulatory frameworks and promote narratives – such as the democratization of finance through tokenization – that deflect criticism and sustain legitimacy. Professions and professionals are thus not peripheral but central to the economic, political and epistemic power of IFCs.

The practices of legal innovation and jurisdictional expansion discussed throughout this chapter underscore the significance of *micro-geographies* and *micro-histories* – localized spaces and temporalities through which these processes unfold and mutually reinforce one another. These dynamics will be examined in greater depth in the following chapter, with particular emphasis on the *expanding territorialities of law*, offering a complementary perspective to this chapter's focus on the evolving role of professional authority in global economic and financial governance.

5

EXPANDING TERRITORIALITIES OF LAW

Enabling legal geographies of offshoring and onshoring

Engaging with legal themes, such as the relationship between law as discourse and law as power, invites critical reflection on how social space is produced, sustained and transformed, particularly in the realm of finance. Social space is saturated with legal meanings, yet these meanings are plural, contested and open to divergent interpretation. Analysing the social – political, historical and cultural – through a spatio-legal lens offers fresh insights into the constitution of social life and the conditions and consequences of socio-economic transformation. Crucially, this approach challenges the notion that law and geography are external forces acting upon a pre-legal, aspatial entity called "the economy". Instead, it posits that the legal and the spatial are deeply entangled – constituting irreducible dimensions of a holistically conceived socio-material reality. This foundational premise of new legal geographic thought may be further explored through two interrelated dimensions of the social: *power* and *discourse* in and through financial centres.

Therefore, to focus solely on the corporation and its business strategy as a means of understanding the complexities of IFCs is both reductionist and increasingly inadequate. Within the social sciences (with some exceptions), the misleading tendency remains to conflate the *firm* with the *corporation*, especially through the ubiquitous concept of the "multinational corporation". As established previously, the corporation is not the firm but the legal structure through which the firm's business strategy is enabled and executed (Robé 2011): the corporation is a *legal creature* – a legal person – that enters into contractual relationships with other legal persons, such as suppliers, employees and clients. It is through these legal operations that the corporation constitutes the foundation of economic exchange, a useful reminder for this chapter. Indeed, the corporation is continually constituted and reconstituted through distinctive legal practices and institutional operations (Delaney 2015). Importantly, the architecture of corporate design often unfolds in strategic legal geographies and places – most notably IFCs – which function, for example, as hubs of legal pluralism. *Legal pluralism*, understood as a legal–spatial strategy, refers to the coexistence of multiple legal systems within a single jurisdiction, often concentrated in IFCs. These systems may derive from diverse sources, creating a heterogeneous legal landscape in which firms may select among different legal traditions to structure transactions or resolve disputes.

Now, the conventional view of the state as a unified legal order with a monopoly on law is, as Tamanaha (2021) argues, another longstanding legal *fiction*. State legal systems are inherently pluralistic in both form and function. This pluralism extends into the heart of corporate law, carrying profound implications for global economic governance. Legal pluralism does not merely introduce complexity; it actively enables firms to navigate and selectively adopt the most strategically advantageous elements of different legal systems – whether common law, civil law or Islamic finance principles – thereby enhancing their regulatory flexibility and capacity for jurisdictional arbitrage creation. In this sense, legal systems do not coexist passively; to some extent, they *compete* for use, relevance and survival.

However, this same pluralism significantly complicates transnational regulatory enforcement and undermines collective oversight. As supranational institutions seek to standardize tax regimes, reporting obligations or sustainability frameworks, legal pluralism often resists these harmonizing efforts, creating openings for legal and financial manoeuvring. The result is a fragmented legal terrain, where achieving normative coherence – particularly in areas such as environmental protection, labour rights and human rights obligations – becomes increasingly elusive. Rather than a tool for resolving problems, *legal difference* becomes an economic resource, strategically leveraged through arbitrage.

In many jurisdictions, corporate law is shaped by a composite of statutory law, case law and regulatory frameworks established by state authorities – structures particularly evident within IFCs. Tax avoidance mechanisms such as the *Double Irish* and the *Dutch Sandwich* have exemplified how multinational companies strategically leverage jurisdictional privileges embedded within legal frameworks.[1] Crucially, however, such corporate strategies rely not solely on firm-level decision-making but on the enabling legal infrastructures of specific jurisdictions.

Large business corporations operate strategically across a patchwork of jurisdictions, each offering distinct legal regimes. This leads to increasing complexity in corporate governance and compliance requirements. Within this fragmented legal landscape, law, legal and accountancy practices, and corporate governance standards play a critical role in shaping both industry norms and international regulatory frameworks. As Delaney (2015: 99) observes, "these innumerable spatially constitutive episodes are clearly fundamental to the makings and unmakings of places". Legal pluralism manifests through the intersection of diverse legal sources and norms, influencing how corporate structures are designed, governed and regulated. This mutual relationship also underscores how jurisdictions themselves shape opportunities for corporate structuring. Accordingly, expertise in corporate law and governance co-evolves with specific locations and institutions, where legal and financial knowledge is closely aligned with economic power (Dezalay 1995).

The expansion of legal jurisdiction beyond the administrative boundaries of the nation-state reflects broader shifts in power and organizational structure. The emergence of archipelago-like zones of offshoring and exclusion – often materialized through special economic zones – illustrates the strategic deployment of zoning practices that have been embedded in neoliberal policy over extended time horizons (Slobodian 2023). Zoning and offshoring are mutually constitutive processes: while *offshoring* refers to the relocation of economic activity beyond territorial jurisdictions – and thus beyond accountability to national authority or civil society (Peck 2017; Urry 2014) – *zoning* defines and facilitates this movement, enabling the commercial expansion of legal territorialities.

Offshoring has become a central mechanism in contemporary financial economies, characterized by deliberate strategies to circumvent regulation, exploit jurisdictional discrepancies and maintain financial secrecy. As Urry (2014) argues, these practices are not accidental but systematically engineered to evade public oversight and cultivate a clandestine financial world, one that undermines the transparency of open economies. The offshore system enables the concentration of wealth by facilitating tax avoidance and evasion, disproportionately benefiting large financial institutions, UHNWIs, family offices and multinational companies. This is achieved through offshore financial centres, which offer tailored legal, accounting and financial services designed to obscure ownership, facilitate the shifts of financial capital and shield private wealth from regulatory scrutiny. Ultimately, zoning and offshoring are socio-legal practices that reflect broader trends in financial governance. Offshore jurisdictions – often governed or strategically influenced by major powers such as the US, the UK, France and China – serve as crucial enablers for the formation of complex, opaque financial architectures that undermine efforts at global regulatory coordination. While the previous chapter examined the expansion strategies of professional jurisdictions, this section shifts focus to *territoriality* as a political technology of both expansion and social control – one shaped by spatial temporalities and legitimized through legal rationales. A decade ago, Urry (2014) identified the banking sector as the principal beneficiary of offshore tax havens, noting that more than half of overseas subsidiaries were then based in what Shaxson (2011) calls "treasure islands" or what Urry (2014: 51) terms "secrecy jurisdictions". Multinational companies are frequently structured like Russian dolls, characterized by multiple layers of concealment, elaborate ownership chains (Pistor 2019) and dense global contractual networks (Robé 2020). The offshore industry emerged as tax avoidance strategies converged with other forms of regulatory fudging, particularly those targeting financial services in their broadest sense.

For the sake of consistency in this book, and drawing on agency theory (Jensen & Meckling 1979), offshore intermediaries – widely employed by financial services – are conceptualized as *legal fictions*. Many international financial companies, for instance, were initially established offshore to circumvent capital controls and, later, to bypass restrictions on authorized investments (Hampton 1996a). The secrecy afforded by these jurisdictions facilitated not only tax avoidance but also evasion, fraud and the concealment of illicit wealth. As offshore finance expanded, these benefits became increasingly accessible, scalable and institutionalized. Professionals – particularly within law and accountancy – leveraged their expertise to spot and exploit regulatory gaps and the absence of coordinated inter-state enforcement (Picciotto 1995).[2]

This complex legal-financial architecture further distorts national economic indicators. For instance, it can misrepresent national accounts (Borio & Disyatat 2015), particularly in response to revised GDP measurement frameworks (Assa 2017). Such distortions are starkly illustrated in the inflated economic statistics of small tax havens and offshore jurisdictions, where reported GDP figures have, at times, surpassed those of entire continents – such as South America – despite the absence of corresponding real economic activity (Tørsløv *et al.* 2022).

The offshore world is a meticulously constructed ecosystem of legal, financial and tax expertise. It operates through *extended statehood* arrangements, wherein major powers indirectly govern offshore jurisdictions, facilitating the global mobility of capital while systematically undermining local economies. These structures are not accidental but embedded in legal-institutional frameworks that reflect the interests of dominant states and professional elites. The fragmentation of large industrial corporations and the growing emphasis on short-term shareholder value have further entrenched such practices. This has led to what Urry (2014: 175) describes as "global gridlocking" – a condition in which ownership is increasingly concentrated in financial institutions focused on short-term gains, thereby stymieing the possibility of coordinated global economic governance (Hale *et al.* 2013).[3]

This intricate web of offshoring is sustained by complexity and secrecy, often enabled by legal frameworks originating in economically powerful states such as the US, the UK, Germany or France. Practices such as *double non-taxation* intensify the opacity of financial flows (Picciotto 1995, 1999). The nation-state, far from being a passive observer, functions as an active facilitator of the offshore system, providing legal and institutional legitimacy at the intersection of neoliberal policy and transnational capital (Slobodian 2023). The implications for the global economy are profound. Beyond facilitating tax avoidance and evasion, offshore centres have become a linchpin of neoliberal globalization, accelerating the circulation of non-productive and fictitious capital and exacerbating global inequality. While recent reforms have introduced greater transparency in some areas, the core mechanisms persist – albeit in modified forms. Innovation, in this context, has not curbed offshoring but reconfigured it, sustaining its role as a cornerstone of the contemporary financial system.

Legal fiction of the firm, continued

As previously outlined, a crucial distinction exists between the firm as a network of socio-technical relations and business strategies, and the corporation (or partnership, etc.) as a legal person with a distinct identity and formal reporting obligations. Accordingly, conceptions of rights and obligations compel us to interrogate the foundational and distributive effects of the specific legal structures and reporting practices adopted by corporations.

This approach diverges – subtly yet significantly – from prevailing conceptions of *control*, which tend to focus on firm governance and operational organization for *profitability* (see Chapter 3). Such approaches often conflate the economic entity (the firm) with its legal structure (the corporation, partnership, etc.), thereby obscuring their respective roles, as not only Leaver and Martin (2021) argue. Crucially, they note that ideas about how the world *should* be often diverge from the structures that later emerge. This relationship is not necessarily linear or performative; rather, it can be "virtualist" (Miller 2000), producing outcomes that are unintended, misaligned or opaque (Miller 2002). Particular understandings of rights and obligations may therefore be advanced by actors who materially benefit from them – even when those advantages are not immediately apparent in the conceptual framework. It is therefore essential to recognize that social relations are mediated not only by financial capital and instruments but also by law and legal practice. All forms of social interaction, including market exchange, are shaped by discursive framing – structures of meaning that influence how individuals perceive themselves in relation to others, and which condition specific forms of social action (Miller 2002). Law operates as a formalized expression of normative and moral expectations, delineating where relationships and obligations are understood to begin and end. Companies offer a clear example of this dynamic: law functions as a codified expression of moral and normative expectations, defining the boundaries of rights and obligations. Take, for instance, the *limited liability company* – a legal form explicitly designed to limit certain relational responsibilities, most notably by capping the debt liability of owners and shareholders. This limitation reflects a moral judgement about where share-holder obligations ought to begin and end. Yet it is the *act of incorporation* – the legal creation of boundaries – that constitutes the corporation as a separate legal person, just as the formal declaration of *citizenship* constitutes the individual as a natural legal person, embedded within a national community with defined rights and duties (see Figure 3.3).

With the rise and implementation of agency theory (Jensen & Meckling 1979), the epistemological imperialism of economics and its orthodoxy have translated the legal fiction of the firm into a range of real-world consequences. One significant consequence lies in the transformation of the monetary system into an object of capitalist speculation, rather than a functional mechanism supporting industry and the broader economy (Stockhammer 2004). Under this shift, capital is increasingly invested in financial assets purely to generate more capital; money begets money, rather than being (re-)invested and channelled into productive or socially beneficial activities. As Urry (2014) argues, finance has thus become decoupled from its industrial origins and reconstituted as an autonomous economic system – an economy in itself.

Legal scholars have long critiqued economic theory's conflation of the firm and the corporation (Klausner 2013; Robé 2011, 2020) – an error amplified by the influence of agency theory. While the legal attributes of the corporation enable it to own assets, enter contracts and limit liability (Schane 1987), agency theory often obscures these structural features by framing the firm as an entity owned by shareholders and managed on their behalf. Critics contend that agency theory entrenches a narrow view of corporate purpose, prioritizing shareholder value at the expense of broader societal and environmental responsibilities (Robé 2020). In doing so, it not only distorts the legal reality of the corporation but also constrains the normative imagination of what corporate accountability might entail.

Financial centres bring together key financial and legal actors, forming dynamic ecosystems that underpin contemporary finance. However, the legal structuring of complex financial instruments not only reshapes global profit flows but also extends the spatial reach of specific legal regimes. Capital, defined and protected through legal frameworks, lies at the heart of wealth creation and preservation – positioning law as not merely supportive, but constitutive of finance. Law is inherently spatial and deeply entwined with the state (Potts 2020): lawyers strategically deploy legal mechanisms to maximize clients' wealth, while states uphold capital rights through coercive authority.

Within this legal-financial architecture, assetization emerges as a key mechanism. It refers to the transformative process – constituted through legal, accounting and valuation practices – by which legal structures or relations are converted into assets that generate long-term cash flows for investors. Crucially, this involves not only the transformation itself, but also the constitution of the asset as a boundary object (Golka 2025) – a necessary condition for aligning diverse service providers in the co-creation of new and expanding markets. At the same time, assetization foregrounds important socio-ecological tensions, exposing the contradictions between value creation, commodification and long-term sustainability. Asset formation produces rent-bearing property, fundamentally dependent on capitalization and projections of future revenue. As Muniesa (2023) explains, the market value of an asset is derived from its estimated future rents, creating a market in tradable, rent-yielding property once capitalized.

My broader argument is that within IFCs, highly efficient clusters of business ecosystems – comprising legal, financial and consultancy professionals – collaborate with a shared goal: the creation or expansion of financial markets. In this context, assetization can be understood as a distinct modality of financialization, wherein legal and professional practices are shaped by and serve purely economic imperatives. The creation of assets becomes a lucrative pursuit, driven by the expansion of epistemic authority, which legitimizes the professional activities that follow. However, this process often strips assets of their social and ecological *substance*, reducing them to monetizable units of exchange.

This logic reinforces the privileged status of the firm as an economic entity operating within the frameworks of unfettered financial capitalism, while also exposing the pressures facing the various FABS sub-industries. These industries are tasked not just with generating assets for managers within IFCs to administer and invest in, but also with incentivizing IFCs to continually reinvest in their own institutional endowments, such as regulatory infrastructure, to signal the robustness of their asset base to the global financial community. As explored in previous chapters, asset management has itself become a distinct and economically viable market. These dynamics reveal the broad network of beneficiaries produced by financialization – and more specifically, by assetization as a particular modality of financialization – whose logics have rippled throughout the economic system, subordinating both society and nature to the imperatives of financial performance and capital accumulation.

IFCs function as pivotal nodes within the global financial system, serving a diverse clientele of asset managers, institutional investors and financial intermediaries. Policymakers remain highly attentive to these centres, drawn by their perceived contributions to employment, income generation and urban dynamism. From a political economy perspective, the rise of the asset economy marks a fundamental shift at the "regime level" (Braun & Koddenbrock 2023), particularly in relation to the expanding influence of asset management companies.

This transformation is exemplified by the so-called Big Three – Vanguard, BlackRock and State Street Global Advisors – whose expansive and diversified portfolios confer significant ownership stakes across leading global corporations. As universal owners, these firms depart from the traditional shareholder-centric model. Their strategic priority lies less in the performance of individual corporations than in maximizing the aggregate value of AUM. This structural reorientation, encapsulated in the concept of *asset manager capitalism* (Braun 2020), is embedded within a broader constellation of financial actors, including leveraged corporations and the major accountancy firms. The pursuit of elevated share prices rewards extractive ownership models and attracts capital from other financial intermediaries, reinforcing cycles of accumulation and concentration. In doing so, it reshapes global patterns of wealth distribution and reconfigures the broader contours of financial wellbeing. IFCs are thus not merely service hubs but central arenas in which this regime of accumulation is orchestrated and normalized.

The strategic importance of incorporation

A longstanding and thorny question in regional innovation studies is whether "the geography of innovation is the geography of innovative regions ... [or of] the entrepreneur – that is, an innovator who may, or may not, be located within an innovative region" (Shearmur *et al.* 2016: 8). This debate has often given rise to the unsubstantiated assumption that innovation is the exclusive privilege of large urban centres. Nevertheless, the claim that financial activity – and by extension, financial innovation – is concentrated in particular places remains robust. Recent scholarship highlights that "large financial centres like New York, London and Paris ... [are certainly an] indicator for a country's or region's capacity to originate speculative capital flows" (Kohler 2022: 1526–7).

Yet, a financial centre's significance in innovation is not defined solely by proximity, concentration or expertise. Crucially, the state plays an active role in enabling financial innovation by supporting the legal coding of capital – "offering their coercive law powers to enforce the legal rights that have been bestowed on capital" (Pistor 2019: x). In this context, capital is not merely a financial resource; it is constituted by two relational foundational components: an *asset* and a *legal code*. The innovative processes through which assets are legally coded are carried out behind the scenes by the so-called "coding masters" – corporate lawyers – who earn substantial fees for structuring assets in ways that maximize their clients' wealth. This legal infrastructure is central to the production and concentration of capital, as it generates and protects vast reservoirs of wealth for asset holders through rights that are state-sanctioned, enforceable and strategically engineered. We have established that property rights are *rights* – not possessions – and that such rights can be incorporated. Legal persons hold these rights, and incorporation has become an incredibly lucrative business for jurisdictions offering favourable conditions to such private legal persons. Over time, corporations were effectively privatized and granted constitutional protections against government regulation, comparable to those afforded to natural persons (individuals). In many countries, the protection of corporate rights has, in some cases, come to outweigh the protection of the public interest (see Robé 2020) – a trend that continues.

Legal coding – the "process that adapts and molds formal law over time, often without explicit *ex ante* sanctioning by a legislature or a court" (Pistor 2022: 344) – enables lawyers to shield assets from taxation and protect them from creditors, all while utilizing the state's own legal frameworks (Pistor 2019). Today, most financial capital is legally coded in the world's dominant financial centres, particularly New York and London, operating under two dominant legal systems: English common law and New York State law. The essence of legal shielding lies in making wealth harder for others to claim. For instance, individuals with assets exceeding $2 million may establish a trust – a legally coded structure governed by precise conditions – to safeguard their wealth. Offshore relocation of assets is another key strategy within this toolkit. Trusts, in particular, exemplify how legal design is deployed to facilitate asset protection. Trusts merit closer attention (see also Harrington 2016). A trust is a legal arrangement whereby a trustor (or settlor) transfers assets to a trustee to manage on behalf of a beneficiary. Trusts typically serve to protect assets from creditors of both trustee and settlor, facilitate tax and estate planning, and enable confidential or discreet intergenerational wealth transfers. In some jurisdictions, investment funds may incorporate trust structures – especially in common law contexts – as a legal vehicle for pooling and managing investor capital. However, financial leverage within such funds is typically achieved through separate investment strategies rather than the trust structure itself.

In asset management, financial innovation is deeply intertwined with legal design. Finance, "defined almost completely by contracts" (Potts 2016: 524), is underpinned by a global web of contracts (Robé 2020), in which rights and obligations are bundled into "successive layers of progressively more liquid legal vehicles" (Haberly 2020: 558). Such structuring is the domain of specialized FABS firms operating within IFCs, which help shape the distinct business profiles and governance structures of these centres in specific jurisdictions. Collectively, IFCs and FABS complexes enable the global relocation of super-profits, often through creative accounting – a shadow counterpart to financial innovation aimed at tax mitigation – as well as through lobbying and other strategic forms of regulatory engagement. These practices not only lower tax liabilities but also intensify the commercialization of financial engineering in response to rising global demand. The ongoing crisis of the welfare state, coupled with the intensifying concentration of private wealth – particularly among large asset managers, UHNWIs and family offices – has drawn increased scrutiny to the global corporate tax system (Zucman 2015). Here, tax competition and creative accounting have produced "synthetic" legal differences that benefit IFCs in nation-states such as the Netherlands, Dubai, Switzerland and Ireland (Marian 2017). These centres act not simply by virtue of their offshore status, but through their legal interdependence with other jurisdictions – or their own *relational positioning* within the international legal system (Roberts 1994). Their effectiveness lies in how they interact with, complement or exploit the gaps and inconsistencies of other jurisdictions, enabling transnational capital to leverage legal differentials for strategic gain.

This strategic use of legal difference is not abstract; it materializes in concrete institutional arrangements. With PE funds, for instance, the GP is the legal person – able to own assets, enter contracts and litigate independently of the natural persons behind its operations, such as directors or shareholders (see Figure 3.3). This stands in contrast to the assumptions of agency theory; in practice, shareholders leverage the corporate form to create discrete asset pools, enabling debt issuance and accelerating capital accumulation. As Durand (2017) observes, this contributes to the production of fictitious capital – value derived not from tangible assets or productive output, but from speculative expectations of future financial profits – highlighting the widening gap between financial wealth and real economic value creation.

These corporate structures are often situated in jurisdictions with favourable tax or regulatory regimes, facilitating tax arbitrage and reinforcing the disconnection between financial markets and the productive economy. The choice of jurisdiction is not merely administrative; it is a strategic decision that shapes access to capital, regulatory exposure and competitive positioning. As Nougayrède (2019) notes, legal frameworks shape financial strategies – and so does jurisdictional choice. It determines governance, taxation and contract enforceability, making it central to the spatial clustering of financial activity.

A legal-institutional approach sees corporations embedded within differentiated legal environments, whereas economic theory tends to treat them as homogenous entities. This distinction is more than semantic – it affects corporate law, liability and structuring. Consider the contrasting incorporation regimes of the US and the UK. Delaware, with its corporate-friendly laws and specialist Chancery Court, has become the preferred jurisdiction for over 60 per cent of Fortune 500 companies (Bullock 2023). Meanwhile, the UK's Companies Act 2006 creates a more disclosure-oriented regulatory environment, often favoured by firms engaging with less liberal European markets. Financial firms operating across multiple jurisdictions require incorporation frameworks that offer legal certainty, regulatory flexibility and access to global capital. Many IFCs are deliberately structured to meet these needs. The Cayman Islands, for example, host over 70 per cent of the world's hedge funds, managing more than $1.4 trillion in assets (Conyers 2023). Luxembourg, meanwhile, has emerged as the EU's premier hub for investment funds, with over €5 trillion in AUM, for example, via the Société d'Investissement à Capital Variable (SICAV) model (ALFI 2024), supported by EU passporting rights. *Dual incorporation* strategies, like the "Delaware–London" hybrid – part statutory corporation, part partnership – are frequently used by FinTechs to optimize both legal protections and investor access: Delaware offers governance flexibility; London provides European market exposure.

Some jurisdictions exert disproportionate influence in the global incorporation market by leveraging sovereignty (Picciotto 1999) and forming alliances across onshore/offshore networks. Singapore, for example, has built its status as Asia's financial gateway through a mix of English legal foundations, tax incentives and bilateral agreements with China and the EU (Dezan Shira & Associates 2023). The British Virgin Islands, with nearly 400,000 active companies registered, draws firms with its flexible and confidential incorporation regime. These early incorporation legacies remain critical to the continued success of offshore financial centres.

These incorporation legacies form the foundation of today's offshore financial centres and continue to shape the global legal-financial landscape (Picciotto 1995, 1999; Roberts 1994). Incorporation competition has only intensified. A relatively stable hierarchy of IFCs (see Figure 3.1), largely based on financial sector GDP contributions, has persisted since the 1980s, dominated by centres like London, New York and Tokyo (the latter being replaced by Hong Kong). However, new players are emerging, reflecting the evolving territorialities of global finance. Dubai has positioned the Dubai International Financial Centre (DIFC) as the Middle East's primary financial hub, adopting an independent common law system and establishing arbitration courts aligned with international standards. Paired with cross-border recognition agreements and regulatory efficiency, these legal endowments have made the DIFC a preferred base for multinational financial firms (DIFC 2024). Shanghai, via the Lin-gang Special Area in the Shanghai Free Trade Zone, has "experimented" with financial liberalization – easing capital restrictions, encouraging foreign ownership and internationalizing the renminbi through initiatives such as the Bond Connect and Stock Connect programmes with Hong Kong (see International Services Shanghai 2025). These developments reflect territorial reconfigurations of finance, driven not just by legal frameworks but by proactive economic diplomacy and national promotion of incorporation activity and investment.

Despite these shifts, the core mechanisms of financialization remain stable. However, the tools facilitating financial expansion are evolving. While the underlying logics of capital accumulation remain, the narrative is shifting – often cloaked in the language of sustainability, innovation and inclusivity – raising concerns about greenwashing and the strategic use of ESG discourse to legitimize new markets. Technological innovation is a key catalyst accelerating change, creating new FinTech markets, while political and regulatory interventions – especially in green finance – are opening up new sectors and emerging financial domains. Regulatory sandboxes in the UK, Singapore and Switzerland, for instance, allow FinTechs to test financial-cum-tech products in controlled regulatory environments. Meanwhile, blockchain regulation has spurred jurisdictional competition in a different arena, with Malta and Estonia seeking leadership in digital assets and digital asset regulation. The European Green Deal and initiatives like the EU's Green Taxonomy are reshaping green finance, with Luxembourg positioning itself as a progressive frontrunner through its Green Exchange (LGX), the world's first platform for sustainable bonds.

In this context, incorporation is a critical lever in shaping strategic positioning, risk and regulatory exposure. Jurisdictions that provide tax clarity, legal efficiency and adaptability continue to dominate. While New York, London and Hong Kong remain powerful, rising centres like Dubai, Shanghai and Singapore reflect a shifting global order. Legal engineering, financial diplomacy and regulatory agility are now essential to maintaining relevance in the global hierarchy of financial centres – and shape the future of global finance.

Amid this dynamism, the financial system itself remains remarkably resilient, anchored by foundational private law principles – especially property rights and incorporation law. Incorporation confers legal personality, enabling asset ownership, contractual capacity and limited liability. These services – often including registration of foreign beneficial owners – are vital in both offshore and onshore centres. Although commonly associated with offshore financial centres, incorporation services also underpin the corporate architectures of major onshore jurisdictions. The US, the UK and Singapore, for instance, have become prominent incorporation hubs by allowing the registration of so-called "naked" shell companies – legal structures with little or no real economic activity that nonetheless enjoy international legal recognition (Nougayrède 2019). By contrast, "real-seat" jurisdictions such as Germany and France impose stricter incorporation criteria, limiting companies' ability to engage in jurisdictional arbitrage. Within the EU, several centres specialize in incorporation infrastructure. The Netherlands functions as a key holding company hub, Luxembourg – as a general incorporation centre – excels in finance and investment funds (including PE), and Ireland has evolved from a centre for asset finance (e.g. aircraft leasing) into a broader hub for financial and tech services (Nougayrède 2019). However, law is not static. Legal practice evolves through negotiation, enabling arbitrage – the exploitation of differences in price, regulation or institutional setup. This fragmentation fuels jurisdiction shopping for incorporation services, as firms pursue synthetically created arbitrage opportunities to exploit regulatory asymmetries for financial gain. Paradoxically, states frequently facilitate these practices by continuously developing attractive financial centres, or "regional assets", in response to relentless inter-IFC competitive pressures. The resulting business-friendly environments often cater to non-productive financial industries, yet remain central to the functioning of modern global finance.

Ultimately, the legal design of financial vehicles determines their economic performance and profitability. As legal and regulatory ecosystems shift, so too does the capacity of financial actors to exploit them – redefining the evolving territoriality of global finance.

Sovereignty of nations: an asset

Nation-states have long leveraged their sovereign rights for commercial gain. A prominent example is Switzerland's tradition of (modern) bank secrecy, originally designed to shield "foreigners from their own governments' sovereign claims" (Palan 2002: 170). In *Transithandel*, Lea Haller (2019) offers a detailed account of Switzerland's transformation from a global hub for transit and commodity trading into a prosperous centre of private financial wealth. This evolution is intricately bound to the actions of legal experts and the strategic deployment of law, legal technologies and responses to shifting geopolitical contexts – demonstrating how Switzerland has repeatedly capitalized on its territorial sovereignty and political neutrality. Financial centres such as Zurich and Geneva helped construct a social order that served both the interests of the nation-state and those of an increasingly integrated global capital market. Contemporary financial innovation remains deeply embedded in these territorial-organizational logics – structures that connect distinct social orders yet retain strong path dependency. The constant competitive pressures placed on asset managers and other FABS providers encourage incremental innovations, often developed as contingencies in response to future uncertainties. While these innovations may appear often minor in isolation, they become cumulatively significant, especially as they co-evolve through the mutual adaptation of state institutions and corporate actors. The practices underpinning and linking these developments are traceable across networks of IFCs.

States' strategies to commercialize and capitalize on their sovereignty have emerged gradually, often in a piecemeal and opportunistic fashion, rather than through deliberate planning. From the nineteenth century onward, the relationship between sovereignty and territoriality became increasingly rigid. The sovereign state, as a legal person, is "constructed, recognised, and formalised by an ultimately changeable series of laws, practices, and traditions, both domestic and international" (Lienau 2016: 124). However, the mounting tension "between the insulation of the state in law and the internationalisation of capital" (Palan 2002: 171) has fostered novel "interpretations" of sovereign space, enabling the rise of offshore jurisdictions. As a result, in the competitive race to attract investment, capital and economic growth, nation-states increasingly treat sovereignty as a commercial asset.

Significantly, due to the fragmented nature of national legal systems, the term "multinational corporation" – although widely used across disciplines such as economics, business studies, economic geography and political economy – has no legal basis. Corporations, despite pursuing unified business strategies, consist of legally distinct structures (such as subsidiaries, affiliates, joint ventures) governed by different national laws. Each unit of the corporation, regardless of its global business integration, is legally domiciled in a specific country. This distinction between a *fragmented* legal structure and a *unified* business reality is crucial, especially for jurisdictions such as London, which host both offshore and onshore financial systems that facilitate and regulate transnational capital flows. To reconcile the conflicting imperatives of state-based legal systems with capital's international mobility, states have gradually come to accept that business structures – as legal persons – may operate across multiple legal systems simultaneously. This recognition carries the risk that such "entities" will exploit regulatory discrepancies between jurisdictions, engaging in jurisdiction shopping (Tamanaha 2021) – a practice rooted in the commercialization of states' sovereignty. International tax planning exemplifies this logic, allowing corporations and wealthy individuals to strategically manage where and how their financial realities are disclosed.

Over time, financial companies, structured as partnerships, LLCs or other legal forms, have adapted their frameworks to increasingly suit economic objectives, often in direct consultation with governments. These adaptations include the use of offshore structures, holding companies and highly complex legal arrangements aimed at minimizing both tax liabilities and legal risks. Governments, motivated by the prospect of revenues from the bulk business income of licence fees or corporate rents, have facilitated these structures by permitting company registration within their jurisdictions. This was instrumental in the early success of offshore financial centres – and remains relevant today, as historically embedded practices continue to shape global finance and wealth protection. Complex international financial arrangements typify this trend and seek to resolve technical legal challenges, such as determining the tax location of intangible assets (e.g. software, services) or mitigating the risk that one state's regulations might erode another's sovereignty. These arrangements have further refined leveraged financing and speculative capital strategies by exploiting the expanding territorial reach of law. Trust law – originally rooted in English common law – spread through colonization and has been extended by the global movement of private and corporate capital-seeking jurisdictions with minimal regulatory resistance (Harrington 2016). Even legal systems and countries that follow the civil law tradition, which had not traditionally recognized trusts, including France, Switzerland, Japan and China, and increasingly Germany and Brazil, have adapted their frameworks to accommodate such structures – providing for trust assets, beneficiaries and trustees. These elements are also essential to the (growing) development of the asset economy.

Trusts, once the preserve of estate planning and asset shielding for the ultra-wealthy, now permeate structured finance. They are used not only by corporations but also within international financial arrangements. In the absence of global governance structures – and amid the competing principles of national sovereignty in a context of mobile capital – law alone cannot eliminate offshore jurisdictions. The OECD's Base Erosion and Profit Shifting (BEPS) project, launched in 2013 and implemented from 2016 onward, marks a significant attempt to tackle these challenges. It may well influence the future legal design of investment and corporate structures (see Christensen 2025). These dynamics highlight the need for a deeper understanding of the co-evolution of legal practices and the jurisdictional extension of legal systems, especially as they increasingly intersect with enabling financial practices in offshore regimes and alternative structures. The global proliferation of corporate law firms both mirrors and reinforces this phenomenon, as legal expertise becomes central to financial innovation and jurisdictional arbitrage. Financial centres have capitalized on legal and financial engineering – often advancing capital accumulation and shielding at the expense of broader economic equity. Law firms today do more than advise states on aligning legal frameworks with emerging international standards. Their early involvement in industry consultations allows them to help shape regulation – effectively transforming regulators into "enablers rather than enforcers" (Committee on Oversight and Government Reform 2008: 2), underscoring the foundational role that legal knowledge plays in contemporary financial architecture.

Beyond traditional legal advice, global law firms – now increasingly integrating AI tools – play an active role in shaping financial innovation. By standardizing template agreements, fund structures and jurisdictional strategies, they contribute to a process of legal "productization" (Kennedy 2014: 48): the transformation of legal constructs into scalable, transferable tools that embed logics of risk management, opacity and tax efficiency into financial practice. Many law firms also engage in early-stage regulatory consultations, helping to draft the very rules they later interpret and apply. In this way, legal expertise is no longer merely advisory – it becomes a proprietary asset, circulated across jurisdictions and monetized within the broader financial services ecosystem. Law firms develop these tools largely in response to high demand – particularly from financial institutions, asset managers and multinational clients.

Once a fund's legal structure has been established by a law firm and handed over to a management company (FMC) for ongoing administration (see Figure 3.3), significant legal responsibility is likewise transferred – marking the fund's entry into the broader business ecosystem where legal, financial and economic functions become tightly interwoven. In practice, this means that the appointed representative – typically a director – of the FMC assumes substantial legal liability, usually in return for a fee. Although FMCs commonly insure their employees against such risks, the collapse of Greensill Bank illustrates the residual legal exposure that can remain despite such precautions.[4]

Indeed, legal partnership agreements (LPAs), specific to the PE and venture capital industry, often span several hundred pages. While these complex documents must be reviewed by the fund's management company or administrative representatives, they often lack both the time or specialized legal expertise needed for thorough analysis. As a result, this delegation of risk – effectively shifting legal liability from the law firm to the management company – can involve intricate challenges that require careful navigation of corporate law, securities regulation, and tax and accounting rules. Legal coding can embed such complexities in ways that, if not meticulously managed, function as a kind of metaphorical "poison pill": hidden liabilities embedded in the legal code with potentially serious financial or regulatory consequences.[5] The Greensill Bank case underscores the importance of rigorous legal oversight and the potential pitfalls of complex financial structures. Despite having insurance and risk management strategies in place, the bank's downfall highlights the residual legal exposures that can persist, emphasizing the need for management companies to conduct comprehensive legal reviews and possess sufficient expertise to effectively mitigate such risks.

Because the legal structure of a fund determines both tax obligations and the allocation of profits and losses, fund promoters seek to design the most advantageous framework to attract global investors. This observation aligns with another empirical trend: the global marketing of funds and the pursuit of investor capital has placed increasing pressure on the FABS sector – including law firms, custodian banks, fund administrators and others – to scale up and expand internationally. This dynamic has driven market consolidation, particularly in global custody banking and among leading law and accounting firms. These firms benefit from leveraging economies of scale and network effects, forging links between specialized financial centres while consolidating legal-financial knowledge within a small number of powerful global law firms.

As these law firms operate across jurisdictions, they become increasingly adept at "coding capital" in various legal systems. According to Pistor, law firms – through years of client interaction and cumulative professional exchange – craft new capital forms and "often *make* new law from existing legal material" (2019: 160, emphasis in original). This illustrates that no single state determines the boundaries of how lawyers operationalize capital within legal frameworks. Consequently, the processes described as *legal innovation* appear both pervasive and ongoing, shaped by administrative territorialities and specific legal-spatial linkages. These dynamics underscore the critical role of law firms within the financial ecosystems of financial centres – a role that is frequently overlooked, particularly in their capacity to actively "make" law. This is especially relevant when considered against the backdrop of the often generic use of the economically derived term "institutions" in social theory (North 1990). Law firms play a pivotal role in co-designing the legal architecture and jurisdictional positioning of financial products and transactions, while also influencing accounting practices, valuation methodologies and administrative procedures. Importantly, these are not one-way processes but mutual and integrative social dynamics: legal structures shape financial practices, and financial innovations, in turn, drive legal adaptation. As such, law firms are central to the political economies of key IFCs, which function as crucial nodes within a global "archipelago" of strategically connected jurisdictions that facilitate the fluid operation of finance. As previously discussed, tightly interwoven company networks span these centres, embedding law firms deeply within the legal and institutional infrastructure of global capital.

Focusing specifically on the legal design of financial business organizations, complex alternative funds (such as PE and hedge funds) that seek to maximize absolute returns often employ a wide range of strategies, including unconventional or illiquid investments, such as derivatives, arbitrage, distressed assets, private credit, real estate and other non-liquid holdings. These funds are typically structured as private partnerships or other bespoke investment vehicles, rather than as mutual funds, largely due to regulatory constraints. For example, hedge funds may use leverage and derivatives to amplify returns, or engage in strategies such as short-selling and high-frequency trading – executing hundreds of trades per day across numerous positions, particularly in the case of some quantitative funds. In many jurisdictions, especially offshore ones, trust law can play a central role in structuring such funds, particularly with regard to investor protection and asset segregation. However, as noted earlier, trust law is not universally foundational in fund structuring. Its relevance is concentrated in offshore jurisdictions such as the Cayman Islands, the British Virgin Islands or Jersey, and is most commonly applied in the context of asset-holding structures or to meet specific regulatory requirements.

The legal design of an alternative fund typically serves two primary functions: first, shielding profits from taxation by ensuring pass-through tax treatment;[6] and second, protecting the owners from legal liability, typically through limited partnership arrangements. While both elements are fundamental, the focus here lies on liability protection – whether for a sole owner or multiple shareholders.

Figure 5.1 presents a basic ("plain vanilla") organizational model of PE funds using a master–feeder structure and illustrates how each asset (A–C) is held through protective legal instruments, typically Luxembourg-based holding companies (HoldCos) (SOPARFIs). While master–feeder structures are more common in hedge funds, this schematic reflects how similar logics of cross-border legal structuring are increasingly employed in PE to achieve asset protection and tax efficiency. These HoldCo structures are often embedded within broader asset protection and tax optimization strategies designed to limit exposure to creditors, facilitate upstreaming of returns and ensure legal separation between portfolio assets. Understanding the organizational structure of PE funds is crucial for several reasons. These funds are generally organized as limited partnerships, wherein general partners (GPs) manage the fund and limited partners (LPs) provide the capital (see Chapter 2). In theory, this structure aligns incentives: GPs are motivated by carried interest to maximize returns, while LPs benefit from professional management and potentially substantial gains. However, this arrangement also introduces well-documented concerns around moral hazard. GPs typically invest only 1–2 per cent of the fund's capital, yet they may receive up to 20 per cent of the profits if performance exceeds a predefined hurdle rate – commonly around 8 per cent – while LPs provide the vast majority of the capital – typically 98–99 per cent. This asymmetry means GPs bear minimal downside risk in the event of losses or bankruptcy, but can capture

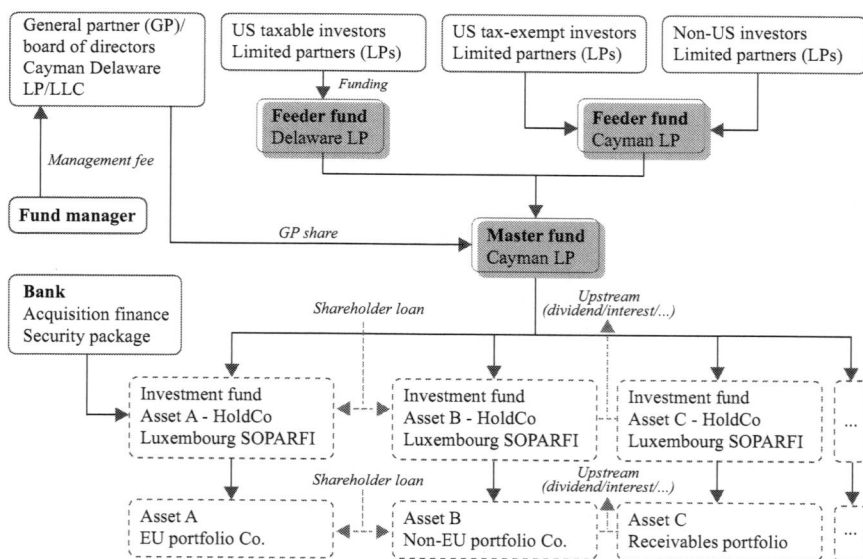

Figure 5.1 A Delaware–Cayman master-feeder fund structure

Source: author, based on material of law firms Ogier and Linklaters.

disproportionately high rewards from successful exits (Appelbaum & Batt 2014). As a result – and despite the strong underlying economics – the incentive structure raises important questions about risk exposure, accountability and fairness in financial governance. Currently, however, compensation structures for GPs in PE and hedge funds are in flux, influenced by regulatory reforms, tax policy changes and shifting investor expectations.

Complex legal structures, such as master–feeder funds, most commonly used in hedge funds but also adapted in PE contexts, typically operate through a two-tiered system: investors commit capital to feeder funds, which then invest in a central master fund (Figure 5.1). The master fund then executes investments in financial markets, generating profits or losses. These structures are designed to optimize tax and regulatory efficiencies, making them particularly attractive to investors from multiple jurisdictions with varying legal and fiscal requirements. For example, US tax-exempt entities can use offshore feeders to avoid unrelated business taxable income (UBTI), while non-US investors benefit from being shielded from US tax reporting obligations.

Liability protection is embedded in the fund's legal architecture through an intricate network of entities – including HoldCos, limited partnerships and special purpose vehicles (SPVs), particularly in PE. These structures serve not only to compartmentalize assets and returns, but also to ring-fence different forms of exposure, whether legal, operational or jurisdictional. Jurisdictions such as Luxembourg and the Cayman Islands are commonly used to design and host these structures – Luxembourg SOPARFIs and Cayman SPVs, for example – due to their flexible corporate laws, favourable tax regimes and robust double tax treaty networks, which help insulate assets from local creditor claims and optimize cross-border cash flows.

While understanding the business – that is, the investment strategies – is crucial, it is equally important to examine the legal infrastructures underpinning financial vehicles and their business strategies. After all, these legal structures determine how returns are processed, allocated and insulated from liability or taxation, and are therefore instrumental in shaping the *economics of circulation* and accumulation of financial wealth. Such legal arrangements therefore contribute significantly to shaping the global financial landscape, directing flows of capital and reinforcing jurisdictional advantages. As a result, legal, accounting and auditing services have become highly concentrated in certain financial centres, in Europe most notably in Luxembourg and Dublin, which in this regard have outpaced larger IFCs such as Frankfurt or Paris (Dörry 2015). This is reflected in their disproportionately large number of law firms and legal staff relative to the overall size of the financial centre. These centres have tailored their legal and regulatory frameworks to attract global funds by offering favourable tax rulings, legal flexibility and access to the EU market – thereby creating vibrant local financial and para-financial economies. Dublin, for example, has massively benefited from EU passporting rights and a regulatory environment that allows for tailored fund structuring within pan-European frameworks.

In summary, IFCs have evolved into critical hubs of financial production, underpinned by the expanding territorial reach of legal systems – particularly English common law and its derivatives, including trust law. These legal traditions have proven indispensable in structuring IFs, PE and hedge funds and other complex financial firms and instruments. Over time, IFCs have strategically refined their regulatory environments to attract mobile capital, often participating in what some scholars have termed a "regulatory race to the bottom": a dynamic in which jurisdictions compete by relaxing or tailoring regulatory standards to capture financial activity. Legal transplants and interlegalities, as discussed previously, are but some examples of financial centres' strategic positioning. However, this legal competition is not solely downward. Some jurisdictions engage in "smart" regulation – balancing investor protection with flexibility – to remain competitive while attempting to preserve credibility (e.g. Singapore or Delaware's Chancery Court). The success of financial innovation within these IFCs is closely tied to legal structuring and regulatory engineering. A jurisdiction's legal frameworks determines not only tax obligations and liability protections but also *enables* jurisdictional arbitrage – the strategic exploitation of regulatory differences across borders. Concrete tools in this arsenal include "check-the-box" rules in US tax law, hybrid mismatches in entity classification and complex SPV arrangements used for tax planning or regulatory light-touch regimes. While these innovations are often economically lucrative and generate considerable fee income, they typically offer limited productive value beyond the financial sector itself. Rather than driving investment in the real economy, such activities frequently serve to extract profit for investors and concentrate wealth, primarily benefiting financial elites and the jurisdictions in which these services are anchored.

To maintain these advantages, IFCs have cultivated robust ecosystems comprising financial and para-financial services clusters. These industries, often concentrated in specialized financial (offshore) centres like Luxembourg, Dublin, Jersey and the Cayman Islands, are essential to the structuring, legitimization and continuous reproduction of cross-border financial flows. Their activities contribute to local economic growth, particularly through employment and fee-based income generation; however, the broader societal impacts are highly uneven. For instance, these business ecosystems may raise incomes for a segment of professionals, but they also contribute to urban distortions, such as inflated housing markets in host cities and beyond, and exacerbate broader patterns of wealth inequality, commuting and transportation pressures, and spatial segregation driven by housing (un)affordability, especially in the era of the asset economy. The intense concentration of financial and legal expertise in a select group of jurisdictions further entrenches the unequal distribution of global economic benefits. Major IFCs disproportionately capture the gains of financial globalization, while peripheral economies remain structurally excluded – yet dependent on capital inflows that have shifted from productive investment to purely financial forms. Moreover, the fee-based nature of these services raises concerns about long-term *durability*, not to be conflated with socio-ecological *sustainability*, as their continued expansion depends on the proliferation of financial structuring rather than on the creation of real economic value or productive investment.

Ultimately, IFCs have become both powerful enablers and beneficiaries of legal and financial engineering, shaping a global economic geography that privileges capital accumulation and fosters regulatory asymmetries. As this chapter has demonstrated, law is not a neutral backdrop to global finance but an active and constitutive force in its expansion and spatial articulation. Financial centres thrive not merely by facilitating transactions but by creating and maintaining the legal environments that render those transactions possible. Practices such as incorporation, trust formation and assetization rely on the *performative power of law* – transforming social and economic activities into ownable, tradable and protected legal constructs. The expanding territorialities of law thus reflect not a passive diffusion but a deliberate and ongoing project of financial world-making – one that consolidates financial power and reinforces *systemic* global inequalities. Through their ability to legally code capital, structure arbitrage opportunities and shape regulatory frameworks more broadly, global law firms (originating most often from the Anglo-American core) and the state via IFCs, act as architects of a financialized global order. This consolidation of legal-financial power stresses the deepening tensions between capital accumulation, distributive justice and socio-ecological sustainability in a world increasingly governed by the logics of asset protection.

6

THRIVING FINANCE, AILING COMMUNITIES

A massive new wave of privatization

A massive new wave of privatization is underway. At the heart of this transformation lies a crucial hypothesis: that legal innovation – as mechanisms linked to the long-term dynamics of privatization and financialization/assetization – has become a central engine of economic growth in contemporary financial capitalism. Yet legal innovation, in this context, defies the textbook understanding of innovation as a societal good intended to benefit the many. Rather than serving the wellbeing of broader society or safeguarding the planet's ecosystems, it has predominantly favoured a narrow elite.

The strong protection of private property has long been a cornerstone of liberal economic systems (Robé 2020), underpinning legal and institutional arrangements oriented toward relentless economic growth. The rise of the asset management industry exemplifies the transformation of capitalism in this direction: no longer merely an economic process, but increasingly a legal and political one. Crucially, legal and accountancy work has itself been subject to increasing economization over recent decades, reflected, for example, in the rapid commercialization of law firms: their growing scale, international expansion and diversification into consultancy and financial services all illustrate this trend. While recent geopolitical shifts may have tempered the momentum of globalization, the broader trend toward the commercial integration of previously non-productive sectors remains evident. Today, legal and accountancy ecosystems have evolved into highly profitable business sectors, despite being largely centred on non-productive economic activities, namely speculative and arbitrage-based practices, facilitated by IFCs. Since the 2007/08 financial crisis, the recognition of all financial activity – including highly speculative transactions – as contributors to national accounts has further reinforced this transformation, embedding financialised logics more deeply into the economic valuation of legal and professional services.

This dynamic is particularly pronounced in economies that have adopted *finance-led growth models*, where national balance sheets increasingly treat legal, accountancy and consultancy services concerned with financial services, products and transactions as generators of economic value. Countries such as the US, the UK, Ireland and Luxembourg – alongside a network of offshore jurisdictions, including Jersey, Vanuatu, Kiribati, the Cayman Islands and Panama (Figure 2.4) – have become key nodes in the global architecture of financial capitalism. Whether onshore or offshore, these IFCs concentrate legal, fiscal and other professional expertise in support of an asset-driven economy. Within this landscape, PE firms have emerged as dominant actors, recently spearheading privatization efforts under the banner of funding sustainable transition programmes, such as Europe's Green Deal. However, their investment strategies are underpinned by financial models that purport "economic viability" and project future cash flows based on present assumptions – models that, as climate economists have warned, systematically *undervalue* long-term ecological risk. In doing so, they entrench a legal-economic framework that privileges short-term financial gains over long-term environmental and social sustainability (Doganova 2024).

Assetization and privatization, although often presented as technical or administrative shifts, are in fact deeply *legal* processes built on evolving legal fictions. Incorporation, legal personhood and ownership have been strategically repurposed by economic orthodoxy to assist rent extraction, regulatory arbitrage and the commodification of public goods. These are not accidental quirks of capitalism, but deliberate legal constructs that facilitate the creation of large volumes of synthetic – or paper – wealth (see McKinsey Global Institute 2023).

The legal infrastructure, which shapes socio-economic relationships, continues to rest on the flawed premise that shareholders are corporates' primary "principals", sidelining broader corporate responsibilities to workers, communities and the environment. As a result, financial markets have become ends in themselves, expanding with little concern for the socio-ecological consequences. The revenues they generate have bolstered the public coffers of states hosting IFCs – many of which have grown structurally dependent on these highly mobile, "footloose" financial and para-financial businesses.

As explored throughout this book, finance-led legal innovation has increasingly permeated domains once considered public or non-commercial. From pension systems and public infrastructure to big data governance and natural resources, the boundary between public and private finance has been redrawn through processes of legal structuring – enabling PE firms, infrastructure funds and other financial actors to capture value rather than reinvest it in communities and local economies. Far from neutral, these transformations systematically redistribute value and risk in favour of globally networked financial actors, while undermining communities' capacity to govern, adapt to and resist socio-ecological and economic exploitation.

The cumulative effects of these transformations are now starkly visible. In essence, parts of economic growth have been synthetically inflated through speculative valuation, GDP has been financialized and legal mechanisms have been co-opted and repurposed to support financial value capture rather than redistribution or reinvestment. Assetization has produced new hierarchies of control, orchestrated through financial centres that concentrate legal expertise, facilitate regulatory arbitrage and channel global capital flows, although counter-initiatives such as the OECD/G20 Inclusive Framework and various IMF assessments have sought to curb these dynamics. Collectively, these IFCs have expanded the reach of finance by cultivating new epistemic authorities and extending the territorial influence of law. As Nicholas Blomley (2005) argues, property is not merely a legal object but a spatial and political force, enabled and justified by legal fictions deeply embedded in mainstream economic theory. These shifts have reshaped rules and institutions and, in turn, the dominant ideas and collective truths internalized by professionals, policymakers and scholars. What is needed is a reorientation of thinking: a forensic disentanglement of legal and economic thought that moves beyond the fetishization of shareholder value and re-centres the role of law – including its enforcement – in shaping equitable collective futures.

The legal innovations that underpin assetization and privatization are neither apolitical nor benign; they may function as ideological instruments with profound material consequences. Confronting the climate emergency requires strong, resilient communities, yet mismatches and incentives within current financial and legal structures can leave them disempowered. Rebuilding community strength requires regrounding the legal foundations of the economy, shifting emphasis from paper wealth to resilience, equity and ecological responsibility. Such a transformation would align with the objectives of a climate-neutral economy committed to *leaving no one behind*, as articulated in the European Green Deal and the Just Transition Mechanism. Robé's analysis (2020: 144–5, emphases in the original) is particularly incisive, calling for renewed attention to the structural foundations that govern the inseparable relationship between state and market economies:

> wherever a State of law exists, that is how the Power System operates. *Violence* has been converted into *power* and the adjudication of the parties' rights is not based either on their relative physical or on their personal strength in the Power System. It is impersonal. And here also, the effectiveness of State institutions is a prerequisite for a somewhat advanced exchange to exist. Mainstream economic analyses adopt the paradoxical and untenable position of taking the State for granted while

neglecting its essential role. Most mainstream economists see the State as a consumer of resources – which it is – forgetting that in return, the State provides services and infrastructure essential to the existence of a market exchange economy. [...] But the State and the market economy have developed *together*. States and markets are historically linked in their development by a relationship in which one is, at least partly, the reason for the existence of the other. The market needs the physical order, the physical infrastructure (roads, ports, canals, all major communication networks etc.) and the intellectual infrastructure (the language, the legal system or standardized weights and measures, in particular) provided by the State which, in turn, requires private monetary exchange for the financing of the services it provides, via the taxes levied on exchange and on the incomes and goods it generates. Both the modern State and the development of a market society are the result of an evolutionary process connecting the two which started many centuries ago. Irrespective of ideological positioning, the market, the State, freedom of contract, the individual and property rights form part of *the same complex institutional arrangement*. So much so that when the State disappears or gets corrupted, the illusion of individual sovereignty fades away rapidly.

The complexities of modern financial instruments – designed in one jurisdiction, linked to assets in another and traded across global markets – reinforce an asymmetrical system of financial power and highlight the deeply intertwined relationship between state and market economies. The expansion of the PE industry (Figure 6.1) exemplifies these co-evolving dynamics, signalling a deeper financialization of legal services and heightening concerns that legal expertise is being co-opted to serve financial interests over the public good. As a result, law risks functioning less as a safeguard of democratic governance and more as a tool of economic and political manipulation, reinforcing entrenched hierarchies of financial power.

The state plays an active role in this transformation. Nation-states hosting prominent financial centres have strategically shaped legal and regulatory frameworks to attract mobile capital activity, securing fiscal revenues and enhancing geopolitical influence. States embedded within the US-centric financial system such as the UK, Ireland and Luxembourg (Chapter 2) benefit from privileged access to global capital flows. This state-finance nexus is particularly visible in the shifting terrain of shareholder accountability. Pension funds, tasked with safeguarding long-term retirement security, have delegated investment authority to PE firms. Yet, the incentives governing PE – carried interest, performance fees and rapid exits – are often misaligned with the long-term interests of fund beneficiaries. While pension funds must balance present and future obligations, asset managers are structurally driven to maximize AUM, reinforcing a bias toward inflated valuations and speculative investment. This dynamic deepens the classic agency dilemma between shareholders and managers, as asset managers' priorities diverge from those of the savers they nominally serve – most notably in the case of pension funds and their beneficiaries (Braun 2022). Nonetheless, asset managers have secured a central position within the asset economy, directing capital flows into high-value sectors – including large-scale green and digital infrastructure – and, in doing so, have become key architects of a trend that might be termed the *financialization of sustainability* itself.

A case in point is KKR's (Kohlberg Kravis Roberts & Co., an American global PE firm and investment company with approximately $553 billion AUM as of end of 2023) global climate strategy, which adopts a risk-based investment approach targeting entire infrastructure systems.[1] This extends beyond the electrification of public transport to include its servicing ecosystems, mobility planning and ticketing infrastructure. The PE business model pursues these investments primarily to maximize financial returns – both immediate and long-term via *exits*. The past decades, particularly since the late 1970s, have demonstrated that earlier waves of privatization – especially in housing, public infrastructure (including energy, utilities and transportation), telecommunications and social infrastructure such as hospitals – have often resulted in higher costs for consumers, chronic under-maintenance of essential services, and exploitative contracts that impede public oversight (Feldman & Kenney 2024). *Materiality*, the concrete physical and social realities of these investments, is scarcely acknowledged by financial firms and investors. Many of these projects were publicly subsidized, yet their profits were largely captured by private financial investors rather than the wider public (Allen & Pryke 2013). These patterns tend to repeat themselves, highlighting the need for closer scrutiny of the legal and financial frameworks governing infrastructure investments.

In this historical context, the current wave of green infrastructure development – initially grounded in the European Green Deal's commitment to a just transition – has increasingly shifted toward a speed-driven agenda dominated by private capital, public subsidies and public-private partnerships (PPPs). Recognizing this shift as a strategic opportunity, Bruce Flatt, CEO of Brookfield Asset Management, has explicitly articulated his firm's strategy as one of securing control over green infrastructure; a trend mirrored across the PE industry. Illustrative of this broader industry approach, he states: "We're in a 50-year transformation of the infrastructure world. We're 10 years in; we have 40 left to go. By the end of that 50 years most infrastructure in the world will be transferred to private hands" (Evans & Smith 2018: np).

Does contemporary financial capitalism risk misaligning with sustainability objectives such as the SDGs, Green Deals and climate legislation? I argue that it does – and, more critically, that it risks actively undermining them. Large-scale "green investment" continues to be shaped by the expanding jurisdictions and territorialities of finance, which govern critical intersections between economic and legal systems (Tamanaha 2021; Braverman *et al.* 2014). While financial actors can mobilize substantial capital for green infrastructure, prevailing investment logics – driven by short-term returns and asset performance metrics – frequently conflict with the long-term nature of sustainability goals (European Commission 2019), putting project durability and lasting impact at risk (Figure 6.1). A closely related concern is the erosion of accountability, as the growing influence of lightly regulated private capital in green infrastructure governance risks subordinating environmental and social priorities to financial imperatives. As a reminder, PE firms have minimal reporting obligations due to their legal structure.

Make no mistake: the $1.8 billion investment in green infrastructure (IEA 2023a, 2023b), including funding for renewable energy and emissions-reducing technologies, is both vital and welcome in shaping a just socio-ecological market economy in Europe. However, earlier waves of privatization, particularly in the US and across the Anglosphere, offer a stark warning. As the epicentre of financial capitalism, the PE model has consistently socialized costs – externalizing harm to society and nature/climate – while generating substantial profits for investors. The consequences have been severe: soaring prices, the displacement of small businesses and residents, the erosion of local economies and the weakening of the social fabric (Feldman & Kenney 2024). These dynamics not only exacerbate socio-economic inequalities but threaten the foundations of democratic governance itself (Figure 6.1; the timelines show only the peaks of each privatization wave; they are ongoing, but PE has shifted its focus). Returns on asset-based income streams have long outpaced earned income (Adkins *et al.* 2020), accelerating the widening divide between rich and poor.

Synthetic wealth, synthetic communities

As Corbridge and Thrift (1994: 15) warned three decades ago, within their critique of neoliberal restructuring, we are witnessing a "restructuring of 'real' communities by the community of money". Financial power, although manifesting differently depending on local political coalitions and institutional configurations, has steadily encroached upon local governance structures. Strikingly, the very communities ostensibly intended to benefit from private (green) infrastructure investments are frequently excluded from decision-making processes – often, as research shows, with little transparency and investor accountability. As shown in cases like Detroit's green infrastructure planning during its municipal

Figure 6.1 Waves of privatization through private equity firms and funds

Source: author.

communities

and more...

companies

energy

Ecological environment

schools

housing

environment

hospitals

Private Equity

Acquisition

Target

Invest to extract

Gain
return on investment

Loss
- ecological
- social
- health
- cultural
- economical

1970 1980 1990 2000 2010 2020

Acquisition
Companies

1.

1970 1980 1990 2000 2010 2020

Acquisition
Real Estate

2.

1970 1980 1990 2000 2010 2020

Acquisition
Green & digital infrastructure

3.

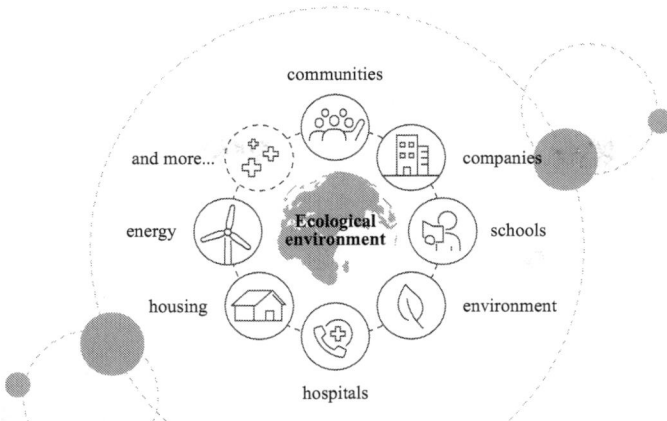

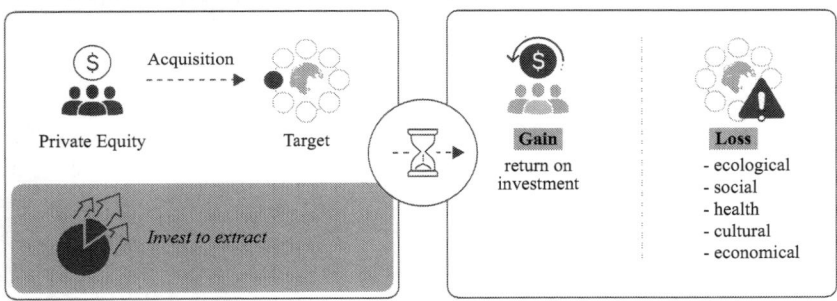

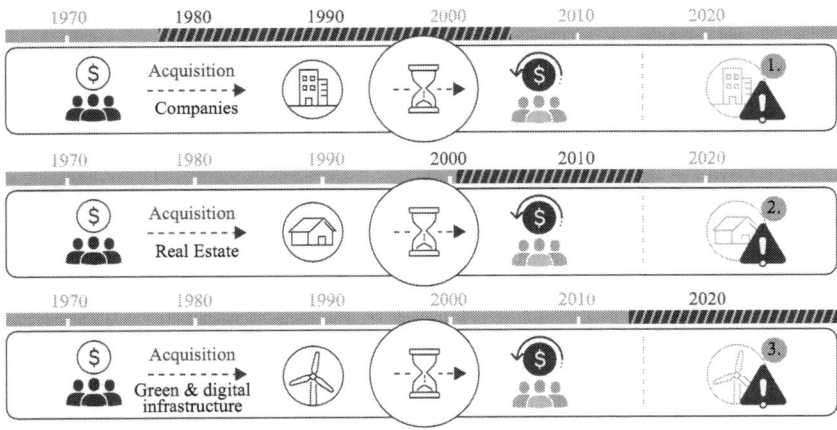

1. companies broken-up and sold, mass layoffs, decision-making transfer

2. acquisition of large-scale public infrastructure, no/low maintenance, high rent/fees for services, forclosures, etc.

3. potential long-term costs for the public: underinvestment, erosion in transparency, compromising environmental performance and purpose

bankruptcy (Cousins & Hill 2021) or the Thames Tideway Tunnel in London (Loftus & March 2019) affected populations are often marginalized in favour of financial actors and technocratic imperatives, even as they bear the brunt of social, environmental and economic risk. Compounding this, communities facing rising debt levels find themselves ensnared in the web of fiscal statecraft (Pike 2023; Pike *et al.* 2019), including instruments such as municipal bonds, PPPs and austerity budgeting, compelled to rely on financial markets to fund essential public services and infrastructure. This shift increasingly transfers power to financial actors, reinforcing market imperatives over public interests. The state must be understood as both an *object* and an *agent* of these dynamics. While governments facilitate financial expansion, global investments driven by private interests frequently generate crises that public authorities must subsequently manage – placing growing fiscal strain on sovereign states (Dymski 2021).

Scholarship has long identified local communities as crucial guardians of climate adaptation strategies (Ayers & Forsyth 2009; Shaw & Theobald 2011; Sareen *et al.* 2024). Amid these dynamics, two ideal types of community can be discerned for illustrative purposes: *organic communities*, rooted in social cohesion and cooperative models, and *synthetic communities*, driven by financial metrics and logics. Both ideal-type categories further reflect a broader tension between competing logics of economic organization and societal values. On the one hand, alternative economic models advocate embedding economic activity within ecological ceilings and social foundations (Raworth 2017), seeking a coordinated and transformative economic transition. On the other hand, green growth – rooted in the paradigm of ecological modernization – remains constrained by financialization, commonly prioritizing economic expansion and aligning with shareholder-driven logics. These competing paradigms represent divergent pathways, each carrying profound and far-reaching consequences for our shared future. Both forms of ideal-type community, however, are embedded in a concrete materiality that is often overlooked – or rendered invisible – within the abstractions of mainstream economic thought.

Financial centres actively compete to attract capital; yet rather than broadly distributing societal benefits, this capital – channelled through complex socio-techno-spatial networks – frequently functions in extractive ways. While financial centres can indeed drive growth and innovation, their success increasingly relies on practices that exert mounting profit pressures on the social and ecological systems they depend on. This extractive dynamic is particularly concerning in the context of a global race to the bottom in regulatory standards (see Miller 1986).

How the nexus between nation-states and global finance is shaped, however, is not inevitable; it is socio-legally constructed. Historian Quinn Slobodian (2018) traces the ideological roots of a long-term transformation, revealing how neoliberalism – reinforced by economic orthodoxy as its intellectual foundation (see Mudge 2008) – has restructured global society and intensified structural divides. These divisions manifest spatially: in zones of financial privilege and wealth extraction on the one hand, and in marginalized communities and degraded environments on the other. This ongoing "perforation" on nation-states operates across multiple territorial levels, fragmenting spaces into governable units (Slobodian 2023). These can take the form of experimental zones and special jurisdictions which, as Slobodian (2023: 4) notes, "set out to model a new end state for all" by starting small – although, as Robé (2020) warns, without the state, the illusion of individual sovereignty collapses.

Indeed, the evidence presented here suggests that global finance is not only eroding societies organized around nation-states but also undermining the nation-state itself by exploiting the very assets upon which financial expansion ultimately depends. One key dimension of this erosion is the growing gap between political and economic democracy (Ringen 2004). In a world increasingly reliant on a privatized and concentrated stock of infrastructure – critical for climate mitigation and adaptation – and dominated by global profit manipulation, local communities risk being systematically disempowered. This progressive erosion of autonomy undermines the capacity for small-scale, context-sensitive solutions, which are vital for resilience, regenerative practices and effective climate action. As economic growth, privatization and the rise of monopolies and oligopolies in tech-driven industries continue, *economic power* has become highly concentrated. Capital holders now wield unprecedented influence, while *political power* remains largely unchanged: each citizen still has only one vote. This asymmetry has allowed private capital to expand into the political realm even as democratic authority retreats from market governance (Ringen 2004).

The contrast between *organic* and *synthetic* jurisdictions helps illuminate this dynamic. Organic jurisdictions are rooted in social cohesion, community-based economies and participatory governance. In contrast, *synthetic* jurisdictions – state-imposed constructs designed to serve economic functions – prioritize efficiency over democratic legitimacy. Populated by transient, market-oriented actors and shaped by market-institutional rather than community logics (Ford 2001), these jurisdictions are created to streamline law enforcement, tax collection, data management or service delivery. Their formal autonomy is conditional – structured to facilitate economic models that privilege corporate and financial interests, particularly those of large businesses.

As Ringen (2004: 20) observes, democratic societies face an enduring tension between *prosperity* and *equality*, since "no political arrangement, even if itself democratic, is democratically feasible unless it is seen to be (reasonably) compatible with economic efficiency". This logic has enabled *economic democracy* – defined by market participation and capital mobility – to overshadow *political democracy*. Offshore finance exemplifies this shift: normalized through professional norms and legal structures that insulates wealth from public oversight, it thrives within a pervasive culture of confidentiality (Shaxson 2018). Regardless of legality, this secrecy reinforces institutionalized privilege and deepens inequality, as access to essential services becomes increasingly tied to private wealth. As market-driven values take precedence, foundational principles of fairness, civic duty and collective responsibility are systematically eroded (Urry 2014).

Synthetic jurisdictions, created for institutional convenience and economic ambition, reframe individuals as the principal political actors while reducing territories to mere utilitarian constructs. Designed to be interchangeable, these jurisdictions cultivate an ethos in which inhabitants are viewed as transient, rational and primarily motivated by profit-seeking and technocratic governance (Ford 2001).[2] Yet this very interchangeability renders them highly vulnerable to near-unconditional global competition. This dynamic is visible in the growing consolidation of local resources and cultural assets by PE firms headquartered in IFCs such as New York, San Francisco, Chicago, London, Hong Kong, Paris and Singapore. These cities have become global command centres for asset management, while PE investors often remain detached from the communities they affect (Allen & Pryke 2013; Goulding *et al.* 2024).[3] In both the US and the UK, financialized growth has increasingly left local communities to bear the brunt of speculative investment, while decision-making power remains concentrated in distant financial capitals:

> In mostly small-town and rural areas of the US, the rise in the populist vote is a consequence of a reaction of communities in which individual losses are strongly identified with collective losses. And social capital may act as one of the transmission mechanisms. Individuals living in these communities know that a loss for one is a loss for all. Therefore, the rise of populism in the US is fundamentally linked to the geography of decline; to places that, despite remaining relatively homogeneous in terms of interpersonal inequality, have witnessed considerable employment and demographic decay over the long term. The Great Recession of 2008 may have ignited the fuse that resulted in the election of Donald Trump as president, but the discontent has roots that are far deeper.
> (Rodríguez-Pose *et al.* 2021: 477–8)

Asset-based decisions that shape communities are now largely made in distant *money communities* – global financial centres disconnected from the social and ecological realities they shape. This near-total separation has contributed to the weakening of local institutions, governance erosion and the steady impoverishment of regions targeted by extractive investment. Rather than investing directly in public services, governments have increasingly subsidized private capital flows (Gabor 2023), thereby effectively promoting *assetization* as a tool of development and industrial policy (Pike *et al.* 2016).

This trend intersects, for example, with the rise of the *smart city* paradigm, where infrastructure and service provision are increasingly shaped by private tech corporations – and positioned as new frontiers for financial investment. Marketed as efficient, sustainable and inclusive, smart cities often reinforce existing inequalities and create new ones. As Jennifer Clark (2020) insightfully argues, the financialization of urban infrastructure intensifies uneven development by transferring control from public institutions to financial actors. Despite rapid technological change, the deeper challenge remains one of governance: ensuring equitable access, local participation and democratic oversight in an increasingly finance-dominated urban environment.

Yet, the epistemological framework supporting these developments shows little sign of change. As explored in Chapters 4 and 5, the legal and accountancy professions continue to operate symbiotically with state-led strategies aimed at financialization and market expansion. While governments advance sustainability initiatives such as the European Green Deal, their reliance on private capital for delivery has grown. PE has emerged as a key intermediary in green infrastructure finance, yet this raises serious concerns around ownership, governance and control. As Christophers (2023) warns in *Our Lives in Their Portfolios*, privatizing green assets risks consolidating decision-making power in the hands of financial actors, whose primary objective is profit, not socio-ecological sustainability. In many cases, the nation-state assumes financial risk while private investors capture the gains – transforming critical infrastructure from public good to private asset.

Global manipulation of profits, uninterrupted

Financial centres of global reach epitomize *synthetic communities*, with Dubai, Mauritius and Montevideo positioning themselves within the evolving financial expansion and private wealth protection landscape. Each operates within OECD or OECD-associated frameworks, leveraging their status to engage in the *global* game of political and economic *perforation* of the nation-state (Slobodian 2023). These emerging financial hubs are forging strategic alliances with asset managers in established global North markets such as Switzerland, while also expanding their operational scope by securing licences for asset custody, trading and fund management. Such alliances may catalyse broader financial infrastructure developments tailored to UHNWIs, often structured as family offices – a rapidly expanding segment of infrastructure investors. Their growing interest in this market is driven by several factors: hedging against inflation in uncertain economic climates, accessing a high-growth sector offering stable long-term returns but also aligning with ESG measures.

A critical factor in developing wealth management in emerging financial centres is OECD affiliation, which signals stability, reliability and safety. A new class of *economic migrants* seeks these jurisdictions not for employment but as protective environments for wealth accumulation, particularly in response to increasingly stringent tax regulations in countries such as the UK, Switzerland, France, Germany and India. These financial centres currently capitalize on two key value propositions: first, addressing a \$100 billion infrastructure deficit, particularly in Africa and South America; second, compensating for the absence of dominant financial centres in regions such as Africa. They offer legal advisory services, non-domicile residency options and secure private wealth environments, aligning finance-led development strategies with state economic policies. The formalization of these centres prioritizes digital asset classes as a strategic approach to wealth management, encompassing pension schemes, offshore investments and estate planning – positioned as an innovative and forward-looking solution.[4] Notably, boutique private banks in the Global South, in partnership with their Global North counterparts, are driving demand for digital assets, extending financial territoriality into virtual realms and further perforating the boundaries of nation-states. This expansion creates alternative zones of inclusion and exclusion, reinforcing the role of financial enclaves in wealth accumulation.

The global architecture of these north-south financial alliances fosters a distinct division of labour: locations in the global South still primarily function as *booking centres*, while their global North counterparts provide ancillary financial services for affluent clients. Although this division remains fluid, it has contributed to the growing detachment of economic activity from social and community contexts, reinforcing the historical separation between ownership and control.

It is crucial to acknowledge the state's role as an *active enforcer* of these economic strategies and local-global developments. Governments facilitate the creation of financial enclaves within OECD countries and related jurisdictions, selected for their political stability and regulatory pragmatism. These enclaves are becoming strategic sites of wealth protection, poised to support the next phase of wealth preservation and expansion. Within this competitive landscape, nation branding has emerged as a key instrument of soft power (Nye 2011). Operating at both macro (national image) and micro (product perception) levels, it seeks to convert political and reputational capital into tangible economic gains – yet another layer in the broader process of economization.

It transforms financial centres into assets, subject to the logic of assetization (Freire 2023), and generates a regime of coexistence between extraction (withdrawing value from assets) and accumulation (generating value through assets), as evident, for example, in the real estate markets of major IFCs. However, nation branding is also a process of co-creation, involving citizens who, as global brand ambassadors (Volcic & Andrejevic 2011), actively promote their nation-state's financial appeal. This serves as an economic development tool and governance mechanism, and fosters cohesion within the global financial ecosystem, but also risks commodifying national identity and state sovereignty. By reframing national identities as strategic assets, *commercial nationalism* prioritizes market logic over political allegiance – a defining feature of synthetic communities.[5]

Nation branding illustrates how states can leverage *economic diplomacy* to foster financial brand loyalty among global stakeholders, including EU regulators, financial policymakers and multinational businesses. Luxembourg and Dublin exemplify this approach in Europe, while Dubai and Singapore serve as prominent counterparts elsewhere. These developments reinforce the expanding territorialities of finance, highlighting the strategic reconfiguration of geographical and social jurisdictions as frameworks for synthetic communities. Richard Ford's (2001) legal analysis of jurisdictional dichotomies is instructive here, distinguishing between *organic/authentic* and *synthetic/convenient* jurisdictions. While this distinction shapes perceptions at any given moment, it does not permanently define a jurisdiction's character. IFCs exemplify this fluidity: synthetic jurisdictions prioritize fungibility and market exchange over claims of uniqueness, managing social relations through bureaucratic policies and impersonal transactions.

These highly agile financial entities prioritize adaptability, particularly in smaller states that serve as global conduits of financial services. Conversely, organic jurisdictions – where social structures take precedence over economic imperatives – align more closely with community-based economies (see Gibson-Graham 2016; Lee 2006). These latter models do not conceive growth as an end in itself but as a transformation of the socio-ecological relations underpinning capitalism. Many governments have sought to support local initiatives by deploying public funds to mitigate the socio-economic effects of decarbonization and ongoing deindustrialization. Paradoxically, these same governments continue to compete for private financial investment, even as both the nature of investment and the profile of investors have evolved. While the state attempts to mitigate the social dislocations caused by globalization, particularly in economically *left-behind* regions (Rodríguez-Pose 2018), it simultaneously upholds an ambivalent investment model that privileges private capital (Pike 2023).

It is not without certain irony that several PE firms, with considerable media attention, now promote their integration of ESG criteria into investment strategies. Firms such as the Carlyle Group, KKR, Blackstone, TPG Capital, Apollo Global Management and Bain Capital have all launched sustainability initiatives, committing to reducing GHG emissions, improving energy efficiency and fostering diversity. The Rise Fund, for instance, is marketed as a global impact investing vehicle (see TPG Rise Climate 2025), designed to generate measurable social and environmental benefits while delivering competitive financial returns. These examples illustrate how PE firms actively narrate their evolution to align with ESG principles, recognizing that sustainable practices can enhance long-term financial outcomes while meeting investor demand. However, despite their professed commitment to sustainability, the fundamental structure of the asset economy and investment fund industry remains inherently unsustainable. Its adverse consequences necessitate systemic scrutiny and disentanglement (Lagoarde-Ségot 2024; Miller 2017); a critique distinct from, yet related to, greenwashing.

This tension is particularly evident in the role of financial centres. Cities such as Dublin, London, Luxembourg, Singapore, New York and Hong Kong frequently brand themselves as green or sustainable (Figure 6.2), aligning with ESG and sustainable finance narratives. Yet these centres remain structurally embedded in extractive investment practices that contradict their sustainability claims. The result is a deepening duality that undermines the credibility and effectiveness of green and sustainable finance initiatives.

The green investment sector is undeniably lucrative for financial centres, serving two distinct political functions. First, they act as conduits for private investment into climate-aligned infrastructure – helping to render initiatives such as the European Green Deal politically viable by framing them in market-compatible terms. Second, they facilitate global capital flows into new markets, with Africa emerging as a primary focus. While ecological modernization and neoliberalism converge in their faith in market mechanisms and technology, they diverge on the role of the state, social equity and long-term governance priorities. For example, the EU Adaptation Strategy (European Commission 2021: 17) emphasizes the importance of "stepping up international action for climate resilience". Yet institutions such as the UK's ODI portray financial centres as neutral platforms for climate finance (Tyson 2019), overlooking the legal competition and economic diplomacy that obscure problematic financial practices and challenge the very notion of finance's purported neutrality.

Financial centres are increasingly central to European sustainable finance policies, linking them to broader shifts in state–market–society relations across EU member states. These policy-making arenas, shaped by coalitions involved in developing taxonomies and ESG criteria (e.g. Tendero & Weber 2025) – are deeply interconnected with parallel transformations in other financial hubs. Shared legal and financial infrastructures, from global law firms to regulatory

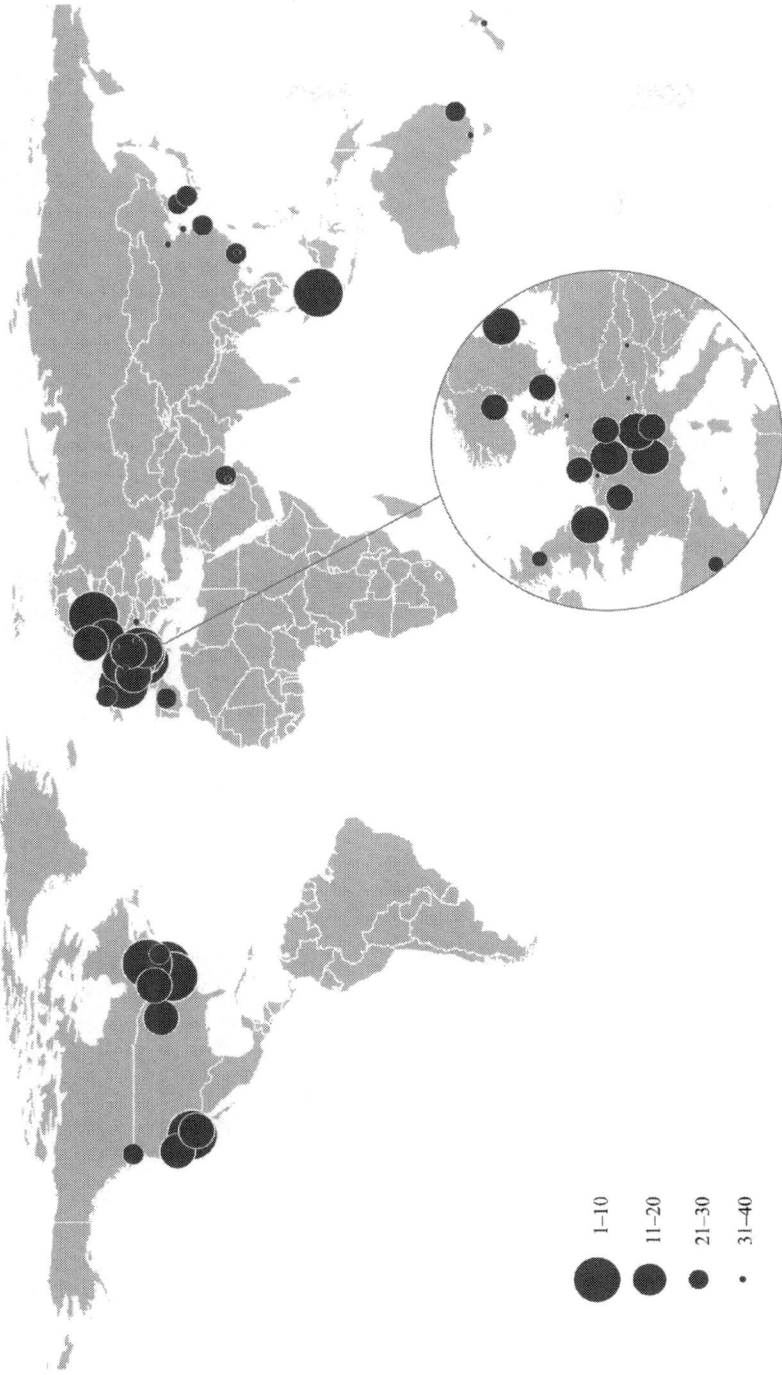

Figure 6.2 The 40 leading green finance centres

Source: Z/Yen 2024a[6].

131

arbitrage, ensure that IFCs respond in largely harmonized ways to market incentives. This complicates efforts to assess the role of IFCs in advancing sustainability, especially when many of the mechanisms supporting sustainable finance rely on legal and accounting manoeuvres that serve much of the system's manipulation for private gain.

The expansion of financial centre ecosystems reflects a broader trend consistent with ecological modernization, but often results in the reproduction of business-as-usual dynamics. Figure 6.2 illustrates how many IFCs now form alliances within the global *sustainable* finance architecture. Among Europe's top 20 green financial centres, cities such as Oslo, Brussels, Vienna and Milan perform well but are not dominant among *traditional* financial hubs (Figure 3.1). In contrast, IFCs such as Dublin and Jersey, although influential in global finance, rank poorly among the top 20 in green finance metrics. Nevertheless, leading conventional IFCs continue to exert structural control over both European and global financial landscapes, reinforced through transnational strategic alliances that create flexible financial spaces within nation-states, often beyond the reach of robust regulation.

The World Alliance of International Financial Centers (WAIFC), in collaboration with the UN-based FC4S Network, seeks to support a transition to sustainable finance. Yet its diverse membership – including centres operating under vastly different regulatory regimes – highlights ongoing tensions. Reconciling high-return financial practices with long-term sustainability remains a fundamental challenge. Despite escalating climate risks, economies such as the US and the Gulf States remain heavily invested in fossil fuel industries, and large volumes of private capital continue to seek returns from carbon-intensive assets.

IFCs operate as strategic nodes in global financial capitalism, shaping networks of legal, political and economic actors that function as de facto policy infrastructure. While often framed as sites of technical expertise and governance innovation, these centres publicly champion ESG and climate-aligned investment strategies, yet their core operations remain structured around financial logics that – as shown – prioritize accumulation over sustainability. This paradox – of facilitating green finance while entrenching private wealth concentration – reveals the structural contradictions embedded within the current green transition agenda.

A façade of sustainability

Legal frameworks have long been instrumental in enabling corporations to exploit tax loopholes, minimize liability and externalize costs onto society.

The structuring of legal entities such as limited liability partnerships and corporations employing base erosion and profit shifting (BEPS) strategies exemplifies how the law is strategically manipulated to maximize profit while shifting financial burdens onto the public. This legal engineering reduces corporate accountability and exacerbates wealth inequality, fostering a system in which financialization prioritizes speculative wealth accumulation over tangible economic productivity. The increasing divergence between paper wealth and real (or productive) value creation further reflects this paradox, as recently highlighted by the McKinsey Global Institute (2023). In an era of escalating planetary crises, marked by climate change, biodiversity destruction and the urgent need for adaptation, the financial industry's role in shaping sustainability narratives warrants critical scrutiny. While the rhetoric of greening finance and achieving sustainability has gained prominence, it often serves as a façade that legitimizes continued resource extraction under the guise of innovation. Resources once freely accessible, such as drinking water, green spaces or even carbon sequestration, are increasingly commodified. Legal–financial mechanisms repurpose them into tradable assets, steadily expanding the geographies of finance and entrenching the dominance of an asset-based economy. Valuation techniques such as discounting and securitization reinforce these logics, producing economic metrics that often distort ecological realities. The paradox is stark: while environmental degradation imposes heavy social costs, those responsible often evade liability. Instead, market-based mechanisms and legal innovations facilitate profit extraction from the very crises they perpetuate, revealing a structural contradiction where destruction begets new markets without delivering meaningful sustainable solutions.

Private property protections have long reinforced socio-economic stratification. As Blomley (2005) notes, property is not merely a legal abstraction but materially embedded in nature, infrastructure and governance. This book has illustrated how financialization reshapes socio-ecological and spatial relationships, complicating the path to net-zero and reinforcing disparities between capital-supplying and capital-dependent regions. Financial centres facilitate "sustainable" investment, yet local economies often struggle to access funding due to valuation models that prioritize large-scale, high-return projects over (often smaller) community-led initiatives.

This asymmetry is amplified by state-led de-risking strategies (Gabor & Sylla 2023), which favour large corporate investors and concentrate capital in financial centres. Legal frameworks do not simply regulate markets; they shape and commercialize them, granting legal and financial elites disproportionate control over economic systems and resources. Property rights – mischaracterized by economic orthodoxy as fixed legal entitlements – have, in practice, become dynamic instruments of commercial governance, particularly in IFCs, where efficient FABS ecosystems further entrench their dominance.

Lessig (2002) argues that in the digital age, property rights empower exclusion – a notion increasingly relevant in the financialization of sustainability. Digital restrictions such as paywalls, patents and encryption limit access to environmental solutions, reinforcing financial hierarchies. The intersection of technology and law presents both opportunities and risks: while technologies such as smart grids and climate analytic tools hold transformative potential, intellectual property regimes and digital controls often obstruct widespread adoption (see Birch & Muniesa 2020 for insightful case studies). In this context, law functions less as a neutral regulatory framework and more as a form of social infrastructure, determining access, participation and control. As a result, marginalized communities and small nations are often excluded from critical climate innovations.

Addressing these barriers to sustainability requires not only technological progress but also systemic restructuring of legal and financial architectures to prioritize accessibility, equity and collective responsibility. As this analysis has demonstrated, the legal structures sustaining financial dominance are deeply embedded in contemporary governance – but critically engaging with these mechanisms offers pathways to challenge and transform the prevailing logic of financial capitalism.

At the same time, the contradictions of financial capitalism are becoming harder to ignore. While facilitating enormous wealth accumulation, it has also amplified systemic risks. Even financial havens such as Dubai, Monaco and Liechtenstein – designed to shield elites from global volatility – remain vulnerable to the structural fragilities of financialization. As the *Economist* (2024b) notes, these enclaves reflect a retreat from uncertainty, but not immunity to it.

Climate-related risks – physical, transitional and legal – are mounting. Insurers, for example, face growing liabilities necessitating higher capital reserves, while asset managers confront the threat of stranded fossil-fuel assets. Legal action, such as lawsuits in Vermont and New York, are increasing accountability while raising financial exposure. PE firms – still heavily invested in carbon-intensive industries – must adapt to shifting regulatory frameworks and growing reputational risks. Yet recent revisions to the EU's Omnibus regulation have softened key requirements, reflecting persistent tension between financial and environmental priorities (European Commission 2025). Although the transition to renewable energy remains underway, the fragile balance between profitability and sustainability leaves firms exposed to legal penalties, reputational damage and accusations of greenwashing (ESMA 2023; Lagoarde-Ségot 2024; Miller 2017). At its core, this reflects a deeper issue: the widening disconnect between financial (paper) wealth and socio-economic and socio-ecological realities.

CONCLUSION: FUTURE FINANCE

The preface of this book began with a pressing question: How sustainable – truly sustainable – can our financial system be, given its structure that enables the creation of financial wealth four times greater than the total annual value of goods and services produced globally (see McKinsey Global Institute 2023)?

Global finance today stands at a defining crossroads. Over the past decades, there has been a proliferation of ESG frameworks, climate finance mechanisms and sustainability-linked investments. And further investment – amounting to trillions of dollars – is both urgently needed and broadly welcomed. Yet, many of these initiatives obscure rather than address the deep *structural* dysfunctions of contemporary global finance. At its core, the system remains oriented toward capital accumulation and speculative value extraction – primarily through asset creation, the rise of asset management as a powerful industry, and the dominance of financial investors whose goal is not long-term reinvestment but short-term gain. Rather than reinvesting profits into companies – and by extension, into communities – these financial investors often channel returns directly to their own shareholders and investors, such as pension funds. This implies that workers across the industrialised world often find their future retirement savings invested in ways that contribute to the very erosion of their own communities and livelihoods.

As this book further explores, *impact* creation is essential – but it is incentivized in markedly different ways across financial actors. Financial investors, in particular, are structurally rewarded for delivering short-term returns. These incentives are not isolated but embedded in broader systemic mechanisms: from the financialization of national accounts like GDP, to asset valuation models that discount future value based on market *expectations*, to dominant economic theories that prioritise monetary value above all else. Wrong incentives trump sustainable values.

These dynamics are sustained and legitimized by concentrated forms of expertise – professional communities clustered in powerful financial centres. These IFCs function as highly networked "islands of knowledge authority", shaping and reinforcing the dominant narratives of the asset economy and institutionalizing practices that prioritize capital accumulation over long-term socio-ecological value. This is not simply a case of misaligned priorities. The problem is structural. With regard to the central question of this book – how sustainable financial investments can truly be – the preceding chapters have shown that the financialization of everything (and everyone, for that matter) is a critical precondition for assigning economic value to nature and everyday livelihoods. For example, only the active creation of categories such as "ecosystem services" enables nature to be priced, and thus made investable. Monetary value, once established, becomes the basis for asset creation – a prerequisite for large-scale investment and the fuel for the asset management behemoths of today's financial system. Yet here, a significant tension emerges: mainstream economists often struggle to account for the systemic complexity and non-linear feedback loops inherent in ecological systems. When these systems are overstretched – as is increasingly the case with climate tipping points – they can amplify risks in unpredictable and irreversible ways, which are difficult to estimate with econometric models.

Paradoxically, such crises generate new categories of risk, which can then be securitized into novel financial instruments – a kind of unstable "assets" in their own right. This trend of framing ecological breakdown as investable risk reflects a troubling trend in financial innovation, where ecological instability is treated less as a warning than as an opportunity for speculative gain.

By contrast, the incentives for non-financial actors – such as public institutions, civil society and communities – reveal a different dynamic. The socio-ecological transformations required to address climate change are slow-moving and often out of step with the accelerating pace of global heating. As extreme weather events intensify, they trigger cascading risks across ecosystems, biodiversity, ocean health and ultimately, human wellbeing. Potential breakdowns are not limited to nature; they extend to our social fabric. Rising inequality across and within regions – particularly in places rendered economically "left behind" – is accompanied by democratic decline. Economic or monetary value alone offers an inadequate framework for understanding the crisis. Ecological, social and cultural values often provide a more meaningful lens through which to define both the problem and its potential solutions – far beyond the econometric models that attempt to quantify nature's worth in monetary terms. In short, and echoing the political critique of large-scale growth strategies such as the European Green Deal, much of what passes for "green finance" today is seamlessly integrated into the very architecture of financial capitalism it ostensibly seeks to reform.

This book further argues that finance must not be seen as a neutral mechanism, but as a socially and politically constructed system: a complex assemblage of legal frameworks, valuation logics, professional ideologies and spatial infrastructures. To unpack this, the book traced the architecture of the asset economy through three interrelated dimensions: (1) the process of assetization; (2) the rise of asset management as a globally dominant industry; and (3) the spatial authority of financial centres in producing and legitimizing economic narratives and financial logics.

Looking at finance through a geographical lens – by connecting abstract financial flows to real places – allows for a deeper analysis of how global finance produces concrete social and ecological consequences. Every financial transaction – whether a local bank loan to a bakery or the use of derivatives by financial investors – has material social and spatial implications. Although often abstracted away, these impacts are concrete and measurable on the ground. The *spatial materiality of finance matters*. Geographers are well-positioned to analyse such systems – not in isolation, but relationally. Just as they study geological, hydrological, economic and cultural systems in relation, they also examine how financial systems interact with and shape social, ecological and political realities. At the outset of this book, I compared financial systems to the production networks of the automotive industry. Consider the electric vehicle: its components are sourced globally, coordinated through multi-tier supply chains and assembled with logistical precision. Financial products – such as investment funds – follow a similar logic. Each stage of their creation is dispersed across jurisdictions to exploit favourable conditions, whether in terms of tax regimes, regulatory environments or concentrations of expertise, that is, "talent". Financial centres must therefore be attractive not just for legal or fiscal reasons, but also for their ability to retain and nurture professional talent.

My point is: like industrial production, financial systems are embedded in real places – cities, towns and regions. These places are home to the people who live and work there, and who sustain them. Just as manufacturing systems connect dispersed production sites, financial investments link disparate geographies. Globalization has enabled the rise of the multinational company, supported by globally integrated networks of consultancy, legal and accountancy firms that manage and facilitate these flows. The notion that finance is disembodied or purely virtual must be critically challenged.

Local investment matters! It plays a critical role in sustaining community wellbeing. Thriving communities depend on continued investment in essential infrastructure – affordable housing, utilities, energy, childcare and other foundational public services. When capital is reinvested locally, it generates a virtuous cycle: economic growth, improved social services, further investment and communal wellbeing. But when this cycle is disrupted – when profits are extracted rather than reinvested – the result is not renewal, but decline. The initial promise of sustainability and prosperity gives way to depletion and social erosion.

In short, financial investment often fails to be productive – not because investment itself is inherently harmful, but because the incentives that drive it are misaligned. When the price signals are wrong, even well-intentioned capital can do harm. As shown throughout this book, communities often decline not despite financial investment, but because of how that investment is designed, incentivised and distributed. The public good becomes a private revenue stream; ecological systems become abstract assets; and value, once grounded in social utility and environmental stewardship, is redefined in terms of liquidity, risk and potential yield.

This is the paradox of *financialized sustainability*: an old logic cloaked in new green promises. It tends to generate returns for the few while undermining the very systems it claims to support. At the heart of this paradox lies the epistemological dominance of financialization and assetization: a worldview that seeks to translate all dimensions of life – ecological, social, temporal – into risk-weighted investable assets.

Meanwhile, the PE industry continues to attract ever more capital from investors seeking diversification and high returns. Buoyed by bullish performance metrics and optimistic projections – and operating within a regulatory landscape still struggling to keep pace – PE's expansion comes at a cost that may ultimately prove unsustainable. The lessons of the past offer little reassurance. In the relentless pursuit of (often illusory) growth – the miracle cure of yesteryear – PE has recast itself as a modern-day economic messiah. Yet what it frequently delivers is *synthetic growth*: seductive, dazzling and ultimately hollow – a gilded promise masking systemic extraction and irreversible depletion.

In the complex machinery of global finance, few instruments have proved as potent – or as opaque – as the PE model. Its advocates tout revitalized businesses, leaner operations and robust investor returns. Yet beneath this reassuring veneer lies a more unsettling reality: the creation of fictitious wealth – paper valuations untethered from real productivity and social value. This illusion of prosperity increasingly shapes everything from high streets and housing markets to pensions, public services and digital infrastructures. Fictitious wealth is wealth in name only. It stems not from tangible economic output but from financial engineering, speculative asset inflation and imaginative accounting. PE, with its reliance on leveraged buyouts, mark-to-model accounting and short investment cycles, is particularly adept at producing such illusions. Even McKinsey – hardly a sceptic of private markets – has cautioned against the proliferation of paper wealth now saturating the sector.

Crucially, legal frameworks underpinning these developments are not neutral facilitators. As this book has demonstrated, law functions as a political instrument, selectively shaped to facilitate and direct processes of capital accumulation. Through mechanisms such as regulatory arbitrage, institutional redesign and legal loopholes, these frameworks support the spatial expansion of financial capitalism, allowing capital to flow, settle and extract value across jurisdictions with minimal constraint.

In fact, financial centres such as London, New York, Singapore and Hong Kong are often mischaracterized as passive marketplaces. In reality, they serve as epistemic and operational command nodes in a sprawling network of capital, regulation and elite expertise. These cities function not just as locations but as strategic infrastructure – where laws are crafted, financial instruments launched and legitimacy manufactured. In boardrooms, regulatory bodies and data-driven labs, the alchemy of fictitious wealth is not only enabled but valorised.

As fictitious wealth expands, so too does the disconnection between capital markets and socio-ecological realities. The climate finance sector now teeters on the same precipice. ESG-labelled funds often favour the optics of sustainability – light-green branding, artful reporting – over measurable environmental benefit. Some even repackage carbon-heavy assets under green façades, earning inflated valuations with little climate alignment. In this way, fictitious wealth is recycled as greenwashed capital. This dynamic extends into the digital sphere. The rise of tokenized assets and blockchain-based financial products offers new terrain for speculative valuation. PE has quickly embraced Web3 platforms and digital infrastructure, transplanting its familiar model into virtual domains. The outcome is predictable: inflated asset values, vague regulation and a growing sense of déjà vu – new visuals, same structural flaws.

The socio-ecological costs are anything but virtual. Fictitious wealth creation builds on real wealth extraction, with tangible consequences. The fallout is borne by communities: job losses, hollowed-out firms, unaffordable housing and "green" investments with minimal or negligible climate benefit. And because many financial investors include public pension funds and universities endowments, the same paper returns that inflate balance sheets today may erode retirement security and public trust tomorrow.

Yet not all is surrender. Regulatory regimes are beginning to respond. In the United States, the Securities and Exchange Commission (SEC) has introduced rules to bolster transparency in fees and valuation practices. In the European Union, the AIFMD framework imposes restrictions on asset-stripping and leverage. Proposals for clawbacks, leverage caps and worker protections are slowly advancing from white papers to parliamentary agendas. More notably, some investors are beginning to explore alternative models. So-called "patient capital" funds, with longer holding periods and a reduced reliance on financial engineering, are gaining traction. Mission-aligned firms are experimenting with employee ownership, democratic governance and more robust forms of ESG integration. Large public pension funds, such as CalPERS, are also pursuing direct investment strategies, seeking to reclaim control from traditional PE general partners (GPs) and to align their portfolios more closely with long-term public interests.

However, these shifts require more than incremental policy reforms. They demand a structural rethinking of the very logics that have shaped financial expansion. The tools that enabled financialization must be reimagined and redirected. Legal and professional actors – once central to institutionalizing opacity and engineering fictitious capital – must become agents of transparency, accountability and public value. Finance must be re-embedded within democratic institutions, not through technocratic adjustments or ESG rebranding, but through a fundamental redefinition of what constitutes value and for whom it is created.

In this light, financial centres must no longer be viewed as neutral marketplaces. They are geopolitical actors in their own right – sites where regulation is shaped, value claims legitimised and economic governance orchestrated. The professional-cum-profession infrastructures concentrated in these centres – finance, law, accountancy, consultancy and tech – must also be held accountable. Ironically, their own financialization has made them more vulnerable to the same extractive dynamics they once enabled. Some of the world's most profitable law firms, as shown, are now themselves targets for acquisition by PE – closing a recursive loop in which enablers of capital accumulation become its assets.

To understand the architecture of fictitious wealth – and to begin imagining viable alternatives – one must move beyond the confines of orthodox economics. While economic reasoning remains a valuable tool, it is not exhaustive and often fails to capture the full social, legal and ecological dimensions of financial systems – dimensions that both shape and constitute one another.

IFCs are unique among economic clusters in that they trade not in physical goods, but – often to a remarkable extent – in fictitious capital: financial claims on future value such as stocks, bonds and derivatives. Unlike clusters in manufacturing or tech, IFCs specialize in engineering these claims through legal, regulatory and financial innovation, enabling the continuous expansion of capital without producing commensurate tangible output, a concern even raised by McKinsey, which reported a fourfold increase in financial assets relative to real economic growth as a troubling structural imbalance (McKinsey Global Institute 2023). As such, IFCs have become powerful instruments not only for markets but also for nation-states, with finance frequently deployed to project geopolitical influence, manage public debt or shape global alignments. European IFCs, despite their global prominence, remain structurally dependent on US-based firms, albeit to varying degrees, reinforcing asymmetries in global financial governance and limiting their autonomy in shaping post-carbon futures. Indeed, IFCs have evolved into *critical relays* of economic transformation and legal-institutional innovation. Yet over time, much of this innovation has drifted away from serving the public interest and collective welfare, toward enabling private accumulation and wealth concentration – although, arguably, still contributing to national GDPs. Crucially, both law and space operate as powerful social technologies within this architecture. Their combined deployment in

IFCs constitutes a distinct legal-geographical formation that remains underexplored, yet is particularly well positioned to illuminate the micro-practices and macro-patterns underpinning the socio-spatial reorganization of contemporary financial capitalism and, crucially, to harness this understanding for shaping more equitable and sustainable futures in times of profound flux.

Contemporary finance has sustained an illusion of endless growth, built on increasingly fragile foundations. In an era of accelerating ecological collapse and deepening inequality, this illusion is no longer tenable. Yet the future of finance is not predetermined. Whether it reinforces inequality or supports regeneration depends on how it is governed, by whom and in whose interest. The current system reflects a set of institutionalized choices – legal, ideological and professional. It can be reshaped by different ones. What is needed is not merely better metrics or smarter regulation, but a collective act of imagination: to build a financial system rooted in justice, sustainability and shared prosperity – one capable of meeting the challenges of climate change and systemic inequality.

The choice is ours. Its consequences will echo for generations.

NOTES

1 Synthetic finance

1. The European Green Deal is the EU's strategy for sustainable growth, aiming to build a fair, competitive and resource-efficient economy. It supports the 2030 Agenda, prioritizes wellbeing and commits to a just, inclusive transition (European Council 2025). The related Green Deal Industrial Plan proposes key measures to boost Europe's strategic autonomy and investment appeal. It also highlights strategic sectors and major infrastructure projects to attract private capital over the long term (European Commission 2023).
2. Several organizations provide regular updates on the world's largest fossil fuel extraction projects, including information on the companies and financial institutions responsible for them such as CarbonBombs.org (www.carbonbombs.org/) or the European Coalition for Corporate Justice (https://corporatejustice.org/publications/report-defusing-carbon-bombs/#:~:text=A%20new%20report%20released%20today,Shell%2C%20RWE%2C%20and%20ENI%20or).
3. Stranded assets are assets that (may) lose their economic value because of market changes, particularly in the context of climate adaptation and ESG.
4. See the 17 SDGs at https://sdgs.un.org/goals.
5. The United Nations Framework Convention on Climate Change (UNFCCC) Standing Committee on Finance defines climate finance as "finance that aims at reducing emissions, and enhancing sinks of greenhouse gases and aims at reducing vulnerability of, and maintaining and increasing the resilience of, human and ecological systems to negative climate change impacts" (UNFCCC nd).
6. In this book, I refer to both epistemic and epistemological authority. The former pertains to professionals' recognized expertise – particularly in professions such as law and accounting – while the latter addresses how these professions' bodies of knowledge are structured, defined and actively defended against competing claims from adjacent professions.
7. The term "non-productive economies" or "non-productive industries" is often attributed to the French economist Frédéric Bastiat (1996 [1845]), who used these terms to describe economic activities that do not contribute to the creation of new wealth or value, and instead, focus on redistributing existing wealth. He contrasted productive industries, which drive economic growth by creating new value, with non-productive industries, which merely circulate wealth without contributing to overall output. Measuring matters – because how we define and quantify value determines what is seen as economically meaningful.
8. The redefinition of GDP has been a contested and politically driven process, shaped by decades of financial influence and institutional power. Financial services, once excluded as non-productive, were reclassified as productive, inflating GDP, particularly in finance-centred economies. These revisions reflect geopolitical shifts more than economic theory, with influence moving from bodies like the UN to institutions such as the IMF and World Bank. The 1993 and 2008 updates to the System of National Accounts marked major

turning points, expanding the definition of productivity to include financial intermediation, risk management and speculative activity (European Commission *et al.* 2009; Assa 2017). While some statisticians questioned the inclusion of activities detached from labour or capital, the European Central Bank argued that any market-paid service and transaction is productive. This shift reveals a broader transformation in economic thinking, where productivity is defined less by material contribution and more by market valuation.

9. In finance, the Euromarkets refers to the market for Eurocurrencies, which include currencies held as deposits by individuals or businesses outside their country of issue. For example, a Eurodollar is a dollar deposit held or traded *outside* the US. A major factor behind the development and continued operation of such a market is its freedom from the regulatory environment, as well as the political or other country-specific risks of the country of origin.

10. A powerful geographical illustration how finance has always been a deeply global, networked and border-spanning phenomenon is indeed the *Atlas of Finance* (Wójcik *et al.* 2024).

11. Empirically, this book draws on extensive research into the asset management industry, incorporating expert interviews conducted since 2013 across major European financial centres, including London, Frankfurt, Dublin and Luxembourg, as well as, to a lesser extent, key US and Asian centres such as New York and Singapore. By integrating both traditional and exploratory methods, including roundtable discussions, document analysis, and engagement with industry practitioners, alongside online sources such as seminars hosted by global law firms and financial think tanks, this study offers a comprehensive understanding of the overlapping processes and competing interests that shape the evolving legal geographies of finance.

2 Dynamic architectures of the asset economy

1. In autumn 2004, Franz Müntefering, then chairman of Germany's SPD, used the "swarm of locusts" metaphor to criticize what he saw as extreme excesses of capitalism. He argued that anonymous investors dismantled companies for short-term profit, disregarding the long-term social costs.

2. For examples see European Commission (nd) and EUIPO (2024) (accessed 30 April 2024).

3. Nearly all asset-price inflation was driven by debt. Money and credit were not used for tangible capital investments or to raise wages. Instead, banks primarily financed existing property and financial assets with the consequence of artificially inflating their prices. This highlights a functional differentiation of credit between "real" and "financial" capital (Bezemer 2014). In such an environment, debt rose nearly as quickly as asset values because of increased speculation on credit (Bezemer & Hudson 2016).

4. This era of "cheap money" is defined by low interest rates, central banks' quantitative easing and high liquidity, all of which was aimed at stimulating economic growth. The two most significant periods of cheap money occurred following the 2007/08 financial crisis and during the Covid-19 pandemic, extending roughly from 2008 to 2022, when central banks started to gradually tighten monetary policies.

5. A limited partnership is a legal business structure characterized by a division of roles and liabilities between two types of partners: at least one GP, who assumes full managerial control and bears *unlimited* financial liability, and one or more LPs, whose involvement is primarily financial and whose liability is restricted to the amount of their capital contribution.

6. The term shadow banking refers to bank-like activities (mainly lending) that occur outside the traditional banking sector, primarily carried out by investment funds (Central Bank of Ireland nd).

7. Other funds include guaranteed/protected funds, real estate funds and other funds. Note: Regulated open-end funds include mutual funds, ETFs and institutional funds.

8. Senator Carl Levin, as chair of the US Senate Permanent Subcommittee on Investigations, led several investigations into offshore tax abuse, including one that examined Enron's use of more than 800 offshore entities, many registered in the Cayman Islands (US Senate Permanent Subcommittee on Investigations 2003). I thank Matti Ylönen for pointing this out to me.

9. However, the underlying "plumbing" at the core of the financial infrastructure has not changed significantly and remains primarily aligned with the interests of the few truly global banks (Robinson *et al.* 2023, 2024). These include, among others, Bank of America Merrill Lynch, Barclays, Citigroup, UBS, Deutsche Bank, Goldman Sachs, HSBC, J.P. Morgan Chase, Société Générale, BNP Paribas and Morgan Stanley.

10. This includes, for example, new crypto-assets. The regulatory environment for cryptocurrencies and related financial products is evolving fast. Although the SEC's stance on these investments is subject to change, it has, for example, approved ETFs that invest directly in Bitcoin futures, such as the ProShares Bitcoin Strategy ETF, which launched in October 2021. These ETFs do not hold Bitcoin directly but instead invest in Bitcoin futures contracts.

11. A notable power shift is underway in the PE industry, as the balance between LPs, such as pension funds, and GPs begins to tilt. Amid rising interest rates, lower valuations and limited exit options, GPs face growing competition for capital, giving LPs – especially pension funds – increased negotiating leverage. This shift is drawing close industry attention (see Barnes & Thornburg 2023).

12. However, recent research suggests that SWFs as LPs tend to yield lower investment returns (Cumming & Monteiro 2023). Previous studies have highlighted the superior performance of endowments in VC and PE funds (Lerner *et al.* 2008), but did not separately consider SWFs, which appear to perform worse than other institutional investors. This finding underscores the distinct decision-making and performance characteristics of SWFs.

13. See industry's global website at www.privateequityinternational.com/global-investor-ranking/.

14. For high-net-worth individuals, life insurance policies serve as wealth protection tools, offering advantages in estate planning, wealth transfer, liquidity management, investment opportunities, tax benefits and more.

15. As of 31 December 2023, Aviva served 16 million customers in the UK, out of a total of 19.2 million globally. Additionally, Aviva Investors managed £233 billion in assets as of 31 March 2024 (Aviva nd).

16. The 'Stichting Pensioenfonds ABP' pension fund is the largest Dutch and European pension fund, and the fifth largest in the world. Managing pensions for government and education employees, ABP manages assets exceeding €500 billion (Thousand Investors 2024).

17. Financial innovations, such as the introduction of new derivative products and trading strategies, expanded the scope and appeal of futures markets and provided investors such as pension funds with more ways to manage risk and generate returns and new opportunities to profit from price movements through futures trading in commodity markets.

18. 50 largest endowment funds (www.visualcapitalist.com/worlds-top-endowment-funds/); 53 largest SWF (https://en.wikipedia.org/wiki/List_of_countries_by_sovereign_wealth_funds); 50 largest public pension funds (www.visualcapitalist.com/worlds-100-biggest-pension-funds/).

19. https://en.wikipedia.org/wiki/List_of_countries_by_sovereign_wealth_funds.

20. Valuable resources for staying informed about the latest developments in the legal industry, law firms, PE and asset management more broadly include Law.com, Funds-Europe.com, and PrivateEquityInternational.com. This section has primarily relied on these sources.

21. 50 largest law firms, by revenue in 2021 (https://en.wikipedia.org/wiki/List_of_largest_law_firms_by_revenue); 10 largest fund providers, by net assets in 2022 (www.visualcapitalist.com/worlds-biggest-mutual-fund-and-etf-providers/); 10 largest asset managers, by AUM in 2023 (www.swfinstitute.org/fund-manager-rankings/asset-manager). Figure 2.5 includes only the top 10 fund providers, whose combined AUM is approximately

$18 trn. The total global figure of $38 trn includes hundreds of additional fund brands beyond these top 10, encompassing regional, niche, and smaller passive and active providers. As such, the figure under-represents the total by omitting the long tail of smaller entities. Further, the $35.4 trn total reflects the combined AUM of the top 10 asset managers. However, global AUM across the top 500 asset managers is estimated at approximately $128 trn. This figure therefore captures only the largest firms, not the full scope of the asset management industry.

22. There are exceptions to this trend, including Slater and Gordon (Australian law), which was the first major law firm to list on the Australian Securities Exchange (ASX) in 2007, but, following a decline in its stock value, was delisted in 2017. In the UK, law firms like Gateley and DWF have also pursued public listings in 2015 and 2019, respectively.

23. In established jurisdictions such as England and Australia, ABSs have been permitted for over a decade, creating frameworks that enable law firms to secure private capital without being bound by conventional constraints. More recently, Arizona began approving ABSs in 2021, further illustrating the growing acceptance of these innovative models. In Spain, for instance, ECIJA's decision to sell a stake to Alia Capital Partners in 2024 demonstrates a strategic move to raise funds, which in turn facilitates the opening of new offices and the attraction of new partners. This case exemplifies how law firms are harnessing PE to drive growth, even within a seemingly restrictive regulatory environment.

3 Assemblages of global authority

1. www.marxists.org/archive/lenin/works/1921/jan/25.htm, from Lenin's Collected Works, 1st English edition, Progress Publishers, Moscow, 1965, Volume 32, pp. 70–107.
2. Much of the current specialization and economic strength of European financial centres can be traced back to their colonial past (Robinson 2002; Van Meeteren *et al.* 2016).
3. The 35th edition of the Global Financial Centres Index (GFCI 35) was published on 21 March 2024. GFCI 35 provides evaluations of future competitiveness and rankings for 121 financial centres around the world. The GFCI serves as a reference for policy and investment decision-makers.
4. See Z/Yen (2025). New indices have been introduced to assess the competitiveness of IFCs worldwide, now incorporating measures of sustainability ("green-ness") and technological capabilities.
5. It is important to note that financial centres have no agency per se, as they are administrative entities made up of multiple groups of actors, each with their own interests and agency – which are not always aligned. However, in efforts to "grow the pie" and assert their interests, these actors can coordinate their actions, thereby effectively endowing the financial centre itself with agency.

4 Expanding epistemologies

1. Boussebaa (2017) examines similar dynamics through the concept of global professional service firms (GPSFs). He argues that professionals within GPSFs reinforce global power imbalances and unequal exchange relationships by engaging in transnational governance both externally (in the global economy) and internally (within their own organizations). This process fosters the cultural and economic colonization of peripheral regions. At the same time, an internal division of labour within these firms allows core professionals to consolidate their dominance by leveraging firm-wide resources to access emerging markets and capitalize on lower labour costs.

2. The literature on conflict of laws (or private international law) is vast and, in essence, examines how jurisdictions determine applicable laws in cases involving multiple territories, highlighting the role of legal professionals in managing cross-border legal complexities (e.g. Crawford & Brownlie 2019; Garner 2019). My intention is not to provide a comprehensive overview of this specialized legal scholarship; rather, I want to encourage readers to draw inspiration from these diverse sources of knowledge and to engage critically with the object of analysis in this chapter – namely, the growing epistemological authority of specific, privileged professions and professionals – from multiple perspectives.
3. Prudential regulation is designed to ensure the safety and soundness of financial institutions, particularly banks and insurance companies. Its primary objective is to mitigate risks to financial stability by imposing requirements related to capital adequacy, liquidity, risk management and governance structures. Regulatory authorities implement prudential regulations to protect depositors, policyholders and the broader economy from financial instability and systemic crises. In contrast, non-prudential regulations such as those requiring the disclosure of effective interest rates or corporate ownership structures are often self-implemented and may be overseen by non-financial regulatory bodies (Christen *et al.* 2003).
4. The Alan Watson Foundation (Watson 1974) lists an enormous list of references that engage critically and in part controversially with the concept of legal transplants and the resulting processes of cross-country diffusion of law, see https://web.archive.org/web/20080930165121/http://www.alanwatson.org/readings.htm.

5 Expanding territorialities of law

1. The "Double Irish" and "Dutch Sandwich" were tax avoidance strategies employed by multinational companies to minimize tax liabilities. The Double Irish involved routing profits through two Irish entities to benefit from Ireland's low corporate tax rates, while the Dutch Sandwich incorporated a Dutch intermediary to further reduce withholding taxes on profit transfers. These structures were widely utilized by technology and pharmaceutical companies until regulatory reforms led to their gradual phase-out in the early 2020s.
2. In a compelling account, Sol Picciotto (1995) illustrates how offshore jurisdictions have actively facilitated the development of favourable legal and administrative frameworks. In 1967, a British tax lawyer amended the trust laws of the Cayman Islands to circumvent changes in the "power to enjoy" rules introduced in British law. Similarly, in 1976, the Cayman Islands strengthened their bank secrecy laws, following American legal advice, in response to the US District Court's ruling in the Field case.
3. Today, this stymying effect arises from several interrelated dynamics. First, and alluding to Chapter 2, financial companies such as globally operating asset managers are primarily accountable to their shareholders, investors and clients, not to public or multilateral governance bodies. This fact limits their responsiveness to global policy goals. Second, their investment strategies are often driven by short-term return maximization, which undermines longer-term priorities like sustainability, social equity but also macroeconomic stability. Third, these companies operate across jurisdictions and frequently exploit regulatory differences, making unified global governance difficult to enforce. Finally, the concentration of ownership in a few powerful asset managers grants them significant influence over global capital allocation, yet this power is exercised without corresponding democratic oversight, further weakening prospects for coordinated and equitable governance at the international level.
4. It should be noted that Greensill's legal structure and the role of its directors were highly unusual and controversial, which may make it an outlier rather than a general example. Greensill Bank, a subsidiary of Greensill Capital, was deeply involved in supply chain financing, particularly through practices such as reverse factoring. In reverse factoring,

a financial institution pays a company's suppliers at a discount, later collecting the full amount from the company, thereby facilitating quicker payments to suppliers while extending the company's repayment period. Greensill expanded this model by introducing innovative "future accounts receivables finance", lending money based on *anticipated* future sales – a practice that introduced significant risk due to its speculative nature. The bank's rapid growth was fuelled by high-interest term deposits from private customers and substantial capital infusions from its parent company, supported by investors such as SoftBank. However, this aggressive expansion led to a complex corporate structure with significant exposure to a limited number of clients, notably the GFG Alliance, resulting in concentrated credit risks. Regulatory scrutiny revealed that Greensill Bank had difficulty substantiating the existence of certain assets on its balance sheet, ultimately leading to its insolvency in March 2021 (e.g. Nelson 2021).

5. The metaphorical "poison pills" also refer to the intricacies and potential pitfalls involved in the cross-border legal structuring of financial products, where even minor errors in legal or regulatory compliance can lead to significant financial or reputational risks.

6. Pass-through taxation ensures that income is only taxed once at the investor level, rather than at both the fund and investor levels.

6 Thriving finance, ailing communities

1. A valuable source for tracking PE industry trends is the podcast *PEI: The Infrastructure Investor Podcast*. Recent examples include KKR's £4 billion ($5 billion) bid for a majority stake in the financially distressed Thames Water, the UK's largest water utility, in February 2025. BlackRock strengthened its infrastructure portfolio by acquiring 43 ports from CK Hutchison for $23 billion, including two at the Panama Canal. Assura, a UK primary care property investor, is set to accept a £1.6 billion buyout offer from a KKR- and Stonepeak-led consortium, reflecting a trend of public-to-private acquisitions in the recovering commercial property sector. Meanwhile, HMC Capital committed $950 million to Neoen's wind, solar and battery assets in Victoria, Australia, as part of its plan to develop a 15GW renewable energy portfolio. These examples (from a long list) highlight PE's crucial role in financing and managing large-scale infrastructure projects to meet future demands across industries.

2. In this context, during the pre-election campaign period, on 4 November 2024, a judge denied District Attorney Krasner's request to halt the Musk PAC's multi-million-dollar, lottery-like voter giveaway. Andy Taylor, representing Elon Musk and America PAC, responded to allegations of unfair vote-buying, stating: "It's an opportunity to earn ... not a chance to win" (*Economist* 2024a).

3. The majority of private capital raised in Europe is domiciled in Luxembourg, the Cayman Islands, Delaware, Ireland and China (Preqin 2024).

4. An insightful and thought-provoking discussion took place during the Z/Yen webinar, "The Emergence of Wealth Management in the Mauritius International Financial Centre", held on 30 September 2024.

5. As this book approaches its conclusion, we observe a "permanent" shift towards interest-driven geopolitics (Pohl 2025: np): "Power is the only universal language." Economic and financial integration, once a mechanism for international cooperation, now appears to function as an instrument of coercion. However, while the financial sector remains well-positioned, the societal costs of adapting to climate change may ultimately prove prohibitively high.

6. The 13h edition of the Global Green Finance Index (GGFI 13) was published on 23 April 2024 and evaluates green finance offerings across 96 major financial centres worldwide. However, while useful for identifying trends, the results of both the GFCI and GGFI should be interpreted with caution, not least because of their underlying methodologies.

REFERENCES

Aalbers, M. 2016. *The Financialization of Housing*. London: Routledge.

Abbott, A. 1988. *The System of Professions: An Essay on the Division of Expert Labour*. Chicago, IL: University of Chicago Press.

Acosta, A. 2013. "Extractivism and neoextractivism: two sides of the same curse". In M. Lang & D. Mokrani (eds), *Beyond Development: Alternative Visions from Latin America*, 61–86. Quito: Fundación Rosa Luxemburg and Transnational Institute.

Adkins, L. *et al.* 2020. *The Asset Economy*. Cambridge: Polity.

Adveq 2013. *Benefits of Private Equity for the European Economy*. Zurich: Adveq.

Alami, I. & A. Dixon 2024. *The Spectre of State Capitalism*. Oxford: Oxford University Press.

ALFI 2024. *SIF (Specialised Investment Funds)*. Luxembourg: Association of the Luxembourg Funds Industry. Available at: www.alfi.lu/en-gb/pages/setting-up-in-luxembourg/alternat ive-investment-funds-legal-vehicles/sif-(specialised-investment-funds).

Allen, F. & G. Yago 2010. *Financing the Future: Market-Based Innovations for Growth*. Philadelphia, PA: Wharton School Publishing.

Allen, J. 2003. *Lost Geographies of Power*. Oxford: Blackwell.

Allen, J. & M. Pryke 2013. "Financialising household water: Thames Water, MEIF, and 'ring-fenced' politics". *Cambridge Journal of Regions, Economy and Society* 6, 419–39. 10.1093/cjres/rst010.

Alves, C. 2023. "Fictitious capital, the credit system, and the particular case of government bonds in Marx". *New Political Economy* 28, 398–415. 10.1080/13563467.2022.2130221.

Amin, A. 2001. "Moving on: institutionalism in economic geography". *Environment and Planning A: Economy and Space* 33, 1237–41. 10.1068/a34108.

Amin, A. & P. Cohendet 2004. *Architectures of Knowledge: Firms, Capabilities, and Communities*. Oxford: Oxford University Press.

Appelbaum, E. & R. Batt 2014. *Private Equity at Work: When Wall Street Manages Main Street*. New York: Russel Sage Foundation.

Arcand, J.-L. *et al.* 2012. *Too Much Finance?* IMF Working Paper. Washington, DC: IMF.

Assa, J. 2017. *The Financialization of GDP: Implications for Economic Theory and Policy*. London: Routledge.

Augar, P. 2000. *The Death of Gentlemanly Capitalism: The Rise and Fall of London's Investment Banks*. London: Penguin.

Aviva nd. *How We're Organised*. Available at: www.aviva.com/about-us/how-we-are-organised.

Ayers, J. & T. Forsyth 2009. "Community-based adaptation to climate change". *Environment: Science and Policy for Sustainable Development* 51, 22–31. 10.3200/ENV.51.4.22–31.

Bair, J. 2005. "Global capitalism and commodity chains: looking back, going forward". *Competition & Change* 9, 153–80. 10.1179/102452905x45382.

Bair, J. & E. Dussel Peters 2006. "Global commodity chains and endogenous growth: Export dynamism and development in Mexico and Honduras". *World Development* 34, 203–21. 10.1016/j.world.dev.2005.09.004.

Bair, J. & G. Gereffi 2002. "NAFTA and the apparel commodity chain: corporate strategies, inter-firm networks, and local development". In G. Gereffi *et al.* (eds), *Free Trade and Uneven Development: The North American Apparel Industry after NAFTA*, 23–50. Philadelphia, PA: Temple University Press.

Balmas, P. & S. Dörry 2023. "Chinese bank networks in Europe: FDI-oriented by legal and strategic design". *Eurasian Geography and Economics* 66, 1–27. 10.1080/15387216.2023.2182805.

Ban, C. & D. Gabor 2016. "The political economy of shadow banking". *Review of International Political Economy* 23, 901–14. 10.1080/09692290.2016.1264442.

Barnes & Thornburg 2023. *LP and GP Relations in Flux: 5 Key Takeaways*. Available at: https://btlaw.com/en/insights/news/2023/commentary-lp-and-gp-relations-in-flux-5-key-takeaways.

Barnes, T. 1988. "Rationality and relativism in economic geography: an interpretive review of the homo economicus assumption". *Progress in Human Geography* 12, 473–96. 10.1177/030913258801200401.

Bassens, D. *et al.* 2024. "World cities under conditions of digitization and platform capitalism: updating the advanced producer services complex". *Geoforum* 152. 10.1016/j.geoforum.2024.104021.

Bassens, D. & M. Van Meeteren 2015. "World cities under conditions of financialized globalization: towards an augmented world city hypothesis". *Progress in Human Geography* 39, 752–75. 10.1177/0309132514558441.

Bastiat, F. 1996 [1845]. *Economic Sophisms*. Irvine-on-Hudson, NY: Foundation for Economic Education.

Baudrillard, J. 1994. *Simulacra and Simulation (The Body, In Theory: Histories of Cultural Materialism)*. Translation Sheila Faria Glaser. Ann Arbor, MI: University of Michigan Press.

Beaverstock, J. *et al.* 2000. "World-City network: a new metageography?" *Annals of the Association of American Geographers* 90, 123–34. 10.1111/0004-5608.00188.

Beaverstock, J. *et al.* 2002. "Attending to the world: competition, cooperation and connectivity in the World City network". *Global Networks* 2, 111–32. 10.1111/1471-0374.00031.

Beer, A. *et al.* 2005. "Neoliberalism and the institutions for regional development in Australia". *Geographical Research* 43, 49–58. 10.1111/j.1745-5871.2005.00292.x.

Berle, A. & G. Means 1967 [1932]. *The Modern Corporation and Private Property*. New York: Harcourt, Brace and World.

Bezemer, D. 2014. "Schumpeter might be right again: the functional differentiation of credit". *Journal of Evolutionary Economics* 24, 935–50. 10.1007/s00191-014-0376-2.

Bezemer, D. & M. Hudson 2016. "Finance is not the economy: reviving the conceptual distinction". *Journal of Economic Issues* 50, 745–68. 10.1080/00213624.2016.1210384.

Binder, A. 2023. *Offshore Finance and State Power*. Oxford: Oxford University Press.

Birch, K. & F. Muniesa (eds) 2020. *Assetization: Turning Things into Assets in Technoscientific Capitalism*. Cambridge, MA: MIT Press.

Blackburn, R. 2006. "Finance and the fourth dimension". *New Left Review* 39, 39–70.

Blomley, N. 2005. "Remember property?" *Progress in Human Geography* 29, 125–7. 10.1191/0309132505ph535xx.

Blomley, N. 2022. *Territory: New Trajectories in Law*. London: Routledge.

Blomley, N. *et al.* (eds) 2001. *The Legal Geographies Reader*. Oxford: Blackwell.

Blyth, M. *et al.* 2011. "Introduction to the special issue on the evolution of institutions". *Journal of Institutional Economics* 7, 299–315. 10.1017/S1744137411000270.

Bogart, D. & L. Chaudhary 2019. "Extractive institutions? Investor returns to Indian railway companies in the age of high imperialism". *Journal of Institutional Economics* 15, 751–74. 10.1017/S1744137419000237.

Boltanski, L. & E. Chiapello 2006. *The New Spirit of Capitalism*. London: Verso.

Boltanski, L. & A. Esquerre 2020. *Enrichment: A Critique of Commodities*. Cambridge: Polity.

Bonizzi, B. & A. Kaltenbrunner 2024. "International financial subordination in the age of asset manager capitalism". *Environment and Planning A: Economy and Space* 56, 603–26. 10.1177/0308518x241227744.

Borio, C. & P. Disyatat 2015. *Capital Flows and the Current Account: Taking Financing (More) Seriously*. Basel: Bank for International Settlements.

Boschma, R. & K. Frenken 2009. "Some notes on institutions in evolutionary economic geography". *Economic Geography* 85, 151–58. 10.1111/j.1944-8287.2009.01018.x.

Bourdieu, P. 1977. *Outline of a Theory of Practice*. Cambridge: Cambridge University Press.

Boussebaa, M. 2015. "Professional service firms, globalisation and the new imperialism". *Accounting, Auditing & Accountability Journal* 28, 1217–33. 10.1108/AAAJ-03-2015-1986.

Boussebaa, M. 2017. "Global professional service firms, transnational organizing and core/periphery networks". In L. Henriksen & L. Seabrooke (eds), *Professional Networks in Transnational Governance*, 233–44. Cambridge: Cambridge University Press.

Boyer, R. 2000. "Is a finance-led growth regime a viable alternative to Fordism? A preliminary analysis". *Economy and Society* 29, 111–45. 10.1080/030851400360587.

Brackley, J. & A. Leaver 2024. *Value for Money and Accountability: A Report on the Birmingham City Council Section 114 Bankruptcy*. Sheffield: Audit Reform Lab at the University of Sheffield.

Braudel, F. 1984. *Civilization and Capitalism, 15th–18th Century, Vol. III: The Perspective of the World*. New York: Harper & Row.

Braun, B. 2020. *American Asset Manager Capitalism*. Cologne: Institute for Advanced Study & Max Planck Institute for the Study of Societies.

Braun, B. 2021. "Asset manager capitalism as a corporate governance regime". In A. Hertel-Fernandez *et al.* (eds), *The American Political Economy: Politics, Markets, and Power*, 270–94. Cambridge: Cambridge University Press.

Braun, B. 2022. "Fueling financialization: the economic consequences of funded pensions". *New Labor Forum* 31, 70–79. 10.1177/10957960211062218.

Braun, B. & K. Koddenbrock (eds) 2023. *Capital Claims: Power and Global Finance*. Abingdon: Routledge.

Braverman, I. *et al.* (eds) 2014. *The Expanding Spaces of Law: A Timely Legal Geography*. Stanford, CA: Stanford University Press.

Brezis, E. & J. Cariolle 2019. "The revolving door, state connections, and inequality of influence in the financial sector". *Journal of Institutional Economics* 15, 595–614. 10.1017/S1744137418000498.

Bridge, G. 2008. "Global production networks and the extractive sector: governing resource-based development". *Journal of Economic Geography* 8, 389–419. 10.1093/jeg/lbn009.

Budd, L. 1995. "Globalisation, territory and strategic alliances in different financial centres". *Urban Studies* 32, 345–60. 10.1080/00420989550013121.

Bullock, J. 2023. *Delaware Division of Corporations: 2023 Annual Report*. Dover, DE: Delaware Department of State.

Burn, G. 2006. *The Re-emergence of Global Finance*. Basingstoke: Palgrave Macmillan.

Cahill, D. & M. Konings (eds) 2017. *Neoliberalism*. Cambridge: Polity.

Calabrese, M. & B. Majerus 2023. "Archaeology of a treasure island: actors and practices of holding companies in Luxembourg (1929–1940)". *Contemporary European History* 33, 1–18. 10.1017/S0960777323000437.

Çalışkan, K. & M. Callon 2009. "Economization, part 1: shifting attention from the economy towards processes of economization". *Economy and Society* 38, 369–98. 10.1080/03085140903020580.

Çalışkan, K. & M. Callon 2010. "Economization, part 2: a research programme for the study of markets". *Economy and Society* 39, 1–32. 10.1080/03085140903424519.

Castree, N. & G. Henderson 2014. "The capitalist mode of conservation, neoliberalism and the ecology of value". *New Proposals: Journal of Marxism and Interdisciplinary Inquiry* 7, 16–37.

Central Bank of Ireland nd. *Explainer: What Is Shadow Banking?* Available at: www.centralb ank.ie/consumer-hub/explainers/what-is-shadow-banking.

Cerny, P. 1993. "The deregulation and reregulation of financial markets in a more open world". In P. Cerny (ed.), *Finance and World Politics: Markets, Regimes and States in the Post-hegemonic Era*, 51–86. Aldershot: Brookfield.

Cerny, P. 2010. *Rethinking World Politics: A Theory of Transnational Neopluralism.* Oxford: Oxford University Press.

Chen, J. 2024. "Private equity explained with examples and ways to invest". *Investopedia.* Available at: www.investopedia.com/terms/p/privateequity.asp.

Chiapello, E. 2024. "So what is assetization? Filling some theoretical gaps". *Dialogues in Human Geography* 14, 43–46. 10.1177/20438206231157913.

Christen, R. *et al.* 2003. *Guiding Principles on Regulation and Supervision of Microfinance.* Washington, DC: CGAP/The World Bank Group.

Christensen, R. 2025. "Harnessing network power: Weaponised interdependence in global tax policy". *Global Policy* 16, 175–89. 10.1111/1758-5899.13456.

Christophers, B. 2011. "Making finance productive". *Economy and Society* 40, 112–40. 10.1080/03085147.2011.529337.

Christophers, B. 2015. "The limits to financialization". *Dialogues in Human Geography* 5, 183–200. 10.1177/2043820615588153.

Christophers, B. 2018. "Risking value theory in the political economy of finance and nature". *Progress in Human Geography* 42, 330–49. 10.1177/0309132516679268.

Christophers, B. 2020. *Rentier Capitalism: Who Owns the Economy, and Who Pays for It?* London: Verso.

Christophers, B. 2023. *Our Lives in their Portfolios.* London: Verso.

Clark, G. 2000. *Pension Fund Capitalism.* Oxford: Oxford University Press.

Clark, G. *et al.* 2015. "Editorial introduction to the special section: deconstructing offshore finance". *Economic Geography* 91, 237–49. 10.1111/ecge.12098.

Clark, J. 2020. *Uneven Innovation: The Work of Smart Cities.* New York: Columbia University Press.

ClientEarth 2024. *ClientEarth Complaint Targets BlackRock Over Misleading Sustainability Claims.* Available at: www.clientearth.org/latest/press-office/press-releases/clientearth-complaint-targets-blackrock-over-misleading-sustainability-claims/.

Coase, R. 1937. "The nature of the firm". *Economica* 4, 386–405.

Coase, R. 1992. "The institutional structure of production". *American Economic Review* 82, 713–19.

Coe, N. & H. Yeung 2015. *Global Production Networks: Theorizing Economic Development in an Interconnected World.* Oxford: Oxford University Press.

Coe, N. *et al.* 2014. "Integrating finance into global production networks". *Regional Studies* 48, 761–77. 10.1080/00343404.2014.886772.

Committee on Oversight and Government Reform 2008. *The Financial Crisis and the Role of Federal Regulators.* Hearing before the Committee, House of Representatives. 110th Congress.

Conyers 2023. *Cayman Islands Investment Funds.* Cayman Islands: Conyers. Available at: www.conyers.com/services/legal-services/investment-funds/cayman-islands-investm ent-funds/?utm_source=chatgpt.com.

Corbridge, S. & N. Thrift 1994. "Money, power and space: introduction and overview". In S. Corbridge *et al.* (eds), *Money, Power and* Space, 1–25. Oxford: Blackwell.

Cornut St-Pierre, P. 2023. "Securitisation from mortgages to sustainability: circulating techniques and the financialization of legal knowledge". *Transnational Legal Theory* 14, 476–98. 10.1080/20414005.2023.2286876.

Cousins, J. & D. Hill 2021. "Green infrastructure, stormwater, and the financialization of municipal environmental governance". *Journal of Environmental Policy & Planning* 23, 581–98. 10.1080/1523908X.2021.1893164.

Crawford, J. & I. Brownlie 2019. *Brownlie's Principles of Public International Law*. Oxford: Oxford University Press.

Cumbers, A. *et al.* 2003. "Institutions, power and space: assessing the limits to institutionalism in economic geography". *European Urban and Regional Studies* 10, 325–42. 10.1177/09697764030104003.

Cumming, D. & P. Monteiro 2023. "Sovereign wealth fund investment in venture capital, private equity, and real asset funds". *Journal of International Business Policy* 6, 330–55. 10.1057/s42214-023-00162-3.

Cutler, C. 2003. *Private Power and Global Authority*. Cambridge: Cambridge University Press.

Delaney, D. 2010. *The Spatial, the Legal and the Pragmatics of World-Making: Nomospheric Investigations*. New York: Routledge.

Delaney, D. 2015. "Legal geography I: constitutivities, complexities, and contingencies". *Progress in Human Geography* 39, 96–102. 10.1177/0309132514527035.

Der Spiegel 2006. "Steinbrück will gegen Heuschrecken vorgehen". *Der Spiegel*, 27 August.

Derudder, B. *et al.* (eds) 2012. *International Handbook of Globalization and World Cities*. Cheltenham: Edward Elgar.

Deruytter, L. *et al.* 2022. "Why do state-owned utilities become subject to financial logics? The case of energy distribution in Flanders". *Competition & Change* 26, 266–88. 10.1177/10245294211025948.

Dezalay, Y. 1995. "Introduction". In Y. Dezalay & D. Sugarman (eds), *Professional Competition and Professional Power. Lawyers, Accountants and the Social Construction of Markets*, 1–21. London: Routledge.

Dezan Shira & Associates 2023. *An Introduction to Doing Business in Singapore 2023: Asia Briefing*. Hong Kong: Dezan Shira & Associates.

Dicken, P. 1986. *Global Shift: Industrial Change in a Turbulent World*. London: Harper & Row.

Dicken, P. & A. Malmberg 2001. "Firms in territories: a relational perspective". *Economic Geography* 77, 345–63. 10.2307/3594105.

Dicken, P. & N. Thrift 1992. "The organization of production and the production of organization: why business enterprises matter in the study of geographical industrialization". *Transactions of the Institute of British Geographers* 17, 279–91.

Dicken, P. *et al.* 2001. "Chains and networks, territories and scales: towards a relational framework for analysing the global economy". *Global Networks* 1, 89–112. 10.1111/1471-0374.00007.

Diemer, A. *et al.* 2022. "The regional development trap in Europe". *Economic Geography* 98, 487–509. 10.1080/00130095.2022.2080655.

DIFC 2024. *Dubai International Financial Centre*. Available at: www.difci.com.

Dingwall, R. & P. Lewis (eds) 2014 [1983]. *The Sociology of the Professions: Doctors, Lawyers and Others*. London: Macmillan.

Dixon, A. *et al.* 2022. *Sovereign Wealth Funds: Between the State and Markets*. Newcastle upon Tyne: Agenda Publishing.

Doganova, L. 2024. *Discounting the Future: The Ascendancy of a Political Technology*. New York: Zone Books.

Donaghy, M. & M. Clarke 2003. "Are offshore financial centres the product of global markets? A sociological response". *Economy and Society* 32, 381–409. 10.1080/03085140303129.

Dorn, F. *et al.* 2022. "Towards a climate change consensus: how mining and agriculture legitimize green extractivism in Argentina". *The Extractive Industries and Society* 11, 101130. 10.1016/j.exis.2022.101130.

Dörre, K. 2015. "The new landnahme: dynamics and limits of financial market capitalism". In K. Dörre *et al.* (eds), *Sociology, Capitalism, Critique*, 11–66. London: Verso.

Dörry, S. 2015. "Strategic nodes in investment fund global production networks: The example of the financial centre Luxembourg". *Journal of Economic Geography* 15, 797–814. 10.1093/jeg/lbu031.

Dörry, S. 2016. "The role of elites in the co-evolution of international financial markets and financial centres: the case of Luxembourg". *Competition & Change* 20, 21–36. 10.1177/ 1024529415623715.

Dörry, S. & S. Heeg 2009. "Intermediäre und Standards in der Immobilienwirtschaft". *Zum Problem der Transparenz in Büromärkten von Finanzzentren* 53, 172–90. 10.1515/ zfw.2009.0012.

Dörry, S. & M. Hesse 2022. "Zones and zoning: linking the geographies of freeports with ArtTech and financial market making". *Geoforum* 134, 165–72. 10.1016/j.geoforum.2022.07.006.

Dörry, S. & C. Schulz 2024. "Green, alternative or business as usual? Critical geographies of sustainable finance". *Tijdschrift voor Economische en Sociale Geografie* 115, 573–81. 10.1111/tesg.12661.

Dumrose, M. *et al.* 2022. "Disaggregating confusion? The EU taxonomy and its relation to ESG rating". *Finance Research Letters* 48, 102928. 10.1016/j.frl.2022.102928.

Durand, C. 2017. *Fictitious Capital: How Finance is Appropriating Our Future.* London: Verso.

Dymski, G. 2014. "The neoclassical sink and the heterodox spiral: political divides and lines of communication in economics". *Review of Keynesian Economics* 2, 1–19. 10.4337/ roke.2014.01.01.

Dymski, G. 2021. "Intersectional inequality and global economic power: self-feeding dynamics within and across national borders". *International Journal of Political Economy* 50, 189–97. 10.1080/08911916.2021.1984729.

Dymski, G. 2024. "Capital accumulation, the separation of ownership and control, and the corporate form: from imperialism to financialization". *The Ritsumeikan Economic Review: The Quarterly Journal of Ritsumeikan University* 72, 376–94.

Economist 2020. "Brex and the city". *The Economist*, 24 October.

Economist 2024a. "The $1m voters". *The Economist*, 23 October.

Economist 2024b. "European millionaires seek a safe harbour from populism". *The Economist*, 27 June.

Economist 2025. "The bequest boom". *The Economist*, 1 March.

Engelen, E. 2008. "The case for financialization". *Competition & Change* 12, 111–19. 10.1179/ 102452908x289776.

Engelen, E. *et al.* 2010. "Reconceptualizing financial innovation: frame, conjuncture and brico-lage". *Economy and Society* 39, 33–63. 10.1080/03085140903424568.

Epstein, G. 2005a. *Financialization and the World Economy.* Cheltenham: Edward Elgar.

Epstein, G. 2005b. "Introduction: financialization and the world economy". In G. Epstein (ed.), *Financialization and the World Economy*, 3–16. Cheltenham: Edward Elgar.

ESMA 2023. *Progress Report on Greenwashing.* Paris: European Securities and Markets Authority.

Esmark, A. 2020. *The New Technocracy.* Bristol: Bristol University Press.

EUIPO 2024. *The EUIPO and Invest Europe Joint Study on Private Equity and Venture Capital.* Available at: www.euipo.europa.eu/en/news/the-euipo-and-invest-europe-joint-study-on-private-equity-and-venture-capital.

European Commission nd. *Investment Funds.* Available at: https://finance.ec.europa.eu/capi tal-markets-union-and-financial-markets/financial-markets/investment-funds_en.

European Commission 2019. *The European Green Deal.* Brussels: European Commission.

European Commission 2021. *Forging a Climate-resilient Europe: The New EU Strategy on Adaptation to Climate Change.* Brussels: European Commission.

European Commission 2023. *The Green Deal Industrial Plan.* Available at: https://commission. europa.eu/strategy-and-policy/priorities-2019-2024/european-green-deal/green-deal-industrial-plan_en.

European Commission 2025. *Commission Proposes to Cut Red Take and Simplify Business Environment.* Available at: https://commission.europa.eu/news/commission-proposes-cut-red-tape-and-simplify-business-environment-2025-02-26_en.

European Commission *et al.* 2009. *System of National Accounts 2008*. New York: United Nations.

European Council 2025. *European Green Deal*. Available at: www.consilium.europa.eu/en/ policies/european-green-deal.

Evans, J. & P. Smith 2018. "Bruce Flatt of Brookfield on owning the backbone of the global economy". *Financial Times*, 22 September.

Evenhuis, E. *et al.* 2021. "Rethinking the political economy of place: challenges of productivity and inclusion". *Cambridge Journal of Regions, Economy and Society* 14, 3–24. 10.1093/ cjres/rsaa043.

Evetts, J. 2003. "The sociological analysis of professionalism: occupational change in the modern world". *International Sociology* 18, 395–415. 10.1177/0268580903018002005.

Evetts, J. 2006. "Short note: the sociology of professional groups: new directions". *Current Sociology* 54, 133–43. 10.1177/0011392106057161.

Farmer, S. & R. Weber 2022. "Education reform and financialization: making the fiscal crisis of the schools". *International Journal of Urban and Regional Research* 46, 911–32. 10.1111/ 1468-2427.13137.

Faulconbridge, J. *et al.* 2007. "Analysing the changing landscape of European financial centres: the role of financial products and the case of Amsterdam". *Growth and Change* 38, 279–303. 10.1111/j.1468-2257.2007.00367.x.

Felber, C. 2021. *Economic growth without GDP growth*. European Envirnmental Bureau (EEB). Available at: https://meta.eeb.org/2021/05/18/economic-growth-without-gdp-growth/.

Feldman, M. & M. Kenney 2024. *Private Equity and the Demise of the Local: The Loss of Community Economic Power and Autonomy*. Cambridge: Cambridge University Press.

Fichtner, J. *et al.* 2017. "Hidden power of the Big Three? Passive index funds, re-concentration of corporate ownership, and new financial risk". *Business and Politics* 19, 298–326. 10.1017/ bap.2017.6.

Fitch Ratings 2021. *Shifting Ownership Patterns of Fossil Fuel Assets and Decarbonisation*. London: Sustainable Fitch.

Folkman, P. *et al.* 2007. "Working for themselves? Capital market intermediaries and present day capitalism". *Business History* 49, 552–72. 10.1080/00076790701296373.

Ford, R. 2001. "Law's territory (a history of jurisdiction)". In N. Blomley *et al.* (eds), *The Legal Geographies Reader*, 200–20. Oxford: Blackwell.

Fourcade, M. & J. Savelsberg 2006. "Introduction: global processes, national institutions, local bricolage: shaping law in an era of globalization". *Law & Social Inquiry* 31, 513–19.

Freire, J. (ed.) 2023. *Nation Branding in Europe*. London: Routledge.

Friedman, M. 1970. "The social responsibility of business is to increase its profits". *The New York Times Magazine*, 13 September.

Gabor, D. 2023. "The (European) derisking state". *Stato e mercato* 43, 53–84.

Gabor, D. & N. Sylla 2023. "Derisking developmentalism: a tale of green hydrogen". *Development and Change* 54, 1169–96. 10.1111/dech.12779.

Galloway, A. 2012. *The Interface Effect*. Cambridge: Polity Press.

Garner, B. (ed.) 2019. *Black's Law Dictionary*. St Paul, MN: Thomson Reuters.

Gereffi, G. 1983. *The Pharmaceutical Industry and Dependency in the Third World*. Princeton, NJ: Princeton University Press.

Gereffi, G. 1989. "Rethinking development theory: insights from east Asia and Latin America". *Sociological Forum* 4, 505–33.

Gereffi, G. & M. Korzeniewicz 1994. *Commodity Chains and Global Capitalism*. Westport, CT: Praeger.

Gereffi, G. *et al.* 2005. "The governance of global value chains". *Review of International Political Economy* 12, 78–104. 10.1080/09692290500049805.

Germain, R. 1997. *The International Organization of Credit: States and Global Finance in the World-Economy*. Cambridge: Cambridge University Press.

Gertler, M. 2018. "Institutions, geography, and economic life". In G. Clark *et al.* (eds), *The New Oxford Handbook of Economic Geography*, 1–17. Oxford: Oxford University Press.

Gibson-Graham, J. 2016. "Building community economies: women and the politics of place". In W. Harcourt (ed.), *The Palgrave Handbook of Gender and Development: Critical Engagements in Feminist Theory and Practice*, 287–311. London: Palgrave Macmillan.

Golka, P. 2025. "Assets and infrastructures". In C. Westermeier *et al.* (eds), *Cambridge Global Companion to Financial Infrastructures*, 75–87. Cambridge: Cambridge University Press.

Goode, W. 1957. "Community within a community: the professions". *American Sociological Review* 22, 194–200. 10.2307/2088857.

Goulding, R. *et al.* 2023. "From homes to assets: transcalar territorial networks and the financialization of build to rent in Greater Manchester". *Environment and Planning A: Economy and Space* 55, 828–49. 10.1177/0308518x221138104.

Goulding, R. *et al.* 2024. "A 'distributional apparatus' for real estate: fair value accounting and the assetization of UK property". *Critical Perspectives on Accounting* 99, 102729. 10.1016/j.cpa.2024.102729.

Greenwood, R. *et al.* 2002. "Theorizing change: the role of professional associations in the transformation of institutionalized fields". *Academy of Management Journal* 45, 58–80. 10.2307/3069285.

Grote, M. *et al.* 2002. "A value chain approach to financial centres: the case of Frankfurt". *Tijdschrift voor economische en sociale geografie* 93, 412–23. 10.1111/1467-9663.00213.

Guthman, J. 2009. "Unveiling the unveiling". In J. Bair (ed.), *Frontiers of Commodity Chain Research*, 190–206. Stanford, CA: Stanford University Press.

Haberly, D. 2020. "Offshore and the political and legal geography of finance: 1066–2020 AD". In J. Knox-Hayes & D. Wójcik (eds), *The Routledge Handbook of Financial Geography*, 552–83. New York: Routledge.

Haberly, D. & D. Wójcik 2015a. "Regional blocks and imperial legacies: mapping the global offshore FDI network". *Economic Geography* 91, 251–80. 10.1111/ecge.12078.

Haberly, D. & D. Wójcik 2015b. "Tax havens and the production of offshore FDI: an empirical analysis". *Journal of Economic Geography* 15, 75–101. 10.1093/jeg/lbu003.

Haberly, D. & D. Wójcik 2022. *Sticky Power: Global Financial Networks in the World Economy*. Oxford: Oxford University Press.

Haberly, D. *et al.* 2019. "Asset management as a digital platform industry: a global financial network perspective". *Geoforum* 106, 167–81. 10.1016/j.geoforum.2019.08.009.

Hadjimichalis, C. 1984. "The geographical transfer of value: notes on the spatiality of capitalism". *Environment and Planning D: Society and Space* 2, 329–45. 10.1068/d020329.

Hale, T. *et al.* 2013. *Gridlock*. Cambridge: Polity.

Haller, L. 2019. *Transithandel. Geld- und Warenströme im globalen Kapitalismus*. Berlin: Suhrkamp.

Hampton, M. 1996a. "Creating spaces: the political economy of island offshore finance centres: the case of Jersey". *Geographische Zeitschrift* 84, 103–13.

Hampton, M. 1996b. "Sixties child? The emergence of Jersey as an offshore finance centre 1955–71". *Accounting, Business & Financial History* 6, 51–71. 10.1080/09585209600000030.

Harrington, B. 2016. *Capital without Borders: Wealth Managers and the One Percent*. Cambridge, MA: Harvard University Press.

Harvey, D. 1996. *Justice, Nature, and the Geography of Difference*. Oxford: Blackwell.

Helleiner, E. 1993. "When finance was servant: international capital movements in the Bretton Woods Order". In P. Cerny (ed.), *Finance and World Politics: Markets, Regimes and States in the Post-Hegemonic Era*, 20–48. Aldershot: Edward Elgar.

Henderson, J. *et al.* 2002. "Global production networks and the analysis of economic development". *Review of International Political Economy* 9, 436–64.

Hendrikse, R. *et al.* 2020. "Strategic coupling between finance, technology and the state: Cultivating a Fintech ecosystem for incumbent finance". *Environment and Planning A: Economy and Space* 52, 1516–38. 10.1177/0308518x19887967.

Hercelin, N. & S. Dörry 2024. "Valuation conflicts in Madagascar's mining reform: a prag-matic inquiry into surplus distribution from strategic transition minerals". *Environment and Planning F* 3, 286–304. 10.1177/26349825241241319.

Hermann, C. 2021. *The Critique of Commodification. Contours of a Post-Capitalist Society.* New York: Oxford University Press.

Hopkins, T. & I. Wallerstein 1982. *World-Systems Analysis: Theory and Methodology.* Beverly Hills, CA: Sage.

Horner, R. 2014. "Strategic decoupling, recoupling and global production networks: India's pharmaceutical industry". *Journal of Economic Geography* 14, 1117–40. 10.1093/jeg/lbt022.

Horton, A. 2019. "Financialization and non-disposable women: real estate, debt and labour in UK care homes". *Environment and Planning A* 54(1), 144–159. 10.1177/0308518X19862580.

Hudson, M. 2014. *Funds: Private Equity, Hedge and All Core Structures.* Chichester: Wiley.

Hui, A. *et al.* (eds) 2017. *The Nexus of Practices.* London: Routledge.

Hunter, B. & S. Murray 2019. "Deconstructing the financialization of healthcare". *Development and Change* 50, 1263–87. 10.1111/dech.12517.

Hyde, J. 2025. "Private equity reshapes UK law firms with record investments". *The Law Soeciety Gazettle.* Available at: www.lawgazette.co.uk/news/private-equity-reshapes-uk-law-firms-with-record-investments/5122494.article.

IEA 2023a. *Net Zero Roadmap: A Global Pathway to Keep the 1.5°C Goal in Reach.* Paris: International Energy Agency.

IEA 2023b. *World Energy Outlook 2023.* Paris: International Energy Agency.

IEA 2024. *Oil Market Report.* Paris: International Energy Agency.

Iida, T. 2023. "Bricolage by institutions: towards the recreation of norms and organizations". In J. Babb & T. Iida (eds), *Dealing with Crisis: The Japanese Experience and Beyond*, 27–45. Cheltenham: Edward Elgar.

IMF 2017. *Global Financial Stability Report October 2017: Is Growth at Risk?* Washington, DC: International Monetary Fund.

International Investment Funds Association 2023. *Industry Statistics.* Toronto: International Investment Funds Association.

International Investment Funds Association 2024. *Worldwide Regulated Open-end Fund Assets and Flows, First Quarter 2024.* Toronto: International Investment Funds Association.

International Services Shanghai 2025. *International Services Shanghai.* Available at: https://english.shanghai.gov.cn.

Investment Company Institute 2024. *Investment Company Fact Book: A Review of Trends and Activities in the Investment Company Industry.* Washington, DC: Investment Company Institute.

Jarvis, D. & M. Griffiths 2007. "Learning to fly: the evolution of political risk analysis". *Global Society* 21, 5–21. 10.1080/13600820601116435.

Jensen, K. *et al.* (eds) 2012. *Professional Learning in the Knowledge Society.* Rotterdam: Sense Publishers.

Jensen, M. 1986. "Agency costs of free cash flow, corporate finance, and takeovers". *American Economic Review* 76, 323–29.

Jensen, M. & W. Meckling 1979. "Theory of the firm: managerial behavior, agency costs, and ownership structure". In K. Brunner (ed.), *Economics Social Institutions: Insights from the Conferences on Analysis & Ideology*, 163–231. Dordrecht: Springer Netherlands.

Jepperson, R. 1991. "Institutions, institutional effects, and institutionalization". In W. Powell & P. Dimaggio (eds), *The New Institutionalism in Organizational Theory*, 143–63. Chicago: University of Chicago Press.

Johns, J. & S. Hall (eds) 2024. *Contemporary Economic Geographies: Inspiring, Critical and Plural Perspectives.* Bristol: Bristol University Press.

Jones Day 2025. *New York Enacts Climate Change Law that Fines Companies for Historical Emissions.* Jones Day. Available at: www.jonesday.com/en/insights/2025/01/new-york-clim ate-change-law-fines-companies-for-historical-emissions?utm_source=chatgpt.com.

Kane, E. 1986. "Technology and the regulation of financial markets". In A. Saunders & L. White (eds), *Technology and the Regulation of Financial Markets: Securities, Futures, and Banking*, 187–93. Lexington, MA: Lexington Books.

Kaplan, S. & P. Stromberg 2009. "Leveraged buyouts and private equity". *Journal of Economic Perspectives* 23, 121–46. 10.1257/jep.23.1.121.

Karwowski, E. & E. Stockhammer 2017. "Financialization in emerging economies: a systematic overview and comparison with Anglo-Saxon economies". *Economic and Political Studies* 5, 60–86. 10.1080/20954816.2016.1274520.

Kauder, E. 2015. *History of Marginal Utility Theory*. Princeton, NJ: Princeton University Press.

Kay, J. 2016. *Other People's Money: Masters of the Universe or Servants of the People?* London: Profile Books.

Kennedy, D. 2014. "The productization of legal services: identifying and implementing new revenue sources based on nonlegal business models". *Law Practice* 40, 48–51.

Keynes, J. 1937. "The General Theory of Employment". *Quarterly Journal of Economics* 51, 209–23. 10.2307/1882087.

Keynes, J. 1971 [1930]. *A Treatise on Money, in Two Volumes: Volumes 5 and 6 of the Collected Works of John Maynard Keynes*. London: Macmillan.

Kipping, M. & O. Bjarnar 1998. *The Americanisation of European Business: The Marshall Plan and the Transfer of US Management Models*. London: Routledge.

Kitson, M. *et al.* 2004. "Regional competitiveness: an elusive yet key concept?". *Regional Studies* 38, 991–99. 10.1080/0034340042000320816.

Klabbers, J. & G. Palombella (eds) 2019. *The Challenge of Inter-legality*. Cambridge: Cambridge University Press.

Klausner, M. 2013. "Fact and fiction in corporate law and governance". *Stanford Law Review* 65, 1325–70.

Knell, M. 2015. "Schumpeter, Minsky and the financial instability hypothesis". *Journal of Evolutionary Economics* 25, 293–310. 10.1007/s00191-014-0370-8.

Knorr Cetina, K. & A. Preda (eds) 2005. *The Sociology of Financial Markets*. New York: Oxford University Press.

Kogut, B. 1985. "Designing global strategies: comparative and competitive value-added chains". *Sloan Management Review* 27, 27–38.

Kohler, K. 2022. "Capital flows and geographically uneven economic dynamics: a monetary perspective". *Environment and Planning A: Economy and Space* 54, 1510–31. 10.1177/0308518x221120823.

Lagoarde-Ségot, T. 2024. "Greenwashing and sustainable finance: an approach anchored in the philosophy of science". *Current Opinion in Environmental Sustainability* 66, 101397. 10.1016/j.cosust.2023.101397.

Lai, K. 2025. "Financial geography II: green finance and climate transition". *Progress in Human Geography* 49, 215–26. 10.1177/03091325251315158.

Lang, M. & D. Mokrani (eds) 2013. *Beyond Development: Alternative Visions from Latin America*. Quito: Fundación Rosa Luxemburg and Transnational Institute.

Langley, P. 2006. "The making of investor subjects in Anglo-American pensions". *Environment and Planning D: Society and Space* 24, 919–34. 10.1068/d405t.

Lapavitsas, C. 2013. *Profiting without Producing: How Finance Exploits Us All*. London: Verso.

Lapier, T. 1998. *Competition, Growth Strategies and the Globalization of Services: Real Estate Advisory Services in Japan, Europe and the United States*. London: Routledge.

Larcker, D. *et al.* 2022. *ESG Ratings: A Compass without Direction*. Stanford, CA: Rock Center for Corporate Governance at Stanford University.

Leaver, A. 2024. "The temporalities of financialized accounting". In H. Vollmer (ed.), *The Handbook of Accounting in Society*. Cheltenham: Edward Elgar.

Leaver, A. & K. Martin 2018. "Creating and dissolving social groups from New Guinea to New York: on the overheating of bounded corporate entities in contemporary global capitalism". In T. Eriksen (ed.), *An Overheated World: An Anthropological History of the Early Twenty-first Century*, 117–33. London: Routledge.

Leaver, A. & K. Martin 2021. "'Dams and flows': boundary formation and dislocation in the financialised firm". *Review of Evolutionary Political Economy* 2, 403–29. 10.1007/s43253-021-00057-0.

Lee, R. 2006. "The ordinary economy: tangled up in values and geography". *Transactions of the Institute of British Geographers* 31, 413–32. 10.1111/j.1475-5661.2006.00223.x.

Leffel, B. *et al.* 2023. "Divergence of the world city system from national economies". *Global Networks* 23, 459–77. 10.1111/glob.12405.

Lerner, J. & P. Tufano 2011. "The consequences of financial innovation: a counterfactual research agenda". *Annual Review of Financial Economics* 3, 41–85. 10.1146/annurev.financial.050808.114326.

Lerner, J. *et al.* 2008. "Secrets of the academy: the drivers of university endowment success". *Journal of Economic Perspectives* 22, 207–22. 10.1257/jep.22.3.207.

Lessig, L. 2002. "The architecture of innovation". *Duke Law Journal* 51, 1783–801.

Lévi-Strauss, C. 1966. *The Savage Mind*. Chicago, IL: University of Chicago Press.

Lienau, O. 2016. "Connecting sovereign debt to questions of justice". *Proceedings of the ASIL Annual Meeting* 110, 123–6. 10.1017/S0272503700102782.

Loftus, A. & H. March 2019. "Integrating what and for whom? Financialisation and the Thames Tideway Tunnel". *Urban Studies* 53, 2280–96. 10.1177/0042098017736713.

Luxemburg, R. 2003 [1913]. *The Accumulation of Capital*. New York: Routledge.

Macdonald, K. 1995. *The Sociology of the Professions*. London: Sage.

MacKenzie, D. 2011. "The credit crisis as a problem in the sociology of knowledge". *American Journal of Sociology* 116, 1778–841. 10.1086/659639.

MacKinnon, D. 2009. "Institutionalism/institutional geographies". In K. Rob & T. Nigel (eds), *International Encyclopedia of Human Geography*, 499–506. Oxford: Elsevier.

MacKinnon, D. 2012. "Beyond strategic coupling: reassessing the firm-region nexus in global production networks". *Journal of Economic Geography* 12, 227–45. 10.1093/jeg/lbr009.

Mader, P. *et al.* (eds) 2020. *The Routledge International Handbook of Financialization*. Abingdon: Routledge.

Marian, O. 2017. "The state administration of international tax avoidance". *Harvard Business Law Review* 7. 10.2139/ssrn.2685642.

Marketfeed 2021. *BlackRock: The World's Largest Asset Manager*. Marketfeed. Available at: www.marketfeed.com/read/en/blackrock-the-worlds-largest-asset-manager?utm_sou rce=chatgpt.com.

Martin, R. 2002. *The Financialization of Daily Life*. Philadelphia, PA: Temple University Press.

Marx, K. 1990 [1867]. *Capital: A Critique of Political Economy, Vol. I*. London: Penguin Books.

Massey, D. 1995. *Spatial Divisions of Labour: Social Structures and the Geography of Production*. London: Palgrave Macmillan.

Massey, D. 2004. "Geographies of responsibility". *Geografiska Annaler: Series B, Human Geography* 86, 5–18. 10.1111/j.0435-3684.2004.00150.x.

Massey, D. 2005. *For Space*. London: Sage.

Massey, D. 2007. *World City*. Cambridge: Polity.

Massey, D. 2008. "A global sense of place". In T. Oakes & P. Price (eds), *The Cultural Geography Reader*, 269–75. London: Routledge.

Mazzucato, M. & R. Collington 2023. *The Big Con: How the Consulting Industry Weakens our Businesses, Infantilizes our Governments and Warps our Economies*. London: Allen Lane.

McKinsey Global Institute 2023. *The Future of Wealth and Growth Hangs in the Balance*. Washington, DC: McKinsey Global Institute.

Merki, C. (ed.) 2005. *Europas Finanzzentren. Geschichte und Bedeutung im 20. Jahrhundert*. Frankfurt am Main: Campus.

Mian, A. & A. Sufi 2014. *House of Debt: How They (and You) Caused the Great Recession, and How We Can Prevent It from Happening Again.* Chicago, IL: University of Chicago Press.

Miller, D. 2000. "Virtualism: The culture of political economy". In I. Cook *et al.* (eds), *Cultural Turns/Geographical Turns: Perspectives on Cultural Geography*, 196–213. Harlow: Prentice Hall.

Miller, D. 2002. "Turning Callon the right way up". *Economy and Society* 31, 218–33. 10.1080/03085140220123135.

Miller, M. 1986. "Financial innovation: the last twenty years and the next". *Journal of Financial and Quantitative Analysis* 21, 459–71. 10.2307/2330693.

Miller, P. & M. Power 1995. "Calculating corporate failure". In Y. Dezalay & D. Sugarman (eds), *Professional Competition and Professional Power*, 51–76. London: Routledge.

Miller, T. 2017. *Greenwashing Culture.* London: Routledge.

Minsky, H. 1982. "The financial-instability hypothesis: capitalist processes and the behavior of the economy". In C. Kindleberger & J. Laffargue (eds), *Financial Crises: Theory, History, and Policy*, 138–52. Cambridge: Cambridge University Press.

Minsky, H. 1986. *Stabilizing an Unstable Economy.* New Haven, CT: Yale University Press.

Minsky, H. 1992. *The Financial Instability Hypothesis.* Levy Economics Institute Working Paper. New York: Bard College.

Minsky, H. 1993. "On the non-neutrality of money". *Federal Reserve Bank of New York Quarterly Review* 18, 77–82.

Minsky, H. 1995. "Longer waves in financial relations: financial factors in the more severe depressions II". *Journal of Economic Issues* 29, 83–96. 10.1080/00213624.1995.11505642.

Minsky, H. 1996. "Uncertainty and the institutional structure of capitalist economies". *Journal of Economic Issues* 30, 357–68. 10.1080/00213624.1996.11505800.

Mitchell, T. 2023. *Carbon Democracy: Political Power in the Age of Oil.* London: Verso.

Molt, E. 2006. "No double-Dutch at sea: how English became the maritime lingua franca". *International Journal of Maritime History* 18, 245–56. 10.1177/084387140601800211.

Mudge, S. 2008. "What is neo-liberalism?" *Socio-Economic Review* 6, 703–31. 10.1093/ser/mwn016.

Muniesa, F. 2023. "Financial value, anthropological critique, and the operations of the law". In I. Feichtner & G. Gordon (eds), *Constitutions of Value: Law, Governance, and Political Ecology*, 169–80. London: Routledge.

Muniesa, F. *et al.* 2007. "An introduction to market devices". *Sociological Review* 55, 1–12. 10.1111/j.1467-954X.2007.00727.x.

Musschoot, J. *et al.* 2023. "Hierarchical tendencies, functional specializations, and (in)stability across European banking centers". *European Urban and Regional Studies* 30, 446–64. 10.1177/09697764231161241.

Muzio, D. *et al.* 2011. "Professions, organizations and the state: applying the sociology of the professions to the case of management consultancy". *Current Sociology* 59, 805–24. 10.1177/0011392111419750.

Nelson, E. 2021. "The swift collapse of a company built on debt". *The New York Times*, 28 March.

Nicolini, D. 2017. "Is small the only beautiful? Making sense of 'large phenomena' from a practice-based perspective". In A. Hui *et al.* (eds), *The Nexus of Practices*, 98–113. London: Routledge.

Noordegraaf, M. 2007. "From 'pure' to 'hybrid' professionalism: present-day professionalism in ambiguous public domains". *Administration & Society* 39, 761–85. 10.1177/0095399707304434.

Norfield, T. 2017. *The City: London and the Global Power of Finance.* London: Verso.

North, D. 1990. *Institutions, Institutional Change and Economic Performance.* Cambridge: Cambridge University Press.

Nougayrède, D. 2019. "After the Panama Papers: a private law critique of shell companies". *The International Lawyer* 51. Available at: https://ssrn.com/abstract=3386623.

Nye, J. 2011. *The Future of Power.* New York: PublicAffairs.

OECD 1998. *Harmful Tax Competition: An Emerging Global Issue*. Paris: OECD.

Ong, A. & S. Collier 2005. *Global Assemblages: Technology, Politics, and Ethics as Anthropological Problems*. Malden, MA: Wiley Blackwell.

Ouma, S. 2015. *Assembling Export Markets: The Making and Unmaking of Global Food Connections in West Africa*. Hoboken, NJ: John Wiley.

Pagano, U. 2010. "Legal persons: the evolution of fictitious species". *Journal of Institutional Economics* 6, 117–24. 10.1017/S174413740999021X.

Palan, R. 2002. "Tax havens and the commercialization of state sovereignty". *International Organization*, 56, 151–76. 10.1162/002081802753485160.

Palan, R. *et al.* 2010. *Tax Havens: How Globalization Really Works*. Ithaca, NY: Cornell University Press.

Pan, F. *et al.* 2017. "How Chinese financial centers integrate into global financial center networks: an empirical study based on overseas expansion of Chinese financial service firms". *Chinese Geographical Science* 28, 217–30. 10.1007/s11769-017-0913-7.

Parfitt, C. 2024. "ESG integration and its derivative logic of ethics: exposing the limits of sustainability capitalism". *Finance and Space* 1, 221–39. 10.1080/2833115X.2024.2358815.

Parnreiter, C. 2024. *The Wealth of Cities and the Poverty of Nations*. Newcastle upon Tyne: Agenda Publishing.

Paterson, I. *et al.* 2003. *Economic Impact of Regulation in the Field of Liberal Professions in Different Member States: Regulation of Professional Services*. Vienna: Institut für Höhere Studien (IHS)/Institute for Advanced Studies.

Peck, J. 2010. *Constructions of Neoliberal Reason*. Oxford: Oxford University Press.

Peck, J. 2017. *Offshore: Exploring the Worlds of Global Outsourcing*. Oxford: Oxford University Press.

Petry, J. *et al.* 2021. "Steering capital: the growing private authority of index providers in the age of passive asset management". *Review of International Political Economy* 28, 152–76. 10.1080/09692290.2019.1699147.

Philo, C. & H. Parr 2000. "Institutional geographies: introductory remarks". *Geoforum* 31, 513–21. 10.1016/S0016-7185(00)00018-x.

Picciotto, S. 1995. "The construction of international taxation". In Y. Dezalay & D. Sugarman (eds), *Professional Competition and Professional Power: Lawyers, Accountants and the Social Construction of Markets*, 25–50. London: Routledge.

Picciotto, S. 1999. "Offshore: the state as legal fiction". In M. Hampton & J. Abbott (eds), *Offshore Finance Centres and Tax Havens: The Rise of Global Capital*, 43–79. London: Palgrave Macmillan.

Pike, A. 2023. *Financialization and Local Statecraft*. Oxford: Oxford University Press.

Pike, A. *et al.* 2016. *Local and Regional Development*, 2nd edn. London: Routledge.

Pike, A. *et al.* 2017. "Shifting horizons in local and regional development". *Regional Studies* 51, 46–57. 10.1080/00343404.2016.1158802.

Pike, A. *et al.* 2019. *Financialising City Statecraft and Infrastructure*. Cheltenham: Edward Elgar.

Pistor, K. 2019. *The Code of Capital: How the Law Creates Wealth and Inequality*. Princeton, NJ: Princeton University Press.

Pistor, K. 2022. "Legal coding beyond capital?". *European Law Open* 1, 344–50. 10.1017/elo.2022.19.

Pohl, J. 2025. *From Neo to Geo: The Collapse of Ideological Politics and the Rise of Interest-Driven Geopolitics*. LinkedIn. Available at: www.linkedin.com/pulse/from-neo-geo-colla pse-ideological-politics-rise-geopolitics-pohl-cmg5f?utm_source=rss&utm_campaign= articles_with_engagement&utm_medium=google_news.

Pollman, E. 2024. "The making and meaning of ESG". *Harvard Business Law Review* 14, 403–54.

Porter, T. 2005. *Globalization and Finance*. Cambridge: Polity Press.

Potts, S. 2016. "Reterritorializing economic governance: contracts, space, and law in transborder economic geographies". *Environment and Planning A: Economy and Space* 48, 523–39. 10.1177/0308518x15607468.

Potts, S. 2020. "Beyond (de)regulation: law and the production of financial geographies". In J. Knox-Hayes & D. Wójcik (eds), *Routledge Handbook of Financial Geographies*, 103–21. London: Routledge.

Potts, S. 2024. *Judicial Territory: Law Capital, and the Expansion of American Empire*. Durham, NC: Duke University Press.

Preqin 2024. *Private Capital Fund Domiciles in 2024*. Available at: www.preqin.com/insights/research/reports/private-capital-fund-domiciles-in-2024.

Private Equity International 2024a. *A Maturing Asset Class: CDPQ's Approach to Private Equity Hasn't Stopped Evolving*. London: PEI.

Private Equity International 2024b. *PEI 300, Largest Private Equity Firms in the World*. London: PEI.

Raitasuo, S. & M. Ylönen 2022. "How legal scholars facilitate tax avoidance: case study on the power of tax consultancy firms". *Public Administration* 100, 507–21. 10.1111/padm.12796.

Raworth, K. 2017. *Doughnut Economics*. London: Penguin.

Reuters 2025. *BlackRock Assets Hit Record $11.6 Trillion in Fourth Quarter*. Reuters. Available at: www.reuters.com/business/finance/blackrock-assets-hit-record-116-trillion-fourth-quarter-2024-2025-01-15/.

Riles, A. 2011. *Collateral Knowledge*. Chicago, IL: University of Chicago Press.

Ringen, S. 2004. "A distributional theory of economic democracy". *Democratization* 11, 18–40. 10.1080/13510340412331294192.

Robé, J.-P. 2011. "The legal structure of the firm". *Accounting, Economics, and Law* 1. 10.2202/2152-2820.1001.w.

Robé, J.-P. 2020. *Property, Power and Politics*. Bristol: Bristol University Press.

Roberts, R. 2008. *The City: A Guide to London's Global Financial Centre*. London: Economist Books.

Roberts, S. 1994. "Fictitious capital, fictitious spaces: the geography of offshore financial flows". In S. Corbridge *et al.* (eds), *Money, Power and Space*, 91–115. Oxford: Blackwell.

Robinson, G. *et al.* 2023. "Global networks of money and information at the crossroads: correspondent banking and SWIFT". *Global Networks* 23, 478–93. 10.1111/glob. 12408.

Robinson, G. *et al.* 2024. "Preserving the obligatory passage point: SWIFT and the partial platformisation of global payments". *Geoforum*, 151, 104007. 10.1016/j.geoforum.2024.104007.

Robinson, J. 2002. "Global and world cities: a view from off the map". *International Journal of Urban and Regional Research* 26, 531–54. 10.1111/1468-2427.00397.

Rodríguez-Pose, A. 2018. "The revenge of the places that don't matter (and what to do about it)". *Cambridge Journal of Regions, Economy and Society* 11, 189–209. 10.1093/cjres/rsx024.

Rodríguez-Pose, A. *et al.* 2021. "Golfing with Trump: social capital, decline, inequality, and the rise of populism in the US". *Cambridge Journal of Regions, Economy and Society* 14, 457–81. 10.1093/cjres/rsab026.

Rodríguez-Pose, A. *et al.* 2024. *Overcoming Left-Behindedness: Moving Beyond the Efficiency versus Equity Debate in Territorial Development*. Washington, DC: World Bank.

Rose, G. 2016. "Rethinking the geographies of cultural 'objects' through digital technologies: interface, network and friction". *Progress in Human Geography* 40, 334–51. 10.1177/0309132515580493.

Rueschemeyer, D. 2014 [1983]. "Professional autonomy and the social control of expertise". In R. Dingwall & P. Lewis (eds), *The Sociology of the Professions: Lawyers, Doctors and Others*, 29–44. New Orleans: Quid Pro Books.

Ryngaert, C. 2013. "Embassy bank accounts and state immunity from execution: doing justice to the financial interests of creditors". *Leiden Journal of International Law* 26, 73–88. 10.1017/S0922156512000659.

Sareen, S. *et al.* 2024. "Watt sense of community? A human geography agenda on energy communities". *Progress in Environmental Geography* 3, 289–310. 10.1177/27539687241287795.

Sani, H. 2020. "State law and legal pluralism: towards an appraisal". *The Journal of Legal Pluralism and Unofficial Law* 52, 82–109. 10.1080/07329113.2020.1727726.

Santos, B. 1987. "Law: a map of misreading. Toward a postmodern conception of law". *Journal of Law and Society* 14, 279–302.

Sassen, S. 2006. *Territory, Authority, Rights: From Medieval to Global Assemblages*. Princeton, NJ: Princeton University Press.

Sassen, S. 2010. "Global inter-city networks and commodity chains: any intersections?" *Global Networks* 10, 150–63. 10.1111/j.1471-0374.2010.00279.x.

Schane, S. 1987. "The corporation is a person: the language of a legal fiction". *Tulane Law Review*, 61, 563.

Schatzki, T. 2017. "Sayings, texts and discursive formations". In A. Hui *et al.* (eds), *The Nexus of Practices*, 126–40. London: Routledge.

Schumpeter, J. 1934. *The Theory of Economic Development*. Cambridge, MA: Harvard University Press.

Schumpeter, J. 2017 [1912]. *The Theory of Economic Development: An Inquiry into Profits, Capital, Credit, Interest, and the Business Cycle*. London: Routledge.

Scott, R. 1995. *Institutions and Organisations*. London: Sage.

Seabrooke, L. & D. Wigan 2018. *Global Wealth Chains: Managing Assets in the World Economy*. Oxford: Oxford University Press.

Sgambati, S. 2019. "The art of leverage: a study of bank power, money-making and debt finance". *Review of International Political Economy* 26, 287–312. 10.1080/09692290.2018.1512514.

Shaw, K. & K. Theobald 2011. "Resilient local government and climate change interventions in the UK". *Local Environment* 16, 1–15. 10.1080/13549839.2010.544296.

Shaxson, N. 2011. *Treasure Islands*. London: Bodley Head.

Shaxson, N. 2018. *The Finance Curse: How Global Finance Is Making Us All Poorer*. London: Vintage.

Shearmur, R. *et al.* 2016. "The geographies of innovation: beyond one-size-fits-all". In R. Shearmur *et al.* (eds), *Handbook on the Geographies of Innovation*, 1–16. Cheltenham: Edward Elgar.

Shove, E. 2017. "Matters of practice". In A. Hui *et al.* (eds), *The Nexus of Practices*, 155–68. London: Routledge.

Sikka, P. 2008. "Globalization and its discontents". *Accounting, Auditing & Accountability Journal* 21, 398–426. 10.1108/09513570810863987.

Sigler, T. *et al.* 2023. "Brokerage as an urban and regional process between systems and scales". *Regional Studies* 57, 209–14. 10.1080/00343404.2022.2093343.

Silbey, S. 2001. "'Let them eat cake': globalization, postmodern colonialism, and the possibilities of justice". In N. Blomley *et al.* (eds), *The Legal Geographies Reader*, 256–75. Oxford: Blackwell.

Sinclair, T. 2000. "Reinventing authority: embedded knowledge networks and the new global finance". *Environment and Planning C: Government and Policy* 18, 487–502. 10.1068/c10c.

Sloan, K. 2024. *Law Firm Profits Soared in Third Quarter of 2024, Report Finds*. Reuters. Available at: www.reuters.com/legal/transactional/law-firm-profits-soared-third-quarter-2024-report-finds-2024-11-11/

Slobodian, Q. 2018. *Globalists: The End of Empire and the Birth of Neoliberalism*. Cambridge, MA: Harvard University Press.

Slobodian, Q. 2023. *Crack-Up Capitalism: Market Radicals and the Dream of a World without Democracy*. New York: Metropolitan Books.

Spigel, B. 2016. "The cultural embeddedness of regional innovation: a Bourdieuian perspective". In R. Shearmur *et al.* (eds), *Handbook on the Geographies of Innovation*, 88–99. Cheltenham: Edward Elgar.

Stern, N. 2008. "The economics of climate change". *The American Economic Review* 98, 1–37.

Stockhammer, E. 2004. "Financialization and the slowdown of accumulation". *Cambridge Journal of Economics* 28, 719–41. 10.1093/cje/beh032.

Storey, D. 2020. "Territory and territoriality: retrospect and prospect". In D. Storey (ed.), *A Research Agenda for Territory and Territoriality*, 1–24. Cheltenham: Edward Elgar.

Storme, T. *et al.* 2019. "Introducing cluster heatmaps to explore city/firm interactions in world cities". *Computers, Environment and Urban Systems* 76, 57–68. 10.1016/j.compenvurbsys.2019.03.004.

Storper, M. 2013. *Keys to the City*. Princeton, NJ: Princeton University Press.

Strange, S. 1997 [1986]. *Casino Capitalism*. Oxford: Blackwell.

Suddaby, R. & R. Greenwood 2005. "Rhetorical strategies of legitimacy". *Administrative Science Quarterly* 50, 35–67. 10.2189/asqu.2005.50.1.35.

Talani, L. 2019. "What is globalisation?". In T. Shaw *et al.* (eds), *The Palgrave Handbook of Contemporary International Political Economy*, 413–28. London: Palgrave Macmillan.

Tamanaha, B. 2021. *Legal Pluralism Explained: History, Theory, Consequences*. Oxford: Oxford University Press.

Tellmann, U. 2022. "The politics of assetization: from devices of calculation to devices of obligation". *Distinktion: Journal of Social Theory* 23, 33–54. 10.1080/1600910X.2021.1991419.

Tendero, M. & C. Weber (eds) 2025. *The European Environmental Conscience in the EU: Finance, Innovation, and External Relations of the EU*. London: Routledge.

Thiemann, M. 2018. *The Growth of Shadow Banking: A Comparative Institutional Analysis*. Cambridge: Cambridge University Press.

Thousand Investors 2024. *List of the 100 Largest Pension Funds in the Netherlands*. Available at: www.thousandinvestors.com/product/list-pension-funds-netherlands/.

Tooze, A. 2018. *Crashed: How a Decade of Financial Crises Changed the World*. London: Allen Lane.

Toporowski, J. 2020. "Financialization and the periodisation of capitalism: appearances and processes". *Review of Evolutionary Political Economy* 1, 149–60. 10.1007/s43253-020-00005-4.

TPG Rise Climate 2025. *Accelerating Capital to Critical Climate Solutions*. Available at: www.tpg.com/platforms/impact/rise-climate.

Trautman, L. 2016. "Following the money: lessons from the Panama Papers: part 1: tip of the iceberg". *Penn State Law Review* 121, 807.

Tyson, J. 2019. *International Financial Centres and Development Finance*. London: ODI.

Ülgen, F. 2014. "Schumpeterian economic development and financial innovations: a conflicting evolution". *Journal of Institutional Economics* 10, 257–77. 10.1017/S1744137414000022.

UNDP nd. *What Are the Sustainable Development Goals?* UNDP. Available at: www.undp.org/sustainable-development-goals.

UNDP 2020. *Financing the 2030 Agenda: The Role of the Private Sector*. New York: UNDP.

UNFCCC nd. *Resources*. UNFCCC. Available at: https://unfccc.int/resources.

Urry, J. 2014. *Offshoring*. London: Wiley.

US Senate Permanent Subcommittee on Investigations 2003. *US Tax Shelter Industry: The Role of Acountants, Lawyers, and Financial Professionals*. Washington, DC: US Government Printing Office.

Van Meeteren, M. & D. Bassens 2016. "World cities and the uneven geographies of financialization: unveiling stratification and hierarchy in the world city archipelago". *International Journal of Urban and Regional Research* 40, 62–81. 10.1111/1468-2427.12344.

Van Meeteren, M. *et al.* 2016. "Can the straw man speak? An engagement with postcolonial critiques of 'global cities research'". *Dialogues in Human Geography* 6, 247–67. 10.1177/2043820616675984.

Volcic, Z. & M. Andrejevic 2011. "Nation branding in the era of commercial nationalism". *International Journal of Communication* 5, 21.

Walker, N. 2022. "Legalising inter-legality". *European Law Open* 1, 216–27. 10.1017/elo.2022.4.

Ward, C. 2022. "Land financialization, planning informalisation and gentrification as statecraft in Antwerp". *Urban Studies* 59, 1837–54. 10.1177/00420980211028235.

Watson, A. 1974. *Legal Transplants: An Approach to Comparative Law*. Edinburgh: Scottish Press.

Watson, S. 2019. "The corporate legal person". *Journal of Corporate Law Studies* 19, 137–66. 10.1080/14735970.2018.1435951.

Weeks, S. 2024. "Channeling the capital of others: how Luxembourg came to be asset managers' 'plumber' of choice". *Environment and Planning A: Economy and Space* 56, 627–44. 10.1177/0308518x221150012.

Whalen, C. 2001. "Integrating Schumpeter and Keynes: Hyman Minsky's Theory of Capitalist Development". *Journal of Economic Issues* 35, 805–23. 10.1080/00213624.2001.11506415.

Wójcik, D. 2013. "The dark side of NY–LON: financial centres and the global financial crisis". *Urban Studies* 50, 2736–52. 10.1177/0042098012474513.

Wójcik, D. *et al*. 2018. "Economic geography of investment banking since 2008: the geography of shrinkage and shift". *Economic Geography* 94, 376–99. 10.1080/00130095.2018.1448264.

Wójcik, D. *et al*. 2022. "Luxembourg and Ireland in global financial networks: analysing the changing structure of European investment funds". *Transactions of the Institute of British Geographers* 47, 514–28. 10.1111/tran.12517.

Wójcik, D. *et al*. 2024. *Atlas of Finance: Mapping the Global Story of Money*. New Haven, CT: Yale University Press.

Wood, A. & D. Valler 2001. "Turn again? Rethinking institutions and the governance of local and regional economies". *Environment and Planning A: Economy and Space* 33, 1139–44. 10.1068/a3472.

Worthington, M. 2022. "Legal personality as licence". *Griffith Law Review* 31, 397–417. 10.1080/10383441.2022.2096968.

Yeung, H. 2016. *Strategic Coupling: East Asian Industrial Transformation in the New Global Economy*. London: Cornell University Press.

Ylönen, M. & H. Kuusela 2019. "Consultocracy and its discontents: a critical typology and a call for a research agenda". *Governance* 32, 241–58. 10.1111/gove.12369.

Z/Yen 2024a. *The Global Green Finance Index, GGFI 13 Rank*. London: Z/Yen Group.

Z/Yen 2024b. *The Global Financial Centres Index 35*. London: Z/Yen.

Z/Yen 2025. *The Global Financial Centres Index*. Available at: www.longfinance.net/programmes/financial-centre-futures/global-financial-centres-index/.

Zhang, C. & C. Morris 2023. "Borders, bordering and sovereignty in digital space". *Territory, Politics, Governance* 11, 1051–58. 10.1080/21622671.2023.2216737.

Zucman, G. 2015. *The Hidden Wealth of Nations*. Chicago, IL: University of Chicago Press.

INDEX

Page numbers with an "n" denote notes.